him both insensitive to and wary of those which rise above a mediocre level.

Another reason for the failure of preaching, says Grasso, is that seminary education is failing to meet the demands of groping young students. Priests pass on to their pastorate what knowledge they have acquired during their years of education; it is, therefore, theology itself that must answer for the lifeless spirituality of so many Christians today.

Seeing the de-Christianization of society as no excuse for the failure of today's preachers to adapt their needs to a changing audience, Father Grasso believes God is needed now as "the only one who can explain and calm the metaphysical anxiety of man." Thus, the preacher's approach to his homily must be a new one, keyed to the demands of a society that appears to have found its own answers but is endlessly searching for an ultimate one. Father Grasso's investigation of this crisis in preaching is no polemic. Rather it is a positive approach to a new theology of preaching. His aim is "to make a contribution to the understanding of the word of God as it is transmitted."

This is the eighth volume in the continuing Liturgical Studies series.

Rev. Domenico Grasso, S.J., is a professor of pastoral theology at the Gregorian University in Rome and has been a visiting lecturer at the University of Notre Dame.

UNIVERSITY OF NOTRE DAME

LITURGICAL STUDIES

VOLUME VIII

Liturgical Studies

DEPARTMENT OF THEOLOGY OF THE UNIVERSITY OF NOTRE DAME

Liturgical Piety
REV. LOUIS BOUYER (OF THE ORATORY)

Church Building and Furnishing
REV. J. B. O'CONNELL

The Bible and the Liturgy
REV. JEAN DANIELOU, S.J.

Worship: the Life of the Missions
REV. JOHANNES HOFINGER, S.J.

The Meaning of Sacred Scripture
REV. LOUIS BOUYER (OF THE ORATORY)

The Early Liturgy
REV. JOSEF A. JUNGMANN, S.J.

Rite and Man: Natural Sacredness and Christian Liturgy
REV. LOUIS BOUYER (OF THE ORATORY)

Proclaiming God's Message:
A Study in the Theology of Preaching
REV. DOMENICO GRASSO, S.J.

PROCLAIMING GOD'S MESSAGE

A STUDY IN THE THEOLOGY OF PREACHING

Liturgical Studies

PROCLAIMING GOD'S MESSAGE

A Study in the Theology of Preaching

BY
REV. DOMENICO GRASSO, S.J.

UNIVERSITY OF NOTRE DAME PRESS
1965

Imprimi Potest: Howard J. Kenna, c.s.c., *Provincial*

Nihil Obstat: Joseph Hoffman, c.s.c., *Censor Deputatus*

Imprimatur: ✠ Leo A. Pursley, D.D., L.L.D.,
                Bishop of Fort Wayne-South Bend
                February 11, 1965

Library of Congress Catalog Card Number 65-14739

Contents

vii

INTRODUCTION

The Theological
Problem of Preaching

Preaching has moved into the center of attention. When one
realizes that spreading the Gospel has always been considered
the prime duty of the Church, this seems a strange statement.
Nevertheless, it is a fact that pastoral care, and theology too, are
presently rediscovering the value of preaching, its nature and its
function in Christian life. Congresses,[1] pastoral reviews,[2] discussions among preachers and listeners[3] and an ever-increasing

[1] See the *Proceedings of the Catholic Homiletic Society* in Chicago in
1958.

[2] The interest in preaching problems led to the founding of various
reviews after World War II: *Parole et Mission* (Paris, 1958), *Catéchèse*
(Paris, 1960), *Sinite* (Salamanca, 1960). In addition such reviews as *La
Nouvelle Revue Théologique* (June 1947), *Lebendige Seelsorge* (1954, Heft
4), *Anima* (1955, Heft 3 and 4), *Orientamenti Pastorali* (1957, nos. 1 and
3), and *Lumière et Vie* (no. 35 [1957] and no. 46 [1960]) have issued
special numbers given over to the problem of preaching. The Liturgical
review *La Maison Dieu* issued two special numbers given over to the problem of preaching, no. 16 in 1948 and no. 39 in 1954. The latter carries a
bibliography of all the articles published in the review on this theme. See
also *Living Light* (1964).

[3] Research into the state of preaching in Europe was published by Silens,
"Le sermon du point de vue de l'auditeur," *Nouvelle Revue Théologique,*
69 (1947), 563–580; "Enquête sur la prédication," *Évangéliser,* 8 (1954),
564–568; "I chierici e la predicazione," *Temi di predicazione,* 24 (1960),
297–324; B. Fischer, "Die Stimme derer unter der Kanzel," *Trierer Theologische Zeitschrift,* 69 (1960), 275–287; and others.

number of important publications point to a hitherto unknown interest in preaching.

The crisis of preaching

A whole series of reasons underlies this newly aroused interest, the problems and demands of which reflect present day pastoral care and theology.[4]

Let us first examine the "crisis of preaching,"[5] a slogan which comes at once to everybody's mind. It is a fact that preaching no longer "pleases" and that sermons have ceased arousing consciences. The faithful do not like to listen, and it is no secret that many priests give to preaching as little as possible. There are even people who hold that preaching as a means of spreading the Gospel has had its day and should be replaced by means more adequate to everyday expressions, such as those employed by press, radio, TV, and the screen. Gone are the days of St. John Chrysostom, who talked of the honor in which preachers were held.[6]

Father Duployé calls contemporary preaching "a misery,"[7] and

[4] In a supplement called "Il problema teologico della predicazione," *Gregorianum,* 40 (1959), 671–744, Fathers Z. Alszeghy and M. Flick examined the principal works and articles on preaching published between 1936 and 1959. They list books and magazine articles which treat of the nature, effect, and necessity of preaching, and evaluate them. This is an indispensable instrument for whoever wants to study the historical evolution and the actual stand of research. We have continued this examination in the supplement "Nuovi apporti alla teologia della predicazione," *Gregorianum,* 44 (1963), 88–118, including in the study also the forms of preaching.

[5] The crisis of preaching is a theme treated widely by all those concerned with the problem. We shall here point only to a few of the more important ones: P. Duployé, *Rhétorique et Parole de Dieu* (Paris, 1955), pp. 9–49. V. Schurr, "Situation und Aufgabe der Predigt heute," *Verkündigung und Glaube,* Festgabe für F. X. Arnold, herausgegeben von Theodor Filthaut und Joseph Andreas Jungmann (Freiburg, 1958), p. 185 ff. with bibliography; H. Fleckenstein, "Die Predigt von Heute im Urteil der Hörer," *Theologie und Predigt* (Würzburg, 1958), pp. 12–32 (discussion included); J. Hamer, "La crise de la predication," *La Revue Nouvelle,* 29 (1959), 137–147; M. Flick, "Riflessioni sulla crisi della predicazione," *La Civiltà Cattolica,* 111 (1960), 225–234; J. Ries, *Krisis und Erneuerung der Predigt. Studien zur Situation der Verkündigung* (Frankfurt, 1961); A. Günthör, *Die Predigt. Theoretische und Praktische theologische Wegweisung* (Freiburg-Basel-Vienna, 1963), p. 1 ff.

[6] St. John Chrysostom, *De sacerdotio,* L. V. in MG 48, col. 667–668.

[7] P. Duployé, *Rhétorique et Parole de Dieu* (Paris, 1955), especially p. 47.

Fleckenstein agrees with him.[8] Father Jannarone speaks of "the general apathy into which preaching has fallen among Christians" and of "the distrust that even priests have for it."[9] *L'Osservatore Romano*, in its January 1, 1963, issue comments on this crisis: "Preaching in the classical manner is today undergoing a real crisis. The material and spiritual desert facing the pulpits has roundly been denounced and analyzed in public-opinion polls, by means of more or less reliable statistics, and through serious studies of a theological and sociological nature. The facts are undisputed; to deny them would reveal a most unrealistic approach; it would even make the situation worse."

This crisis is felt and discussed by laymen as well, and the opinions of I. Goerres and François Mauriac are well known. The former expressed surprise that today "a decorous sermon" is the exception,[10] while Mauriac, in answer to the question of what he expected from a priest, said that a good preacher had nothing to tell him and that there was not one of them with whom he would not disagree from the third sentence on. He said the only real preaching is found in the liturgy.[11]

The reproach raised against preaching is specific: it is too abstract and unreal; it is fragmentary and lacking in sincerity; its character is mainly moralistic. The preacher does not make contact with the situation of modern man and therefore cannot impress him. The preacher's words, like anachronisms from another age, are bloodless and lifeless; as a result, they leave their hearers cold. Modern preaching does not appear to touch on vital concerns. Today's Christian looks upon the sermon as something which has to be endured because of convention, as a sort of admission price to the festive table, to prepare for Holy Communion or for marriage. Yves Congar has given a half-serious description of the condition of modern preaching: "The sermon is a more or less brilliant announcement of what has been decided, could be said and should be said in this special place which is the Church, from the height

---

[8] H. Fleckenstein, "Förderungen an eine zeitgemässe Verkündigung," *Mittelalterliches in der Kirche von Heute?* (Würzburg, 1962), p. 61.

[9] Jannarone, "I cherici e la predicazione," *Temi di predicazione,* 24 (1960), p. 297.

[10] Quoted by Scherer in "Wer ohren hat zu hören," *Beiträge zur Frage der Predigt* (Freiburg, 1948), p. 45.

[11] *La table ronde,* 1949.

of this platform which is the pulpit, in the course of a special cere-
mony, and—so often—in a special language."[12] To sum up, the
sermon has all too often become a mere "rite" which is enacted
almost automatically.[13]

R. Scherer, the German theologian, has indicated[14] that in
today's sermon a subterranean tension exists between clergy and
laymen "which is the more disturbing because it is found among
the most religiously open faithful. This tension causes many of
them to seek out Masses without a sermon or where preaching
is held to a minimum."[15]

This crisis has not only affected Catholicism; we also find it in
Protestantism, which likes to refer to itself as "the religion of the
word." In a book on homiletics, concerned specifically with the
difficulties that preaching reveals among the members of his
church, L. Fendt[16] wondered if it would not be advisable to pay
more attention to the liturgy, since the Catholic Mass, in spite of
four centuries of assault, still seems to exercise a great deal of
attraction. A few years later the Swiss Shaedelin made the same
observation.[17] During the general synod of Lutheran churches in
Hamburg, May 19 to 23, 1957, Bishop Lilje, referring to the Protestant doctrine of preaching as the Church's chief duty, said, "It
is apparent that this very thesis is the one which arouses not only
distrust but probably outspoken opposition among modern men."[18]

[12] Yves Congar, "Pour une liturgie et une predication réelles," *Maison Dieu*, 16 (1948), 85.

[13] *Ibid.*, 85.

[14] R. Scherer, *op. cit.*, p. 45.

[15] Many have pointed this out, and Segneri has complained: "I have to speak especially to the heads of families who send their wives to the Mass in which the priest harangues the people, but themselves go to another one where nothing is said" (*Il cristiano istruito*, in *Opere di Paolo Segneri* [Turin, 1840], p. 13).

[16] L. Fendt, *Homiletik, Theologie und Technik der Predigt* (Berlin, 1949), p. 16.

[17] A. Shaedelin, *Die rechte Predigt. Grundriss der Homiletik* (Zürich, 1953), p. 5.

[18] D. Lilje, "Was und wie sollen wir heute predigen?", *Die Predigt. Das Gespräch über die Predigt auf der Lutherischen Generalsynode 1957 in Hamburg.* (Berlin, 1957), p. 10. *Time,* in the March 16, 1962, issue, published opinions by leading American Protestants on the difficulty of preach-
ing in the U.S.A.

The situation with the Orthodox does not seem to be much better.[19]

The cause of the crisis

The crisis has its roots in the situation of modern man and in the situation of Christianity itself. This crisis of preaching is one aspect (and also a consequence) of the over-all crisis of religion which is besetting all creeds today, though it shows up more sharply in Christianity. Over and over again we are reminded that religion is in crisis, that it no longer means anything to contemporary man, who has turned to science and technology as a substitute for the happiness which he once demanded from God. There are people who think that the evolution of science has already atrophied (or that it will atrophy) religious feeling in man.

There is a kernel of truth in this assumption. It is certain that twentieth-century man does not need God in the same measure that men of past ages did. Until only a few decades ago a veritable miracle was necessary to recover from certain maladies. Today all that is needed is a physician who is a good practitioner of his profession. Man has become the master of nature and increasingly makes her serve his own well-being. Hence, he does not need God as once he did. But it might be better to say that this has purified, not atrophied, man's religious feeling. Science has by no means rendered God useless, but by developing the potentialities of secondary causes has returned to God His function as prime cause. Thus, while God may no longer be needed to heal sickness or to produce the rain that will save drought-stricken crops, He is needed as the only one who can explain and calm the metaphysical anxiety of man. In this sense scientific progress has helped, not hindered, religion.

For those who have erroneously been taught to turn to God as the answer to all their material problems, science has produced a weakening of the religious sense. Since they no longer have to turn to God for everything, the divine reality has, in their eyes, diminished almost to the vanishing point. To listen to any talk about

[19] Moeller writes that the Orthodox likewise feel the necessity for a renewal of their catechesis. Then he continues: "La coutume de placer la homilie a la fin de la liturgie abouti souvent a une desertation de l'Eglise par les fidèles: la plupart on quitte le sanctuaire à ce moment." "Théologie de la Parole et oecumenisme," *Irenikon,* 24 (1951), 322.

God under those circumstances leaves an impression of heightened unreality.

That progress of science which has everywhere raised modern man's standard of living has also created in him a state of mind which is unfavorable toward religion. Intent on achieving, at all costs, a high position in life, men see in religion only an obstacle to their ascent up the social ladder. Oriented towards the beyond, religion does not seem to offer solutions to the problems of the here and the now, the problems of the real world around us.

Evidently he who thinks this way is sometimes, without knowing it, deeply distrustful of preaching. In his eyes the priest does not understand his circumstances and is not aware of the conditions under which he must live and work. The priest who delivers a sermon appears to hover on the border of reality, and Christianity seems to be a religion which exacts too many renunciations. Hence, his badly concealed aversion to preaching, which often leads him to exaggerate the defects from which it suffers. There is often a psychological undercurrent to this accusation of unreality and moralism, an undercurrent that is characteristic of the Christian of today.

Then, too, we have the inflation of the word. Once the preacher had a monopoly of the word; this is not so any longer. Contemporary man is constantly exposed to a bombardment of words which leads him to put all on the same level, the word of God included. The "nausea" of the word is the real tragedy behind today's pastoral care.[20]

This inflation of the word not only has made hearers insensitive but it also has made them diffident. It is generally assumed that our contemporaries no longer believe in words; instead, they want to see facts. For them the criterion for a value judgment is not truth, but utility; not the abstract principle, but concrete efficiency.

The exigencies of contemporary spirituality

Even though the reasons mentioned above have helped make today's Christian aware of the defects in modern preaching, they are not the only reasons, or the most profound ones. The com-

[20] Louis Bouyer, *Initiation Théologique* (Paris, 1956), vol. IV, p. 589. Lilje, in the work cited above, also speaks of the "inflation of the word," p. 10.

plaints of hearers do indeed betray a discomfort which has its roots in more than the religious crisis or the inflation of the word. Scherer has told us that there is a certain tension between clergy and laymen, which is found particularly in the "religiously open" faithful.[21] This is an important observation. The reasons cited above would explain the disfavor in which preaching is held by Christians whose religious life is only marginal. But the fact that the severest critics are to be found among the most fervent Christians proves that preaching, as practiced today, fails to meet the needs of a spirituality which seeks sustenance in a sermon. The reproaches of abstractness, unrealism and moralism currently leveled against preaching may indicate not a religious crisis, but a progressively mature spiritual life which has at length rejected the threadbare outlines and sterile language that are presently evident.

Contemporary spirituality is searching for the essential; it endeavors, above all, not to get lost on the periphery. The many devotions handed down from the past find little favor with today's faithful; the pious books and prayers which used to pass through everybody's hands no longer satisfy. The modern Christian has tired of the fragmentary manner in which the different aspects of the Christian mystery—such as liturgy, Scripture, the Church, dogma and morals—have been presented to him. He is looking for a center around which to regroup these elements, because he is convinced that there is no spirituality without unity. This need seems to betray a desire, sometimes unconscious, for a closer contact with the very sources of spirituality, that is, with the Bible and the liturgy.

Unfortunately, in everyday pastoral care, preaching has not yet adapted itself to this new need. It continues to rotate around the anchor of devotion; it continues to ignore the profound message of the Bible; it continues to see the moral in a light more ethical than Christian. Meanwhile, it clings to shop-worn themes and uses a language no longer pleasing to a world accustomed to going straight to the essential.

Thus, for one and for all, preaching has become a butt of criticism: for some the reason is the use of an abstract, outmoded language; for others it is because it lacks a content which could provide food for the soul and thus rise above mediocrity.

[21] Scherer, *art. cit.*, 45.

The intrinsic causes

In addition to these contingent and extrinsic causes there are those inherent in preaching considered as a means of communication.

Communication, as is well known, is always an adventure and a risk. Phenomenology shows us the difficulty of contact between persons and makes clear how hard it is to lower those barriers which hinder the revelation of one to the other. The more we progress, the more we realize that others remain a mystery to us. Just as we think we understand them, we are forced to admit that we are mistaken.

Granting that all communication between men is a mystery, in preaching the mystery is even greater, for here man encounters God. In any other form of communication man can reserve for himself a small corner of his personality from which he can eye the stranger. But in the meeting with God this cannot happen; the message means all or nothing. Faith, to which man is called, results from a conversion, a metanoia, an unhinging of his own personality and a reconstruction around a new center. This cannot take place without a severe wrenching. The enterprise is truly difficult, and it is difficult each and every time it occurs. Therefore, preaching is subject to a continuous crisis which external circumstances may heighten or lessen but which at any rate must take place according to preaching's very nature. For the moment let us say that the philosophy of communication has helped to render actual the problem of preaching: it has contributed to our understanding of the crisis by discovering its most profound root.

In addition, there is the most important fact that the content of preaching is a message of salvation destined by its nature to transform the life of man. But a message, as is well known, is transmitted by testimony based on living experience. The encounter with God can be brought about only when the innermost being of the preacher has contacted that of Christ. And who can assert that he ever reached such a point? That is why the preacher's word may so easily ring false. If he does not live what he preaches, if his life is not a living expression of the word which he is proclaiming, his words will seem unreal, conventional and without meaning. Herein lies the mystery of preaching: to make man realize that in the Gospel his destiny is at stake, for better or for worse.

Because preaching is so terribly serious, it is readily exposed to the danger of appearing ridiculous. The "foolishness of our preaching" of which St. Paul speaks (1 Cor. 1:21) becomes clearly evident as soon as the preacher's word is divorced from the sanctity which alone makes it credible.

The crisis in preaching is, however, not new, even though modern times have served to point it up dramatically.[22] It has always existed. Through all the ages we can hear the lament of preachers who find it difficult to win a hearing, and the lament of the faithful who fail to find in preaching sustenance for their souls. Even St. Paul speaks of those who abandon the Gospel for fables (2 Tim. 4:4) and exhorts Timothy not to lose courage but to continue without fear and compromise in his work as a preacher. In St. Augustine's time the deacon Deogratias asked the great doctor what to do to overcome the boredom of his listeners,[23] and St. Augustine himself tells us that the people preferred the circus spectacles to his sermons. In his time Dante[24] lashed out against preachers who had nothing "but wind" for their sheep; more recently, preachers talk of "crisis" whether the people throng the churches or leave them deserted.[25]

The crisis has therefore had the effect of forcing theologians and preachers to ponder what preaching is, what happens during a sermon, what its content should be and what are its scope and its dimensions. If preaching really is in a permanent state of crisis, investigators want to discover the crisis today, and in what way it differs from the difficulties other modes of communications are facing. Only reflection on the word of God will yield an answer to this problem.

[22] Arnold examined the historical roots of today's crisis of preaching in his two volumes, *Dienst am Glauben, Das vordringlichste Anliegen heutiger Seelsorge* (Freiburg i.B., 1948) and *Grundsatzliches und Geschichtliches zur Theologie der Seelsorge* (Freiburg, 1949).

[23] St. Augustine, *De catechizandis rudibus*, 1, 1.

[24] Dante, *Paradise*, XXIX, 106.

[25] Massilon, in his sermon on the Word of God held the first Sunday of Lent, talks about the masses which throng under the pulpits so that all the places of entertainment seem deserted. But right after that he adds that of all the mysteries of the Church none seems as useless as preaching because conversions are so rare (*Ouevres de Massilon* [Paris, 1825], vol. II, pp. 178–179).

The phenomenon of dechristianization

The *crisis* of preaching is not the only point which has drawn the attention of theologians and pastors of souls. Other factors have played roles in revealing preaching's importance and complexity. First among these is the phenomenon of dechristianization.

Up to a few decades ago missions and missionaries were associated with people who had not yet been converted; these expressions immediately called to mind foreign countries and peoples to win for Christ. Then, quite without recognizing it, Christian Europe discovered a kind of paganism within its own borders. This is not only a practical paganism—that of a man who thinks as a Christian but lives at war with the principles which he constantly professes—but a life and a world of vision which has nothing Christian about it whatsoever. Recognition of this phenomenon has forced pastoral care to face the problem of re-evaluation and has given rise to a missionary movement which represents one of the most dynamic practiced by the Church today.

This missionary movement, conceived as a means of reconquering the dechristianized masses, came to life in France as a result of the publication of a book which since has become a classic: *France, pays de mission?*[26] by Fathers Godin and Daniel. It was crystalized in confrontation with a situation which until then had not been evaluated in all its depth, and it inspired the urgency to find its own remedy. It was the first time in centuries that the distinction between Christian countries and mission countries had lost its significance. An impression was created—which later became a conviction—that Christian Europe, too, had its mission territories.

An analysis of this disquieting situation led directly to a consideration of preaching, that great means instituted by Jesus Christ for the dissemination and strengthening of Christian life (Matt. 8:18–20). If one was forced to recognize the existence of paganism in regions which for centuries had been Christian, one was likewise forced to recognize that preaching either had been insufficient or had actually failed altogether. Since it was preaching which had Christianized the countries of Western Europe, it was weakness in preaching or the lack of it altogether which had dechristianized them.

[26] Godin and Daniel, *France, pays de mission?* (Paris, 1943).

This was the situation in the time of Bishop Dupanloup, who in 1830 stated, somewhat bitterly, "Thirty-thousand sermons every Sunday in the churches of France—and France still has the Faith!" Even though the expression was, at the time, considered nothing more than the ill-humor of a man who deplored the state of things, it turned out to be an accurate diagnosis of an ill still in the state of incubation in France and elsewhere as well. Boulard's research has given us a proof of this. He points to either the lack of preaching or its deficiency as the most potent cause of the dechristianization of vast rural areas in his native country. "The great deficiency of our apostolic work in the past," he writes, *was a lack of evangelization.*[27] Very often this lack was to be taken literally: it was rare but by no means unheard of in the country that a tired and discouraged priest had ministered to a parish for twenty or twenty-five years without *ever* preaching a sermon. In other cases the lack has to be understood in a more formal way: evangelization had not actually taken place because the preaching had lacked realism. Religious instruction had consisted of teaching by rote the formulae of the catechism without any explanation being given, while sermon and homily remained meaningless, heavy and moralistic. Not the great themes of Revelation, but a residue of natural religion was preached, which meant nothing to the man of the industrial revolution. Godin, in his book cited above, made the same observation regarding the lack of evangelization.[28]

In contrast, the same sociological research reveals that wherever there had been real preaching, Christian life resisted the process of dechristianization. Boulard, who asked himself why some dioceses retained the Faith while others of the same social and economic conditions became dechristianized, finds his answer in preaching. "It seems that one can say these exceptional regions were firmly evangelized in the seventeenth and the eighteenth centuries. They were not satisfied with simple religious practice, but were profoundly evangelized. These people wanted to be instructed in their religion and to live it in their complete life: firmly, professional and social."[29] It was the word of holy mission-

---

[27] Boulard, *Problemes missionaires de la France rurale* (Paris, 1945), pp. 185–186.

[28] Godin and Daniel, *op. cit.*, p. 60.

[29] Boulard, *Premiers itineraires en sociologie religieuse* (Paris, 1954), p. 48.

aries which implanted the Faith in the souls of these people and thus enabled them to resist the forces of dechristianization.

But if preaching, because of its deficiencies, was "the deep-seated cause of dechristianization," it should also be the prime factor in the mission of recovery. There is nothing like the word of the Gospel to lead the dechristianized masses back to faith. Today, just as in the time of the Apostles, the Church will have to proclaim the Word of God to convert the pagans, because faith comes from preaching (Rom. 10:17). But what is preaching, this fundamental reality which taken in one way causes faith, taken in another way causes that faith to dwindle and die? What does it mean to preach? What is the Word of God or the Gospel which the priest proclaims? These are problems to which only theology has an answer.

It is in this way that the missionary movement, which holds so important a place in the considerations of the Church, poses the theological problem of preaching; the very importance of preaching makes a solution to the problem absolutely essential. Because of the problem, the necessity of closer ties between preacher and theologian has been emphasized, since each can avail himself of the experience and knowledge of the other.

The biblical, patristic, and liturgical movement

The necessity for more profound preaching in the theological sense has not only arisen from the shadows which overlay Christian life today but it has also resulted from the light of that life, from those movements which characterize the spirituality of the modern Christian. We are thinking of the liturgical, biblical and patristic movements.

The liturgical movement, which had its beginnings under Pius X and spread to a greater or lesser degree over all nations, demands intense thought on the part of its followers if they care to penetrate the intimate nature of a complex reality like the liturgy. The movement, too, has contributed to the discovery of the close relationship between liturgy and preaching. Preaching proclaims the same mystery of salvation which the liturgy realizes. The liturgy cannot exist without preaching because it cannot be without the faith which comes from preaching (Rom. 10:17). It was only natural, therefore, that the effort to understand the liturgy brought questions concerning preaching in its wake, especially of liturgical preaching, the homily. "Theorists and practical people know," says Fleckenstein, "that the rediscovery of the homily has introduced a new taste for preaching both in the preachers and in the listeners."[30]

It is indeed to the liturgists that we are indebted for some outstanding writings on the Word of God and its place in the liturgy.[31] They are the ones who have rediscovered the close link between liturgy and preaching and have upheld it with the force of their arguments. Thus has the liturgical movement brought about a rethinking of all preaching, and not only the homily, in its function in the process of faith and the life of the Church.

The same holds true for the biblical movement. It is well known how alive the study of Scripture is, and how diligently scholars work to make it accessible to the greatest possible number of the faithful. But Scripture is inseparable from preaching not only because it furnishes preaching's subject but also because, at least for the New Testament, it is its source. The Gospels and the Epistles constitute the catechesis of the Apostles. The New Testament, as exegesis make abundantly clear,[32] is nothing else than the development of a primitive nucleus of preaching, that is, of the kerygma which St. Paul says belongs to all the Apostles without distinction (1 Cor. 15:11). If this is so, the problem of preaching becomes a question which sheds light on biblical exegesis. He who wants to know the real nature of the New Testament has to consider the nature of preaching and the exigencies which it presented to the Apostles. Like the liturgy, Scripture in turn poses the problem of preaching.

Biblical research, in turn, has enabled preaching to rediscover unity in the multiplicity of its forms. In the Church of the early

[30] H. Fleckenstein, op. cit., p. 61.

[31] Especially Fischer's "Liturgiegeschichte und Verkündigung," Die Messe in der Glaubensverkündigung (Freiburg i.B., 1950), pp. 1–13; V. Warnach, "Menschenwort und Gotteswort," Liturgie und Mönchtum, 12 (1953) 14–34; ibid., "Wort und Sakrament im Aufbau der christlichen Existenz," Liturgie und Mönchtum, 20 (1957), 68–90; L. Agustoni, "Das Wort Gottes als kultisches Wort," Anima, 10 (1955), 272–284; Parole de Dieu et Liturgie, Congrès de Strasbourg 1958, 2nd ed., esp. Chap. XXIV. See also the special issues on preaching in the liturgical magazines already cited.

[32] C. H. Dodd, The Apostolic Preaching and Its Development (London, 1956).

centuries three distinctive forms of preaching were to be found:
the missionary type, directed to pagans with a view to their conversion; that for catechumens, in preparation for Baptism; and that
intended for the members of the Christian community. The study
of the New Testament's beginnings has shown the originality of
missionary preaching and its normative function with regard to the
other two forms.[33] It showed that the primitive catechesis, as we
find it in the Gospels and in the symbols of the Apostles, comes
from the development of the kerygma, from that complex of facts
which comprised the primitive preaching of the Apostles to non-
Christians. We have some examples of this in the Acts and in some
of St. Paul's letters. It was an important discovery, because it made
it possible to follow the whole cycle of preaching and discern a
great variety of forms. The discovery of missionary preaching's
originality has thus played an important role in the evangelization of the pagan world, or of one reverted to paganism. This
discovery is in great part due to the study of the Book of Acts.[34]

Biblical research, in studying about the transmission of faith,
has demonstrated the complexity and the richness of the phenomenon of preaching by furnishing a basis for reflection. The study
of terms like $\kappa\eta\rho\acute{v}\sigma\sigma\omega$, $\epsilon\acute{v}\alpha\gamma\gamma\epsilon\lambda\acute{\iota}\zeta\omega$, $\mu\alpha\rho\tau\acute{v}\rho\rho\mu\alpha\iota$, $\lambda\acute{\epsilon}\gamma\omega$, in different dictionaries, above all in the one by Kittel, has proved indis-
pensable for understanding a reality such as preaching, and the
New Testament makes use of thirty verb forms to convey these
realities.[35]

Nor can the weight of patristic research be underestimated. The
Fathers were not only great pastors of souls and preachers who

[33] This was treated in our article, "Il kerigma e la predicazione," *Gregorianum*, 41 (1960), 424–450.

[34] The study of The Acts has helped a great deal in clarifying the problematics of preaching. A. Rétif, *Foi au Christ et mission* (Paris, 1953); P.
Hitz, *L'Annonce missionaire de l'Evangile* (Paris, 1954), Chap. II; see also
the English translation of Hitz, *To Preach the Gospel* (New York, 1963);
Y. B. Tremel, "Du Kerygme des apôtres à celui d'aujourd'hui," *L'Annonce
de l'Evangile aujourd' hui* (Paris, 1962), pp. 19–116, are some of the most
recent studies in the field.

[35] K. H. Schelkle, *Jüngerschaft und Apostelamt. Eine Biblische Auslegung
des priesterlichen Dienstes* (Freiburg i.B., 1957), p. 57. Important for the
influence of Bible research on the theology of preaching are also R. Asting,
*Die Verkündigung des Wortes Gottes im Urchristentum, dargestellt an den
Begriffen "Wort Gottes," "Evangelium," und "Zeugnis."* (Stuttgart, 1939.)
Many subsequent studies are based on this one.

showed clearly how one should proclaim the Word of God[36] but they also bequeathed to us samples of evangelization, catechesis, and homelitics, thus permitting us to perceive the principles underlying their activity as propagators of the Faith. The various forms of preaching cannot help but profit by their work.

It was catechetics in particular which, through contact with St. Cyril of Jerusalem, St. Ambrose, St. John Crysostom and St. Augustine, discerned the line of salvation history. This helped the Church Fathers to achieve that synthesis between thought and Christian life which made Christianity's earliest practitioners so happy in their Faith. It is due to the study of the Fathers that modern catechetics has been able to give us a work like the German catechism.

Thus the liturgy, Scripture and patristics have again placed the focus of theological attention on the problem of preaching, to which insufficient attention had been paid previously.

Ecumenism

We must add a word about the influence of ecumenism, one of Catholic theology's most profound concerns today.

For a long time Catholic and Protestant theologians fought among themselves. Their polemics led both parties to exaggerate the elements of contrast in their theologies, and heightened the tension already present. Because these elements were denied by the other, each party felt obliged to keep them constantly in the forefront of attention. Thus it happened that Catholic theology provided a doctrine of the sacraments which is complete in every detail, but nothing equally complete has been forthcoming concerning preaching. Since preaching was never controversial, there seemed to be no necessity to concentrate on the strength of reflection.

Karl Barth has reproached Catholic theologians for this lack in words of great severity. "As to preaching," he writes, "Catholic

[36] A bibliography of the preaching of the Fathers was put together by P. B. Mehr in *Collectana Franciscana* 12 (1942) 7–16. Since then the bibliography has grown. Let us mention here only A. Schorn, "Das Wort Gottes bei den Vätern," *Vom Hören des Wortes Gottes,* already cited, pp. 19–33; L. Bopp, "Die Heilsmächtigkeit des Wortes nach den Vätern," *Theologie und Predigt,* (Würzburg, 1958), pp. 190–226; B. H. Vandenberghe, *St. Jean Chrysostome et la parole de Dieu* (Paris, 1961).

dogmatic theologians maintain complete silence (altissimum silentium). After having treated grace or the Church, they immediately pass on to examine the sacraments, develop the sacramental doctrine of the *ordo*, talk endlessly about the magisterium of the Church, just as if the sermon did not exist—a sermon which is considered an indispensable means of grace. What interests them in a sermon, and this only in a cursory manner, are juridical questions such as the question of the primary and secondary subject of legitimate doctrine, the question of the necessity of a *missio canonica*, and so forth. Catholic dogmatics, and the normative declarations of the ecclesiastical magisterium, which can be very precise in its explanations when they treat things which in their opinion are important, cover themselves with an impenetrable veil when it comes to the sermon. . . . Preaching is in no way an essential element in the Catholic notion of priesthood, and in this sense is completely distinguished from the sacrament."[37]

Barth's reproach is not wholly justified. Research has shown how much importance great theologians like St. Bonaventure[38] and St. Thomas[39] assigned to the theological problem of preaching. Even after the Council of Trent, in the midst of Protestant polemics, there was no dearth of theologians who made preaching the object of their investigation.[40] Nor must we forget in this connection the importance the nontheologians—that is, the preachers—have attached to the theology of preaching. They were always conscious of the primary importance of their ministry and the particular effect of the Word of God.[41] But it cannot be denied that theological research has never paid the same attention to preaching that it has to the sacraments.

The ecumenical movement has exerted its influence in closing

[37] Karl Barth, *Dogmatique,* I, vol. I (Geneva, 1953), pp. 64–65.

[38] E. Eilers, *Gottes Wort. Eine Theologie der Predigt nach Bonaventura* (Freiburg i.B., 1941).

[39] A. Rock, *Unless They Be Sent. A Theological Study of the Nature and Purpose of Preaching* (Dubuque, 1953); E. Robben, *Il problema teologico della predicazione* (Rome, 1962).

[40] We mention here Suarez, of whom we shall say more in the third chapter of the first part of this study. See also what Pohlmann writes about the theologians of the Baroque age: "Die theologischen Konzepte der Barockpredigt," *Theologie und Predigt,* pp. 258–271. For mediaeval theologians see Z. Alszeghy, "Die Theologie des Wortes Gottes bei den mittelalterlichen Theologen," *Gregorianum,* 39 (1958), 685–705, with bibliography.

[41] J. B. Schneyer, "Die Heilsbedeutung der Predigt in der Auffassung der Katholischen Prediger," *Zeitschrift für Kath. Theol.,* 84 (1962), 152–170.

this gap. At a time when Catholics and Protestants examine their positions to find points of contact, preaching has emerged as one of the privileged problems on which the scholars of both parties can establish a dialogue.

This fact was remarked on especially by Moeller during the interconfessional meeting held at Chevetogne in 1950. "The necessity of a theology of the word—that is, of preaching—reveals also another problem. Such a theology is part of ecclesiology, and it is on the plane of ecclesiology that the greatest divergence between the Christian confessions comes to light."[42] Since it concerns a mutually interesting problem, the working-out of a theology of preaching might furnish a better basis for the discussion of controversial problems. The fact is that the most important writings on the problem of preaching come from those theologians most actively engaged in the ecumenical movement. Thus Schlier has dedicated a brief but very valuable biblical essay to preaching,[43] and Semmelroth in his works has often touched on the problem of preaching.[44] He is one of those German theologians who are in constant contact with their Protestant counterparts. This can be seen in the fact that he is a collaborator in the review *Catholica*, where he has published the basic ideas developed in the works cited above.

The Philosophy of communication

Finally, let us touch in passing upon the influence which the development of a philosophy of communication may exert on the problem of preaching, even in the theological sense. This philosophy, from Max Scheler to Buber, to Le Senne, Marcel and Nédencelle, has tried to penetrate the mystery of the encounter between persons. Preaching is a form of communication: God and man meet through the mediation of the human word. A study of what happens in the meeting between persons should prove of help in comprehending what happens in a meeting with God.

The philosophy of testimony has here a special importance. Jesus told the Apostles to be his witnesses "to the very ends of the

---

[42] "Théologie de la parole et oecumenisme," *Irenikon*, 24 (1951), 333.

[43] H. Schlier, *Wort Gottes, Eine Neutestamentliche Besinnung (Würzburg, 1958); Die Verkündigung im Gottendienst der Kirche* (Köln, 1953).

[44] O. Semmelroth, *Das Geistliche Amt. Theologische Sinndeutung* (Frankfurt, 1958); also *Wirkendes Wort. Zur Theologie der Verkündigung* (Frankfurt, 1961).

earth" (Acts 1:8). Preaching transmits a message which is communicated by witnesses.[45] It contains values which are destined to influence human life decisively. Thus the philosophy of values cannot help but contribute to the understanding of preaching.[46]

Kerygmatic theology

The problem of preaching thus arises from different directions and from different necessities. Among the causes cited here, priority—at least in the order of time—must be assigned to the crisis of preaching. Fathers Alszeghy and Flick note correctly that a theoretical analysis of preaching is "a necessity derived from practice."[47]

Actually it is this crisis of preaching, and the necessity of solving it through a theological examination of its nature and function in the life of the Church, which is touched upon in Father Joseph Jungmann's now-famous book, *Die Frohbotschaft und unsere Glaubensverkündigung*,[48] later reissued under the title of *Glaubensverkündigung im Lichte der Frohbotschaft*. This it was which kindled the controversy of the so-called *Verkündigungstheologie*, or kerygmatic theology.[49]

We do not want to expatiate here on this movement which has so influenced the theological orientation of the last decade, because others have already done so at length,[50] and the contro-

[45] See among others: J. Guitton, *The Problem of Jesus* (New York, 1955); M. Buber, *I and Thou* (New York, 1958); R. Mehl, *La recontre d'autrui* Neufchatel-Paris, 1955; Gusdorf, *La Parole* (Paris, 1956).

[46] Fathers Alszeghy and Flick, in the supplement cited in note 4 above, call attention to the reasons which have caused the emergence of the theological problem of preaching.

[47] *Ibid.*, p. 672.

[48] Regensburg, 1936. See also *The Good News and Its Proclamation* (synopsis translation of Die *Frohbotschaft*) (New York, 1961).

[49] Innsbruck-Vienna-Munich, 1963. Though this book is only a revision of the preceding one, it points up how much theology was discussed and elaborated from 1936 to today.

[50] E. Kappler, *Die Verkündigungstheologie* (Freiburg, 1949) contains a good bibliography of the question. See also "Saggio bibliografico sulla teologia della predicazione," *La Scuola cattolica*, 78 (1950), 350–356. Even more up to date is *XV Semana Espanola de Teologia*, pp. 387–409, published by the Francisco Suarez Institute in Madrid in 1956. In his book, *Predicacion viviente ad dia* (Madrid, 1956) A. Avelino Esteban Romero has written a critique of the controversy. A short summary was given recently by A. de Villalmonte, *La teologia kerygmatica* (Barcelona, 1963).

versy may be considered closed since the last intervention of Jung-mann.[51] We mention it only to show what great influence the polemic had upon the genesis of the problem of preaching.

The fundamental idea of the book is well known. In the many years of his pastorate in the Tyrol, Father Jungmann had occasion to analyze the Christian life of many faithful and found this life lacking in joy and enthusiasm. "For many," he wrote, "Christianity is not the Good News joyfully accepted, but a heavy law to which one submits to escape damnation."[52] The faithful are especially lacking in "a sense of unity, a view of the whole, a certain compre-hension of the wonderful message of divine grace. All they retain of Christian doctrine is a number of dogmas and moral precepts, menaces and promises, uses and rites, tasks and duties which are imposed on the unhappy Catholics, while the non-Catholics enjoy freedom."[53]

The Innsbruck theologian attributed to preaching a major share in the blame for this state of things. The faithful actually live the kind of Faith they read about in their catechisms and hear in their Sunday sermons. If the result is an anemic and fragmented Faith, it must, in part at least, be the fault of the manner in which the Faith is proposed by catechists and preachers.

Going even further, Jungmann lays the fault at the door of the-ology as it is taught in seminaries. The preachers pass on to the people the religion they have learned during the years of their formation. It is, therefore, theology itself which has to answer for the lifeless spirituality of so many Christians in our times. Preoc-cupied with historical or polemical problems, or with the specula-tive aspect of Revelation, theology has neglected its very pastoral and kerygmatic aspect. This has become obvious in preaching, which has long been considered a vulgarization of theological tracts. When we compare a catechism based on such a concept with the presentation of the Faith as it was done in Christian antiquity, we immediately note the difference. "On one hand, a simple message, a graphic picture; on the other, a complicated

---

[51] J. A. Jungmann, "Kerygmatic Theology," *Handing On the Faith* (New York, 1959), pp. 398–405.

[52] J. A. Jungmann, *Die Frohbotschaft*, p. 7.

[53] J. A. Jungmann, "Le probléme du message à transmettre ou le prob-leme kerygmatique," *Lumen Vitae*, 5 (1950), 272. The article may be con-sidered a synopsis of the book made by the author himself.

edifice of concepts, divisions and distinctions."[54]

Proceeding from these premises, the author concluded that preaching should not be a vulgarization of theology but the announcement of the kerygma, that is, of the Gospel, the Good News: "Here is the basic difference between preaching and theology. Theology serves knowledge, above all; it investigates religious reality to the extreme limits of the known (verum), and strives to obtain the smallest piece of truth that can be known without any reference to the importance this may have for life. In contrast to this, preaching is entirely oriented towards life and therefore considers religious truth as the motivating aim for our efforts (bonum)."[55] These words make a neat distinction between theology and preaching. Whereas the former seeks to understand, systematize and defend the Word of God in the theoretical concern of men, the latter announces the message of salvation, which is not "knowledge but life, not theology but sanctity."[56]

While Jungmann himself never went beyond this, but only pointed to the necessity for preachers to be prepared adequately for their ministry, other theologians at Innsbruck continued to clamor for a legitimate theology of preaching (*Verkündigungstheologie*) which should be different from a strictly scientific one. They seek to justify their demand by means of Scholastic ontology.[57]

The reaction of the theologians

Jungmann's ideas, and even more those of other kerygmatists, caused a controversy which turned out to be very fruitful. For the first time in our days theologians addressed themselves with great interest to the question of preaching.

The reaction of scholars to this attempt to formulate a theology of preaching different from the scientific one is well known. Many of them expressed their opposition in unmistakable terms. They declared either that this would be a definite break between theology and life, or that it would open the way to subjectivism, or

---

[54] J. A. Jungmann, *Die Frohbotschaft*, p. 53.

[55] *Ibid.*, p. 60.

[56] *Ibid.*, p. 61.

[57] Among the best known people in this attempt were Fathers Hugo Rahner, Lotz, and Dander. A presentation of their doctrines can be found in the works of Kappler and Avelino cited above.

that it would bring an imbalance between the emotional and the intellectual element, or that it would find an outlet in irrationalism. The latest reactions are more moderate: the attempt has been termed "not necessary."[58]

But even though there was unanimity of dissent with regard to a double theology, there was also unanimity of consensus in admitting the existence of a kerygmatic and pastoral dimension in theology. If theology had until now paid little attention to the problems of Christian life, the fault lay not with theology's nature, but with the polemics which theologians had to endure. Theology is the science of Revelation, of a reality which by its very nature is regulated by faith and the supernatural life. "Every scientific theology," says Schmaus, "must in some way also be a theology of preaching unless it wants to run the risk of ceasing to be scientific theology."[59]

These reactions may seem negative with regard to Jungmann. But they underlined the fundamental idea that he expressed, that theology must not lose interest in the problems of preaching. In a reply to Schmaus he says: "Theology, as Schmaus says, must shake off its hardening of the arteries, must plant itself firmly on the soil of history, of the history of salvation which puts us in touch with the historical Christ, dead, risen, and glorified. In this way Schmaus requests also a Christocentric structure for scientific theology: he introduces Christ into the definition of theology and assigns to it as its object not 'God in Himself,' but God 'such as He has put Himself within our range in Christ, and in this divine disposal He is continued and realized through the ages in the Church.' " Such a concept of theology corresponds, by and large, to what one would expect from a theology of preaching. Hence, we can, it seems to me, forget the appellative.[60] With these words the author has given the whole controversy a new dimension and brought it back to its starting point, that is, that there must be a concrete, pastoral, Christocentric dimension in theology, open to the questions of Christian life.[61]

[58] Avelino, *Predicaccion viviente al dia,* p. 378.

[59] Schmaus, *Katholische Dogmatik* (Munich, 1962), vol. II, Preface.

[60] J. A. Jungmann, *Handing On the Faith,* p. 401.

[61] Modern theology takes its bearing more and more from the story of salvation. A work which indicates this direction is *Il Creatore,* 2nd ed. (Florence, 1962) by Fathers Alszeghy and Flick.

A theology of preaching

But there is another conclusion to be drawn from all this controversy, and that is the necessity for theological reflection on the nature of preaching, for itself and in the story of salvation. A crisis in a reality so basic to Christian life cannot be overcome without knowing what it is. That the crisis was able to assume such proportions that even priests do not hesitate to label preaching an outmoded means, indicates that nobody knows precisely what preaching is, what its place is in the development of faith, what is its content and intent, and what relationship exists between the message and the hearer of the message.

If one wishes to overcome this crisis, the first step to a solution would be a theology of preaching. The first to say so was Jungmann in the work just cited," In questions of great importance there is nothing more practical than a good theory, a reliable orientation, to find the right ways."[62] Since then, the expression "theology of preaching" has become a household word among theologians. In enumerating all the difficulties in which present-day preaching finds itself, Father Hitz writes, "It is therefore necessary to have a theological view of preaching and its major needs, as revealed by the Word of God."[63] Schlier is even more to the point: "The crisis of preaching has not come about through external or personal difficulties, or through insufficient methodology, but mostly because no one is aware any longer of what happens in preaching. This depends also on the lack of a theology of the word of salvation, and of the word in general, which is making itself felt more and more."[64] According to Hamer the crisis cannot be overcome until we arrive at "a clear vision of the function of God's Word in His divine plan."[65] He also asserts that the principal preoccupation of the scholars should be not the technique of the word or its adaptation, but a reply to the question, "What is the Word of God? What function has it in the Church and in the world?" And he concludes. "Only Scripture, the magisterium and theology hold an answer to these and can show . . . the truth of the Apostle's

[62] J. A. Jungmann, *Die Frohbotschaft*, p. vii.

[63] Hitz, "Théologie et Catèchèse," *Nouvelle Revue Théologique*, **77** (1955), 922.

[64] H. Schlier, *Wort Gottes*, p. 11.

[65] J. Hamer, "La crise de la prédication," *Le Revue Nouvelle*, 29 (1959), 146.

word: 'Woe is me if I do not spread the Gospel!' "[66]

Such a theology does not yet exist in complete synthesis. It was not until a few decades ago that preaching had been considered too obvious and elementary to interest theological thought. What happened to Revelation also happened to it. The former is a fundamental fact of the supernatural order, a basic concept of theology. And yet, until the recent publication by Father Latourelle[67] there was no systematic and profound theological reflection on its intimate nature.

The same can be said for preaching, which is Revelation in transmission. It has always been an object of study, but what interested scholars was its formal aspect, its practical problems, its methodology, in short, the "how" of preaching. This has given rise to a considerable number of tracts on sacred eloquence destined to prepare priests for the ministry of the word.[68] In these tracts theology is presupposed. It seemed unnecessary to support preaching with theology, since everybody knew, or seemed to know, what preaching is. What had to be learned and taught was how to preach, and to this end the authors of the tracts were content to follow St. Augustine, who treats this topic in the fourth book of his *De doctrina christiana*. However, under the impetus of the facts mentioned above, the theological aspect of preaching has come more and more to the fore. This came about especially in connection with the relationship of preaching and sacrament, which has occupied Scheeben[69] and Kuhn.[70] Today the question is of great immediacy, and we find it treated a bit by everybody, Söhngen, Schmaus, Betz and Schillebeeckx among them.[71]

The first essays

Though the problem of preaching is not yet clearly outlined, there has been no dearth of attempts at a synthesis. The first was

---

[66] *Ibid.*, p. 147.

[67] R. Latourelle, *Théologie de la Révélation* (Paris, 1963).

[68] Among others G. Zocchi, *La predicazione, Vizi e Rimedi* (Siena, 1970); A. G. Sertillanges, *L'orateur chrétien* (Juvisy, 1930); L. Paquet, *Cours d'eloquence sacrée* (Quebec, 1925).

[69] W. Bartz, "Verkündigung und Sakrament im Kirchenbegriff Scheebens," *Theologie und Seelsorge*, 4 (1944), 184 ff.

[70] J. Kuhn, "Zur Lehre von dem Worte Gottes und den Sakramenten," *Theologische Quartalschrift*, 37 (1855), 3–57.

[71] We shall speak more about these theologians and their works in Chapter VII.

made by Soiron in 1943.[72] In the first two parts of his work Soiron gives us a theology of the Word of God and its transmission, while in the other two parts he treats the problem of the listener and the preacher according to St. Bonaventure's theology and in view of what Protestant theologians had already written on this theme. The work might be considered a summation—even though somewhat uncertain in view of the state of research twenty years ago—of the theological and practical elements of preaching. The merit of Soiron's work was the statement and the theological proof—so soon after Jungmann—that preaching was the announcement of salvation history, a history centered entirely on the person of Christ. The carefully chosen and well-developed examples showed how the preacher could present the doctrine of the Church in a more concrete and pastoral perspective.

More recently other articles have filled a need to which the publication of Soiron's work called attention. P. O. Semmelroth, already mentioned, wrote probably the most compelling book,[73] though his attention is focused largely on the undoubtedly important topic of efficacy. The work falls into two parts: in the first the author gives us a sample of a theology of the Word of God, which he traces from the heart of the Trinity to its communication to the soul in grace; he then discusses its efficacy. It is a work full of new concepts, original in development, but it skips over all the problems which do not fit in with the line of thought pursued by the author. Semmelroth writes in the German tradition, for which the theology of preaching consists in determining the effectiveness of the word in relation to the effectiveness of the sacraments. Other questions have less importance. Thus, Semmelroth pays little attention to the subject and the object of preaching, which to our mind are indispensable for the understanding of this very effectiveness.

Another attempt at synthesis was undertaken by P. A. Günthör, O.S.B.[74] He too pays much attention to the effectiveness of preaching, an approach which comes close to Semmelroth, but he re-

[72] Th. Soiron, O.F.M., *Die Verkündigung des Wortes Gottes* (Freiburg, 1943).

[73] P. O. Semmelroth, *Wirkendes Wort. Zur Theologie der Verkündigung* (Frankfurt, 1962).

[74] Anselm Günthör, O.S.B., *Die Predigt. Theoretische und Praktische Wegweisung* (Freiburg i.B., 1963).

serves a long chapter to the problem of the aims of preaching, especially to its object, in which he agrees with the Christocentrism of present theology. A considerable portion of the volume is given over to Sunday preaching and to popular mission preaching. The volume is a happy blend of conceptual and formal elements of preaching and is useful both to theologians and to pastors.

In a short volume Sandro Maggiolini[75] has likewise treated the object, the sources, the aim and the effectiveness of preaching, and he sums up what has been written so far on this topic. The same can be said about P. R. Spiazzi's book,[76] which is useful for everybody who is interested in the history of preaching and catechesis. Finally, we shall mention the short resumés of Regan[77] and Kampmann.[78]

Our intention

We wish to continue this work by endeavoring to clarify the problematic in those points which still remain obscure. We propose to do this by projecting a research which, though clinging to the elements already acquired, will tend, perhaps, to develop them and to indicate new paths to tread.

We intend to examine preaching in its function in the divine plan of salvation and in itself while we leave to another study still to be made the examination of the forms which it may adopt in its dynamics.

What we want to do is to make a contribution to the understanding of the Word of God as it is transmitted. This will differ from the contribution by Father Latourelle, to whom we are very grateful. By examining one of the two branches of the problem, he has made our own research easier.

---

[75] *La predicazione nella vita della Chiesa. Lineamenti di riflessione pastorale sul problema della proclamazione della parola di Dio* (Brescia, 1961).

[76] Raimondo Spiazzi, O.P., *Scientia salutis* (Rome, 1963).

[77] Augustin Regan, "The Word of God and the Ministry of Preaching," *Studia Moralia* (Rome, 1963), vol. I, pp. 389–449.

[78] Theodor Kampmann, "Das Wesen der christlichen Predigt," *Liturgie, Gestalt und Vollzug*, ed. Walter Dürig (Munich, 1963), pp. 154–170.

CHAPTER I

The Object of Preaching

I N ORDER to know what preaching is, we have first to determine its object, or content. What is being preached? This may seem too general a question, because it could bring one to question what Christianity is; nevertheless, it must be discussed because it is precisely this object which constitutes the prime characteristic of preaching and makes it a special form of communication.

For an answer to the problem we must first see what the object of preaching was in the time of the Apostles, for preaching in all its forms is but a continuation and prolongation of the Church of the Apostles. The New Testament uses several expressions superficially different from each other in this respect. The most common among them are *Kingdom of God, Word of God, Gospel* and *Mystery*. The first occurs most frequently in the Synoptic Gospels, the last in St. Paul, and the others in the Book of Acts and in the Gospels. In order to determine the object of preaching, we must first determine meanings of these formulae.

The Kingdom of God

The Kingdom of God is the object of Christ's preaching. He began His public ministry with its proclamation, "The time is fulfilled, and the kingdom of God is at hand. Repent and believe in the gospel" (Mark 1:14–14).Traveling through Galilee and teaching in the synagogues, Christ concentrated on preaching "the gospel of the kingdom" (Matt. 4:23). When He sent His disciples forth to preach during the time of His own public career, He told them to say, "The kingdom of heaven is at hand!" (Matt. 10:7). This is the kingdom of which He speaks in all His sermons, outlining its nature in the parables and indicating the inner disposition required of those who would enter it. He discusses it again in the Sermon on the Mount, revealing its external and social elements.

The Old Testament concludes with the proclamation of the Kingdom of God (Luke 11:20); the prophecies are fulfilled (Luke 7:22–23), and the dominion of the Devil is weakened (Luke 11:20). This kingdom, therefore, is a reality intimately linked to Christ. If it is already in existence, it is because Jesus has cast out the devils (Matt. 12:28). If the Messiah has already come, it is because Jesus in His actions has fulfilled the signs the Prophets foretold would pertain to the Messiah (Luke 7:22). If the disciples are glorified, it is because they have seen what the Prophets would have liked to see (Luke 10:23–24).

We should state here that the Kingdom of God is Jesus Himself, whose coming and whose actions have initiated a new relationship between God and man, a new alliance destined to replace that of Sinai. This identification appears evident in various Gospel texts. "And everyone who has left house, or brothers, or sisters, or father, or mother, or wife, or children, or lands, for my name's sake, shall receive a hundredfold, and shall possess life everlasting" (Matt. 19:29). Luke renders the text as follows: "Amen I say to you, there is no one who has left home, or parents, or brothers, or wife, or children, for the sake of the kingdom of God, who shall not receive much more in the present time, and in the age to come life everlasting." (Luke 18:29–30). Jesus and the Kingdom of God are one and the same thing: there is no difference between renouncing everything one has for the sake of Christ or for the sake of the Kingdom of Heaven. In another place Jesus compares the Kingdom of God to ten virgins, some foolish, others prudent, who go to meet the bridegroom with their lamps lighted (Matt. 25:1–13). Luke explains that the bridegroom whom one must always expect is the Son of Man, who may arrive at the moment when He is least expected (Luke 12:35–36).

This identification makes it clear why the person of Jesus is the focal point of the Gospel narrative: because by preaching the

Kingdom of God, Jesus invites men to follow Him and take up their own crosses (Matt. 16:24), because He calls blessed those who suffer persecution for His sake (Matt. 5:11) and are not scandalized in Him (Matt. 11:6), and because he promises to call to eternal life those who, seeing Him in the poor, have helped them, and to exclude those who have refused to do so (Matt. 25:34–46).

The object of Jesus' preaching is, therefore, Himself in His person.[1] An examination of the next expression will lead us to the same conclusion.

The Word of God

The expression *Word of God* is widely used in the Old Testament. According to Grether's statistics[2] it occurs 242 times if we include 10 uncertain texts. As many scholars have acknowledged,[3] the ancient Oriental peoples were unlike the Greeks in this respect. For the Greeks the "word" indicated the intelligible element of an object, the idea of which the intelligence can grasp as it strives to penetrate the nature of things. The Orientals, on the contrary, see in the "word" an expression of the will more than of the intelligence; it indicates a fact rather than an idea, a command rather

[1] It is generally admitted by scholars that the person of Jesus is at the center of the Kingdom of God preached by Him. See, among others, R. Schnackenburg, *Gottes Herrschaft und Reich*, (Freiburg, 1959), p. 49 ss.; Déville-Grelot in *Vocabulaire de théologie biblique* (Paris, 1962), col. 953–956, spec. col. 956; J. Alfaro, *Fides, Spes, Caritas. Adnotationes in tractatum de virtutibus theologicis* (Rome, 1963), p. 132 ss.

[2] O. Grether, *Name und Wort Gottes im A.T.* (Giessen, 1934), p. 64 ff.

[3] The theme is common among scholars concerned with the Word of God who try to determine it in the light of ancient culture both Greek and oriental. See, among others, L. Dürr, *Die Wertung des göttlichen Wortes im A.T. und im antiken Orient* (Leipzig, 1938); H. Ringgren, *Word and Wisdom*, (Lund, 1947); W. Eichrodt, *Theologie des A.T.* (Berlin, 1948), pp. 32–38; B. Barsotti, *Il mistero cristiano e la parola di Dio* (Florence, 1953), pp. 9–35; P. Van Imschoot, *Théologie de l'A.T.* (Tournai, 1954), vol. I, pp. 200–227; E. Jacob, *Théologie de l'A.T.* (Neuchatel-Paris, 1955), pp. 103–109; J. L. McKenzie, "The Word of God in the Old Testament," *Theological Studies*, 21 (1960), 183–206; H. Schlier, *Wort Gottes* (Würzburg, 1958); R. Bultmann, "Der Begriff des Wortes Gottes im N.T.," *Glauben und Verstehen*, I (Tübingen, 1958), pp. 268–293. See also the dictionary articles of C. Procksch in *Kittel*, IV, pp. 89–140; of Robert in *Supplement au Dictionnaire de la Bible*, V, pp. 425–465; and Feuillet-Grelot in *Vocabulaire de Théologie Biblique*, col. 750–60.

than an instruction. It is a means of action. Through the word God creates the world (Gen. 1; Psalm 32(33):6); through the word He creates the Law which He imposes upon His people, and through the word He directs history toward the chosen objects.[4] The word is essentially dynamic; it possesses a particular force which cannot be halted once it has been pronounced. Especially is this true in the case of benediction or malediction.[5]

The dynamism of the word comes from its close relationship to the person. "The Hebrew," says Schillebeeckx, "does not distinguish between the word and the person who speaks. The word is a mode of the person himself. The strength of the word is the strength of the person who pronounces it; hence the potency of the Word of God."[6] As presented in the Old Testament, the Word of God is God Himself insofar as He acts outside Himself, insofar as He creates and turns to man by notifying him of His will.[7] The word speaks and sets up a reality; it is dianoetic as well as dynamic. McKenzie says that it "invests a thing with intelligibility and manifests the character of him who speaks."[8] For Mowinkel[9] the word is, so to speak, "God's being in His Activity *ad extra*. In its proper nature, however, the word is directed to something or somebody; it is communication and tries to arrange a meeting between him who speaks and him who listens."[10]

The New Testament continues the meaning of the Old. The Word of God is the Verb, the Second Person of the Trinity, which becomes Man and dwells among us (1 John 1:14). By expressing Himself, the Father generates the Son, for whom He creates

[4] Jacob, *op. cit.,* p. 106; Barsotti, *op. cit.,* p. 10; Van Imschoot, *op. cit.,* 204.

[5] Jacob, *op. cit.,* p. 103. The dynamism of the word also appears in its etymology, on which the scholars, however, do not agree. According to Jacobs, *dabar* means "the forward projection of what is behind, that is, the passage to the act from what is in the heart" (p. 104). Roberts thinks that *dabar* has a double root, one of which means "speak"; the other, "to be behind" (*art. cit.,* col. 442).

[6] "Parole et sacrement dans l'Eglise," *Lumière et Vie,* 46 (1960), 25.

[7] Bultmann, *op. cit.,* p. 271.

[8] J. L. McKenzie, *op. cit.,* p. 205.

[9] Mowinkel, *The Old Testament as Word of God* (New York, 1952), p. 42.

[10] Says Bultmann: "Und zwar ist das Wort gesprechen zu . . . es ist *Anrede,* nicht Urteil im Sinn der Logik; und als Wort Gottes ist es Befehl." *Op. cit.,* p. 269.

everything (John 1:3). Things are substantiated words of God.[11] Rightly, then, can the New Testament use the expression *Word of the Lord* alongside *Word of God,* or simply *the Word.* These three expressions occur in the New Testament seventy-eight times: the first forty times, the second thirty, and the third eight.[12] They are especially frequent in the Acts of the Apostles, where they indicate the content of apostolic preaching. Thus, the Acts state that "many of those who had heard the Word believed" (Acts 4:4), that the Apostles announced the Word of God with courage (Acts 4:31), and that Paul and Barnabas evangelized the Word of the Lord (Acts 15:35). In his letters St. Paul also speaks of proclaiming the Word (1 Thess. 1:6), that the Thessalonians had accepted not as the word of men, but as the *Word of God* (1 Thess. 2:13). The Apostle also uses the formula of *Word of the Lord* (1 Thess. 1:18), or *Word of Christ* (Rom. 10:17).

But what did the Apostles mean when they declared they would preach the *Word,* or the *Word of God,* or the *Word of the Lord?*

In the Johannine Gospel, especially in the prologue, the Word is identified with the Incarnate Word. Jesus is the Word. The whole Gospel's aim is to show that Jesus is the Word. As Bultmann says, "All his action is one with the word: His works are his words and His words are his works."[13] And Jesus indeed says, "He who rejects me, and does not accept my words, has one to condemn him" (John 12:48). Instead we read, "Amen, amen, I say to you, he who hears my word, and believes him who sent me, has life everlasting, and does not come to judgment, but has passed from death to life" (John 5:24). It is one and the same thing to reject Christ and not to believe in His words; the reverse is likewise true: to listen to His words and to believe in Him who sent Him mean essentially the same thing. Since Jesus is the life (John 14:6), so also are His words (John 6:64); as He judges (John 8:15), so does His word judge (John 12:48).[14] In his very first letter John declares that he announces the word of "life," which he has seen with his own eyes and touched with his own hands (John 1:1–4), the word is the Word of Christ.

---

[11] For Mowinkel the Incarnation of the Word is the novelty of the New Testament compared to the Old. *Op. cit.,* pp. 43–44.

[12] *Kittel,* IV, p. 115 (In this compilation the Johannine writings [*ibid,* 116, note 13] are not included.)

[13] Bultmann, *op. cit.,* p. 291.

[14] *Ibid.*

We must say the same for the Synoptic Gospels. For them God's Word is God's will inasmuch as the word demands its fulfillment in the will. This we can deduce by comparing two texts. Whereas Mark says, "Behold my mother and my brethren. For whoever does the will of God, he is my brother and sister and mother" (Mark 3:35), St. Luke says, "My mother and my brethren are they who hear the word of God, and act upon it" (Luke 8:21). The Word of God, therefore, is the will of God, God Himself as He demands obedience from man. The same goes for the Word of Christ. "For whoever is ashamed of me and of my words in this adulterous and sinful generation, of him will the Son of Man also be ashamed when he comes, with the holy angels in the glory of his Father" (Mark 8:38). And St. Luke says: "And I say to you, everyone who acknowledged me before men, him will the Son of Man also acknowledge before the angels of God. But, whoever disowns me before men will be disowned before the angels of God" (Luke 12:8). As will be seen, the Word of Jesus is one and the same thing as His person.

Therefore, the object and content of preaching is Christ, the Word in which the Father expresses Himself and communicates His will to man. Rightfully, then, can the Book of Acts say that instead of the Word of God Christ Himself (Acts 8:5), or Jesus Himself (Acts 9:20),[15] should be preached.

The Gospel

The term "gospel" ($\epsilon\dot{v}\alpha\gamma\gamma\acute{\epsilon}\lambda\iota o\nu$) is often used in the New Testament to indicate the object of apostolic preaching.[16] It is called "the gospel of God" (1 Thess. 2:2–8,9; 2 Cor. 15, 16 passim), "gospel of Christ" (1 Thess. 3:2; 2 Cor. 9:13; Gal. 1:17 ff.), "our gospel" (1 Thess. 1:5), "my gospel" (Rom. 2:16 and 16:25), "gospel of the glory of Christ" (2 Cor. 4:4), "gospel of peace" (Eph. 6:15), "word of the gospel truth" (Col. 1:6), "gospel of the glory of the blessed God" (1 Tim. 1:11), or simply "the gospel" (1 Thess. 2:4; 1 Cor. 4:15, 9:18; Gal. 2:5, 14; 2 Tim. 1:8 ff.).

[15] All the scholars on the subject arrive at these conclusions. See R. Asting, *Die Verkündigung des Wortes Gottes im Urchristentum* (Stuttgart, 1939), pp. 295–296. The same conclusion in *Kittel*, IV, p. 121 ff.

[16] For meaning and etymology of the word "gospel" see Mollat's article in *Dictionnaire de spiritualité*, 4, col. 1745–1762. See also Friederich in *Kittel*, II, pp. 718–735.

In the Synoptic Gospels (Mark 1:15; Matt. 4:17, 9:35), as well as in the Acts, the content comprises the coming of the Kingdom of God, preached by Philip the Deacon in Samaria (Acts 8:12) and by Paul the Apostle in Asia Minor (Acts 14:21) and in Rome (Acts 28:23). But this content is always the good news of Jesus (Acts 8:35). For St. Paul "the gospel of God" which he spreads is always that regarding "his Son, Jesus Christ, our Lord, through whom we have received the grace of apostleship" (Rom. 1:2–5). Hence, as often as the object of the verb "evangelize" (εὐαγγελίζομαι) is God or the Kingdom of God (Luke 4:43, 8:1, 16:16; Acts 8:12, 14:15), it is even more often Christ or some aspect of His mystery or His life. Thus the Apostles evangelize "Jesus" (Acts 8:35), "Jesus as the Christ" (Acts 5:42), "the Lord Jesus" (Acts 11:20), "the word of the Lord" (Acts 15:35), "peace through Jesus Christ (who is Lord of all)" (Acts 10:36), the "riches of Christ" (Eph. 3:8), "Jesus and the resurrection" (Acts 17:18), "the cross of Christ" (1 Cor. 1:17). This proof acquires greater importance when we examine the objects of the other words which have some relationship with (εὐαγγελίζομαι). Hayward has compiled a very accurate list of these in his thesis. From it we see that with the exception of the verbs which have a testimonial as their object, Christ forms the object twice in the Gospels and forty-seven times in the preaching of the Apostles, God twenty times in the Gospels and twenty-four times in the rest of the New Testament, and on seven occasions God and Christ are found together in the same sentence.[17]

The content of the Gospel, therefore, is a person, God in Christ, or simply Christ in whom God reveals Himself and saves: from Him comes the message of salvation. To know Christ means to know God (John 14:20). The knowledge of Christ and of the Father is inseparable; in it consists the eternal life (John 17:3).

The *Gospel* as the object of the Apostles' preaching is identical with the *Word of God*. For St. Paul the Gospel which he has preached to the Thessalonians (1 Thess. 1:5) is the *word* which they have received in the midst of great tribulations (1 Thess.

[17] The verbs examined by Hayward are derived from εὐαγγελίζω, κηρύσσω, παραδίδωμι, διδάσκω. His unpublished thesis is called *God and Christ: Duality and Synthesis in the Faith of the New Testament* (see p. 144).

1:6). In his Epistles to the Ephesians he is even more explicit: "And in him you too, when you had heard the word of truth, the good news of your salvation and believed in it, were sealed with the Holy Spirit of the promise" (Eph. 1:13). Again, the Gospel is identical with the Kingdom of God. Matthew tells us that Christ announced "the gospel of the kingdom" (Matt. 4:23).

Examination of the three terms thus far has brought us to the same conclusion: the object and content of the preaching of Jesus and of the Apostles is the person of Christ.[18]

The mystery

The three expressions examined up to now become more significant when connected with the notion of mystery which St. Paul uses to illuminate his preaching. This expression is not found so frequently but it is more meaningful, and it helps us to place preaching in the role which it fulfills in the history of salvation. This is why we wish to give it special attention here.[19] Dr. Deden, who in 1936 wrote a still-valid article, on the Pauline mystery,[20] tells us that the term occurs twenty times in the Epistles of the Apostle. In six cases St. Paul speaks of a great mystery which God has revealed to him and which he, in turn, is obliged to proclaim:

[18] To show this identity, R. Hardawirjana establishes in his thesis an interesting comparison between the verb forms relating to preaching and its content. From this it appears that the same verbs have as complement either logos or evangelion (*Notio praedicationis in epistolis paolinis*, p. 93).

[19] There is an enormous literature on the Pauline mystery. We want to point out only a few: D. Deden, "Le mystère paulinien," *Ephemerides Theologicae Lovanienses,* 13 (1936), 405–422; K. Prümm, "Mysterion von Paulus bis Origenes," *Zeitschrift für Katholische Theologie,* 61 (1937), 391–425; C. Spicq, *Saint Paul, Les epitres pastorales* (Paris, 1948), esp. c. V, pp. 116–26; L. Cerfaux, *La Théologie de l'Eglise suivant Saint Paul* (Paris, 1948), pp. 229–267; J. T. Trinidad, "The mystery hidden in God," *Biblica,* 31 (1950), 1–26; Prümm, "Zur Phaenomenologie des Paulinischen Mysterium und dessen seelische Aufnahme, Eine Uebersicht," *Biblica,* 37 (1956), 135–161; R. E. Brown, "The semitic background in the New Testament 'Mysterion'," *Biblica,* 39 (1958), 426–484; J. Coppens, "Le mystère dans la theologie paulinienne et ses parallèles Qumraniens," *Recherches Bibliques V,* (Bruges, 1960). See also the encyclopedia articles: G. Borkmann, art. "Mysterion" in *Kittel,* IV, pp. 809–834; Prümm, art. "Mystères," *Supplement au Dictionnaire de la Bible,* VI, fasc. 30, 10–225; Rigaux-Grelot, art. "Mystère," *Vocabulaire de la Théologie biblique,* col. 664–670.

[20] Deden, *art. cit.,* 406, an article which has been our inspiration.

in 1 Cor. 2:7; in Rom. 16:25–26; in Col. 1:26–27; and in Eph. 1:8–10; 3:3–7; 3:8–12.[21]

The meaning of the word "mystery" has been an object of heated dispute among scholars in recent decades, but for us there is no need to advert to that.[22] One point, however, emerges clearly from these discussions: the Pauline mystery is the plan of salvation, hidden in God in the beginning and then revealed and proclaimed. The Apostle distinguishes three phases:

(1) The mystery of God. From all eternity God conceives a plan, a design for our glory (1 Cor. 2:7), but He keeps it hidden from the "rulers of this world" (1 Cor. 2:8), from the angels (Eph. 3:10), as well as from men (Eph. 3:5). But God so arranges this plan that He can reveal it at a predetermined moment which St. Paul calls "the fullness of the times" (Eph. 1:10).

(2) The mystery revealed. In the fullness of the times God reveals His plan through the Spirit (1 Cor. 2:4–5), first obliquely in the Old Testament, then more clearly in the New Testament. The revelation is made to the Apostles and the Prophets (Eph. 3:5), and also to the Principalities and Powers of Heaven (Eph. 3:10). On St. Paul was bestowed a special privilege, which concerned the call of the Gentiles to the Faith (Eph. 3:8–9).

(3) The mystery proclaimed. The revelation of the mystery, of course, precedes its proclamation, at which time it is brought to the attention of men. This latter phase is brought about by means of the apostolic preaching (Titus 1:1–3). Thus, the "mystery of worship," as St. Paul calls it, is a vision seen by the angels and preached to the Gentiles: Christ in time, accepted in faith; Christ in eternity, taken up in glory (1 Tim. 3:16).

For St. Paul the mystery is not something hidden, or is it something reserved to a few initiates, but it is meant to be widely spread, to be proclaimed before angels and men, Jews and Gentiles. It is called *mystery* because it was revealed not at conception, but only after long preparation when men were ready to receive it.

The content of the mystery

What interests us most is the object, or the content, of the mystery. What does the plan of salvation mean?

---

[21] *Ibid.*, 406.

[22] T. Filthaut makes a clear exposition of these discussions in *Die Kontroverse über die Mysterienlehre* (Warendorf, 1947).

St. Paul expresses himself in various ways. The content of the mystery is the participation in the divine good already promised by Isaias (Isa. 64:3), a good that is proper to the Messianic times, that is, to the eschatological good designated in theology by the name "everlasting life" (1 Cor. 2:7–10). Or it is the calling of the Gentiles to participate in this good (Rom. 16:25–27; also Eph. 3:6–8). In the Epistle to the Colossians the reconciliation of mankind through the blood of Christ is declared the object of the mystery (Col. 1:20 and 1:26). In Christ, enmity among men and enmity of men for God and the celestial powers, the result of original sin, are dissolved and harmony is re-established. The same concept appears under slightly different form in the Epistle to the Ephesians. The mystery is "to re-establish all things in Christ, both those in the heavens and those on the earth" (Eph. 1:10). This means to re-establish in the universe the unity which was destroyed by original sin, to draw all things on earth and in heaven under a single head, to a single center which is Christ.

These terms are basically the same: the content of the mystery is Christ. He it is who shows how to partake of the divine good (1 Cor. 2:7–10), and who also does it for the Gentiles (Rom. 16:26); He it is who restores the harmony and unity of all things which were destroyed by original sin. The Epistle to the Colossians is even more explicit in identifying the mystery with Christ. St. Paul speaks of the mystery of God the Father and of Jesus Christ "in whom are hidden all the treasures of wisdom and knowledge" (Col. 2:2–3). He has been commanded by God to make known to us the mystery of his will (Eph. 1:9), and he has put that plan into action through Christ (Col. 1:27).[23]

Because Christ is the object of the mystery and thus of the Pauline preaching, would it be possible for the Apostle to summarize it all by saying that he "might preach him among the Gentiles?" (Gal. 1:16), or preach "Jesus Christ as Lord" (2 Cor. 4:5), or simply preach "Christ Jesus" (Col. 2:2) without knowing anything "except Jesus Christ" (1 Cor. 2:2), nor wanting anything except Christ dwelling in the hearts of his listeners through faith, so that they will be filled with all the fullness God can give (Eph. 3:17–19).

It is clear, therefore, that the expressions *Kingdom of God, Word of God, Gospel,* and *mystery* mean the same thing: the

[23] Deden, *art. cit.,* p. 406.

object and the content of apostolic preaching is Christ. They complete and define each other in turn: the Apostles preach Christ, that Word which God expresses in Himself from the beginning of time and which at a definite moment in history was made flesh. This Word is the Good News, the Gospel which God sends forth to all men in the fullness of time so as to establish with them a kingdom and a community of salvation. Thus can St. Paul properly identify the mystery with the *Word* of God (Col. 1:25) and with the Gospel (Eph. 6:19).

The paschal Christ

That Christ who is the object of the Word of God, of the Gospel, and of the mystery, is essentially the paschal Christ, dead but risen from the dead. The Acts testifies to this on every plane.[24] It is the Christ who died and arose from the dead that St. Peter preaches in his sermons to the people of Jerusalem at Pentecost (Acts 2:22–36), to the multitude after the healing of the man who was lame (Acts 3:13–15), before the rulers and elders (Acts 4:10; 5:30–3), and before Cornelius (Acts 10:39–40). It is the paschal Christ whom St. Paul preaches to the Jews of Pisidian Antioch (Acts 13:27–30) and to the Gentiles of Athens (Acts 17:31).

St. Paul does the same thing in those evangelizing sermons wherein he synthesizes the Gospel, retaining only the fundamental facts.[25] Never does he omit the Death and Resurrection of Christ. Whenever he has to concentrate on a single fact, the Resurrection is that fact. Christ was "foreordained Son of God by an act of power in keeping with the holiness of his spirit, by his resurrection from the dead" (Rom. 1:2–5). He has risen from the dead for our justification (Rom. 4:24–25). To obtain salvation we must believe that God has raised him up from the dead (Rom. 10:8–9). Death and Resurrection form the core of the longest and most important kerygmatic passage of the Pauline Epistles (1 Cor. 15:1–11). The

---

[24] For the object of apostolic preaching in the book of The Acts see A. Rétif, *Foi au Christ et mission,* c. 4; P. Hitz, *L'annonce missionaire de l'Evangile* (Paris, 1954), Chap. 2, esp. p. 93 ff.; Y. B. Tremel, "Du kérygme des apôtres à celui d'aujourd'hui," *L'annonce de l'Evangile aujourd'hui* (Paris, 1962), p. 19 ff.

[25] For the kerygmatic passages in the letters of St. Paul see C. H. Dodd, *The Apostolic Preaching and Its Development* (London 1956), Chap. I; A. M. Hunter, *Un Seigneur, une Eglise, un salut* (Paris, 1950), esp. p. 28 in which he completes Dodd's texts with others.

Apostle confirms that if Christ had not risen from the dead, his preaching would have no content.

Hitz writes that "all the other facts of the story of salvation are grouped around the center of the paschal mystery."[26] These facts range from the first announcement of the Prophets to the final parousia, when the Lord will return on the clouds of Heaven to judge the living and the dead and thus to put an end to history. The vision of the Apostles reaches from the Old Testament to the public life of Jesus and, finally, extends even beyond this point, to where Christ sits at the right of the Father.

The meaning of Christocentrism

A theology of history that is important for preaching is implicit in the concept of mystery that is found in the Pauline Epistles. According to the Apostle all history is a complex of facts, a warp of happenings, foreordained by God and following in order, so that the Revelation and the communication of Christ may be realized. Before the Incarnation, history is directed towards Him, while after the Incarnation it streams from Him. Christ is the center and the meaning of history. Through Him man can understand the Old and the New Testaments: Christ it is who brings about their unity. The New Testament is the completion and perfection of the Old. Compared to the Old, the New Testament represents fulfillment (Gal. 4:4; Eph. 1:10), reality as compared to shadow (Heb. 10:1). The Law is a tutor unto Christ (Gal. 3:24), who has susperseded it (Rom. 10:4).

In the light of this, St. Augustine could write, "In veteri testamento est occultatio novi, in novo testamento est manifestatio veteris"[27] or that "in veteri novum latet, et in novo vetus patet."[28] The Old Testament is veiled in a manner that does not permit its

[26] These are common concepts in modern theology, in great part due to the Biblical renewal. See, among others, O. Cullmann, *Christ and Time* (Philadelphia, 1950); E. C. Rust, *The Christian Understanding of History* (London, 1947); J. Daniélou, *The Lord of History* (London-Chicago, 1958); H. Urs von Balthasar, *A Theology of History* (New York, 1963). An over-all critical look about the state of various currents in the theology of history can be found in the shrewd supplement by Alszeghy and Flick, "Teologia della Storia," *Gregorianum,* 35 (1954), 256–298.

[27] St. Augustine, *De catechizandis rudibus,* 4, 8.

[28] St. Augustine, *Quaestiones in Hept.,* 2, 73.

intimate nature to be penetrated; Christ lifts the veil and discloses its real content.

Thus, Christ is indeed the Alpha and Omega, the beginning and the end (Apoc. 1:8), He through whom all things came into being (John 1:3). St. Paul calls him "the image of the invisible God, the first born of every creature. For in him were created all things in the heavens and on the earth, things visible and things invisible, whether Thrones, or Dominations, or Principalities, or Powers. All things have been created through and unto him, and he is before all creatures, and in him all things hold together" (Col. 1:15–17). "For it has pleased God the Father that in him all his fullness should dwell" (Col. 1:19).

The history of salvation

But Christ cannot be separated from man. The mystery is not Christ contemplated separately, but "Christ in you, your hope of glory!" (Col 1:27). The mystery, or plan of God, concerns Christ in His relationship to man. The Incarnation did not take place for mysterious reasons that in God's wisdom were to remain hidden, but for our salvation. The Kingdom of God which Jesus preached, the Word which He addressed to men, is essentially a kingdom and a gospel of salvation. Christ is basically the Savior (Matt. 1:21; Luke 1:31) come to earth to save what was lost (Luke 19:10), to give life eternal (John 3:16), to give His own life as ransom for the lives of many (Matt. 20:28), to rescue us from the powers of darkness and transfer us to the heavenly kingdom (Col. 1:13), thereby making us sons by adoption (Gal. 4:6; Titus 2:11, 3:4; Rom. 1:16 ff.). In summing up Revelation, St. John could say: "And this is the testimony that God has given us, eternal life; and this life is in his Son. He who has the Son has the life. He who has not the Son has not the life" (1 John 5:11). The completeness which is Christ must be communicated to others, because it is the completeness of a head which must be shared by its members. "Again, he is the head of his body, the Church; he, who is the beginning, the first born from the dead, that in all things he may have the first place. For it has pleased God the Father that in him all his fullness should dwell and that through him he should reconcile to himself all things, whether on the earth or in the heavens, making peace through the blood of his cross" (Col 1:18–20).

Hence, history is the history not only of Christ but also of Christ the Savior, of the encounter of God in Christ and man, the history of salvation.

But what *is* salvation?

Salvation

In the Old Testament the word "save," σώζειν, as translated from the Hebrew yš' means to liberate from temporal ill or dangers (Judges 15:18; Sam. 10:19), to rescue the people from slavery (Isa. 45:17; 46:13; etc.). But this material liberation serves only as a springboard for another, more important liberation, the Messianic salvation (Isa. 33:22–23; Ezech. 36:28–29), which comprises all the gifts brought by the Messiah (Isa. 45:17; 49:6).[29] In the New Testament "σώζειν" means the Messianic salvation understood as liberation from sin and possession of the eschatological goods which God has prepared for our glory. Jesus will save His people from their sins (Matt. 1:21); God sent His Son into the world that people might find salvation through Him (John 3:17); Jesus has come to save the world, not to pass sentence on it (John 12:47); everyone who calls on the name of the Lord shall be saved (Acts 2:21). Though this salvation confers upon us the Messianic good already on this earth, it is essentially eschatological, and will find its full realization only in another life. In fact, once reconciled, says the Apostle, we shall find salvation (Rom. 5:10; 1 Cor. 3:15). Salvation will come in the day of "our Lord Jesus Christ" (Phil. 3:20). He who saves us is God, called "our Savior" (1 Tim. 1:1, 2:3). But salvation is also attributed to Jesus Christ. He is the "Savior" (Luke 2:11; Acts 5:31), the "Savior" of His mystical body (Eph. 5:23), "the Savior of the world" (John 4:42), "our Savior Jesus Christ" (2 Tim. 1:10), and also "our Lord and Savior Jesus Christ" (2 Pet. 1:11).

According to the concept implicit in these texts salvation includes, first, a negative element, preservation or liberation from danger; next, a positive element, the pursuit of a good which constitutes the end of man, the termination of all his struggles, one which will satisfy his need for happiness and eternal life; and, finally, a Savior who can grant the good in which happiness consists

---

[29] S. Lyonnet, "De notione salutis in Novo Testamento," *Verbum Domini*, 36 (1958), pp. 6–7. This article has served us as an inspiration. See also Cerfaux, "Saint Paul nous parle du salut," *Lumière et Vie*, 15 (1954), 83–112.

by removing those dangers which could prevent attainment of the end. Salvation, therefore, means that man is not self-sufficient or autonomous, that the aim of his existence does not lie within himself, that he cannot by his own efforts satisfy the need for happiness which underlies all his activities.[30] Salvation presupposes that the aim of life is outside man, outside this visible world's limits, in a beyond where happiness can be obtained. It supposes that the aim of life is in an Other, in an Absolute, in God, to whom life is directed by the law of nature and who alone can give eternal life. Therefore, human life, in order to make sense, must lean upon another, upon God. It is in God and with God that man can overcome the obstacles that arise in pursuing eternal life, and obtain the absolute good without which there is no full happiness.

The obstacles are two: death, which is the destruction of the being, the occurrence of which renders impossible the realization of happiness; and sin, which is the attempt of man to save himself by himself alone, seeking outside of God that which God alone can give. Only an absolute and eternal God can give eternal life; to find this life without Him is impossible, just as it is impossible to discover a means of vanquishing death independently of God. Salvation consists, therefore, in a life wholly oriented to God, in a union with God.

The new creature

Beyond these things which reason can comprehend, Revelation tells us that God, in order to save man, has devised a plan which goes far beyond the imaginative power of the human mind. To placate man's longing for happiness, God Himself meets man, invites him to touch Him, to participate in a dialogue which from all eternity has been carried on among the three Divine Persons, to form with Him a community of life and love. To satisfy our thirsting for happiness, God, the Supreme Good, delivers Himself into our keeping and admits us to His confidence, first in an obscure but nonetheless real way in this world, and then when death has been overcome, fully and totally in another life. All this is done through Christ, the only real mediator between God and

---

[30] The notion of salvation is fundamental to all religions. See Dhanis in *Introductio in problema Christi* (mimeographed) (Rome, 1960), p. 25 ff. with bibliography. Also A. Brunner, *Die Religion* (Freiburg, 1956), Chap. IX.

man (1 Tim. 2:5), He who through His own blood reconciled us with God after the tragedy of original sin (Col. 1:20; 2 Cor. 5:19), who admits us, as sons by adoption (Gal. 4:5), to the possession of the eschatological goods of eternal life (Titus 1:2).

Thus there is established between God and man not a simple metaphysical rapport such as exists between the relative and the absolute, but an intimate rapport such as that between father and son. To do this, God creates us anew. "If then any man is in Christ," St. Paul says, "he is a new creature: the former things have passed away; behold they are made new!" (2 Cor. 5:17). And elsewhere: "For in Christ Jesus neither circumcision nor uncircumcision but a new creation is of any account" (Gal. 6:15). Here, then, is a new being which means a new beginning, a new life. "Redemption," says Guardini, "is not only a righting of existing failures with the help of teaching and a model, or another religious recognition which corrects the one which was faulty, but an advancement of the rank of creation. It has nothing in common with what is in the world, but represents a new foundation of existence. . . . Redemption elevates the whole existence to a new beginning."[31] The Epistle to the Ephesians states, "We are created in Christ Jesus, in good works, which God has made ready beforehand. . . ." (Eph. 2:10). This creation cannot take place without that death of the old man and the birth of the new which occurs in Baptism. Through this sacrament man is clothed in Jesus Christ, justified and sanctified through truth (Eph. 4:23).

The man saved is the man who is reborn in Christ, and for whom Christ is the inspiration of his life and thought. So much so, that this man can say with St. Paul, "For to me to live is Christ" (Phil. 1:21).

Therefore, if we say with St. Paul that all history is the history of salvation, we are also saying that all historical events tend to make man aware of his condition as a creature, and of his need for the Absolute, that he may be led to anchor his life in it. And since, in the order of providence, salvation is actually offered us by Christ and in Christ, it must be said that the center of history is Christ, inasmuch as what happened before the Incarnation is the result of His coming and His Revelation, and what happened afterwards, the consequences of His proclamation and communication.

[31] R. Guardini, *L'essenza del Cristianesimo* (Brescia, 1950), p. 47.

In the so-called time of the Church, which stretches from the Ascension to the parousia, the aim of history is "the building up of the body of Christ until we all attain to the unity of the faith and of the deep knowledge of the Son of God" (Eph. 4:13). All the events of history thus make no sense unless seen in the perspective of Christ. This is truly a majestic concept: all was created for Christ and His Mystical Body—the history of civilization, the results of artistic efforts and thought, the wars which fill the annals of humanity, the sins, the virtues which were present in all times—all were an indication and an anticipation of Christ. According to this concept God has shown—though sometimes in mysterious ways—His love for humanity, and He has prepared it for the greatest revelation of this love, the Incarnation of His Son. The same can be said for history after the Incarnation; here, too, God's love for man is gloriously evident. God seeks to make man aware of His Mystical Body and of the necessity of belonging to it. This is an essentially Christocentric and ecclesial vision.

The economy of salvation

If we want to draw conclusions that apply to preaching from what has been said so far, we see that Revelation is not only, and not primarily, the manifestation of a truth, or of a series of truths, or of a system. Nor is it an answer to the problems of human thought, as is so often claimed in books of apologetics. Revelation is, above all, a fact, an event, God's intervention in history to save man, to free him from sin and from death, to admit him to participation in His divine nature, to begin a dialogue with him which will attain its fullness in the Beatific Vision.

But Revelation, of course, is also doctrine, mostly because God cannot intervene in human history without giving man the reason for His intervention, without explaining the significance of the facts in which He reveals Himself. Without God's clarifying word history would be mute and unable to reveal the mystery of God's love that hides within. Speaking of the Old Testament, St. Augustine declares that the true reality which it contains is hidden by a veil; it is the Word of God which lifts the veil and shows us its meaning.[32] Revelation is doctrine in another sense as well: it presupposes a metaphysics and contains a series of intellectual and moral propositions, which, when developed and organized, can

---

[32] These concepts are widely treated by Latourelle, *op. cit.*, p. 372 ff.

lead to a coherent system of truth. Important as this is, it is not the main concern. Revelation, or Christianity, is a complex of facts which together constitute a history, the history of God's interventions designed to show man His love and to call him to participate in His divine nature. In the Bible the narration of historical events begins with Paradise, continues with Abraham and the history of the Chosen People, culminates in Christ, continues in the Church, and will end in the parousia and life everlasting.[33]

Christianity, therefore, is not a *Weltanschauung*, but a Gospel, or News, the Good News of our salvation, of our call to the divine life. Putting it technically, Christianity is not a system but a message. This is a rather common concept, but it can bear examination.

Message and system

A system usually consists of a certain number of rational truths which can be organized and reduced to one self-evident principle. It is a knowledge of reality through reality's ultimate causes such as Aristotle, and after him the Scholastics, call philosophy. The system is the answer to problems of human thought, an effort to interpret reality and to penetrate the manifold aspects of phenomena in order to discover the laws which govern them. This is why it is also called *Weltanschauung*, or vision of world. By its very nature every system is impersonal and eternal: impersonal because the laws of reality are independent of man—man discovers them, but does not create them—eternal because these laws have always existed, at least in the divine essence. Once discovered, a system can be communicated to others. The one who communicates it is called "professor," and the form in which this communication proceeds is called "teaching." Such systems are, for instance, Aristotelianism, Thomistic Realism, Rationalism, Idealism, Empiricism, and so on.

Although we may assume a message to be an interpretation of reality, a system, and while we may further assume that the message is founded on this interpretation, the message goes further than mere interpretation. When the philosopher has penetrated reality to its innermost structure, he must halt there, admitting that the reality is determined and that he can do nothing to

[33] See also Vagaggini's explanation of a concept of sacred history in his book quoted above, 2nd ed., chap. I, *op. cit.*, p. 79.

change it. The laws of reality are universal and necessary. The message, to the contrary, is a revolt against reality, an attempt to transform it, to change the course of things.

A convincing example of a message today is Marxism. It is founded upon a system, materialism, which is an interpretation of reality. As Mehl says:[34] "It wants to be scientific, that is, founded upon an objective analysis not of the human condition, but of the becoming of humanity: it goes so far as to repudiate any utopian thought as wasteful and pretends that its conception of the future is rigorously determined by past history." But after this analysis Marxism proclaims that man *can* change the course of history: he can oppose it if the proletariat is aware of the need for it and engages in the fight against capitalism. The moment Marxism proclaims the possibility of a revolution to create a new order, a new society, it becomes a message and not only, not even principally, an interpretation of reality. For them it seeks to transform history. Therefore, Feuerbach's materialism is a system, while the materialism of Marx is a message.[35]

While the system is thus static and conservative because it limits itself to seeing reality as it is, the message is dynamic and revolutionary because it attempts to upset an existing situation in order to create another. The system creates resignation; the message, hope. It is a Gospel, the Good Tidings, the Good News that the reality of things can become better.

Christianity is a message

Christianity, just as Marxism, presupposes a doctrine, a system, an interpretation of the world and man. It supposes, for example, the immortality of the soul, the existence of God, the possibility of communicating with Him and of discerning His presence in the world. But it is not satisfied with this interpretation. It wants to transform the life of man by making him a participant in the divine life. Man, as the existentialists see him, is unhappy, desperate, miserable, dedicated to death, incapable of giving his existence a direction which makes it worth living. Through Christ, God urges man to put this situation behind him: He offers men a

[34] Mehl, *La rencontre d'autrui* (Neuchatel-Paris, 1955), p. 25.
[35] Karl Marx's phrase is well known: "Until now the philosophers have done nothing but interpret the world; now we have to transform it." (Thesis on Feuerbach, 11)

community of life, whereby they may jointly overcome loneliness, sin and death. Christianity is a message of salvation, an offer to man to unite his destiny with God, the sole source of a meaningful life, the sole means of overcoming death.

God waited many centuries after original sin before proclaiming this message, so that man would feel his misery and engender the desire to overcome it. This is why salvation was conceived according to a plan, according to a history which has consumed thousands of years. Before God would activate the plan, man had to realize the impossibility of saving himself by his own strength.

When the Apostles began to preach the Gospel in the Roman empire, they often heard the Gentiles object: if Christ is the only means of salvation, why did He not come sooner, why did He leave so many people in ignorance? The answer was simple: Christ came when men were disposed to receive Him.

This explains why in their sermons the Apostles dwelled on descriptions of human misery: they wanted their listeners to feel this misery and to long for its end. They presented men as slaves to sin (Rom. 6:20), convicted of sin (Rom. 3:9), given over to wrath (Eph. 3:3), and in the power of evil (1 John 5:19). God had compassion on them, and in His infinite love sent His Son to save them. "For God so loved the world," says St. John, "that he gave his only-begotten Son, that those who believe in him may not perish, but may have life everlasting. For God did not send his Son into the world in order to judge the world, but that the world might be saved through him" (John 3:16–17). And St. Luke says, "For the Son of Man came to seek and to save what was lost" (Luke 19:10), and St. Paul says, "For there is no distinction, as all have sinned and have need of the glory of God. They are justified freely by his grace through the redemption which is in Christ Jesus . . ." (Rom. 3:23–24).

Unlike all other messages, the Christian message is identified with the Messenger, with the person of Christ. The Christian message, the Gospel, is Christ Himself.[36] He does not show us the way of salvation; He is Himself salvation. He is the one who, overcoming death and sin, takes up to Him and becomes for us our sense of existence. "Come to me, all you who labor and are burdened and I will give you rest. Take my yoke upon you, and learn from me for I am meek and humble of heart; and you will find rest for

---

[36] R. Guardini, *op. cit.*

your souls" (Matt. 11: 28–29). "If anyone thirst, let him come to me and drink" (John 7:37); "I am the light of the world. He who follows me does not walk in the darkness, but will have the light of life" (John 8:12); "I am the way and the truth, and the life" (John 14:6).

Jesus, therefore, does not differ from His message. He Himself is the way; He Himself is truth; He Himself is eternal life. We have to accept Him, to make common cause with Him, so that our life may be full and may make sense—in short, that we may be saved.

The problem of preaching

Here is the true nature of the problem of preaching. If it were only a case of transmitting a system of ideas, like philosophy, or a complex of facts, which, though true in themselves, have no direct relation to life, preaching would be nothing other than teaching. It is through teaching that philosophic systems and historical facts are passed on to us. He who has discovered, through active thought, the laws of reality can present the results of his research to his disciples and indicate the reasons which led him to think of things in a particular way. His thesis will be accepted or rejected according to the validity of the reasoning by which he attempts to demonstrate it. Little does it matter if the professor is good or bad in his private life; all that matters is the proof.

The same can be said about teaching history. The professor is required to show proof that the facts happened the way he has presented them. This means an examination of sources, discussion and evaluation. His teachings, too, will be accepted on the strength of their underlying reasoning.

Not so with preaching. What is transmitted and what one seeks to have accepted is a person. And the goal to be obtained is adherence to a person. It emphasizes that the real problem of preaching consists in discovering how to transmit the knowledge of a person, how to effect the meeting of persons, or, more factually, how to establish between God and man a community of life, so that man will not think of or see himself except in the light of God, as His adopted son, as a being in dialogue with Him. Even though analogies between teaching and preaching exist, preaching is not teaching.

Here is our conclusion: the object of preaching is Christ in His role as Savior of man or, what amounts to the same thing, Christ in the history of salvation. All that pertains to this does so because it is Christ or has a relationship to Him. Hence, there is no human activity which can not be the object of preaching. Politics, art, economics, sociology—everything can form the object of preaching because everything concerns Christ, for whom all things came into being (John 1:3) and in whom all subsist (Col. 1:17), and because everything concerns man (1 Cor. 3:22). Man in the totality of his existence and relationships is called to divine life. The biblical text which best explains this totality of the object of preaching is Ephesians 1:10, in which the Apostle speaks of *istaurare omnia in Christo*. In Christ everything is unified because there everything finds its center of origin and gravity.[37]

The object of preaching is, therefore, not an object but a subject. Further illustrations of this conclusion will be given in the next chapter.

[37] D. Lilje, "Was und wie sollen wir heute predigen?" *Die Predigt* (Berlin, 1957), pp. 19–18.

CHAPTER II

The Principal Subject:
God Speaks

To INQUIRE about the subject of preaching means to ask who utters the "Word" or the "Gospel" which Scripture indicates is the object of preaching. Is it God Himself, is it man, or is it both according to different causalities?

The answer can be obtained only from a re-examination of the expression "Word of God," or "Gospel." By that means we can determine if the genitive "of God" has a subjective or objective sense. In the former case it would mean *word said by God;* in the latter, word said by man *about God.*

The Word of God

Though scholars more and more tend to agree in this area, one cannot say that the question is resolved. There are still those who see in the expression *Word of God*, or *Gospel of God*, a subjective genitive, and those who see only an objective one.

In the first group Schlier may be found. In his excellent small volume, *Wort Gottes,*[1] which studies the Word of God in the New Testament, Schlier based his opinion on various biblical texts. He maintains that the genitive of God, Τοῦ θεοῦ, indicates mainly the source of the word and not the one of whom we speak, nor the nature of the word spoken. "God is the one who speaks the

---

[1] Schlier, *Wort Gottes* (Würzburg, 1958).

word."[2] In preaching it is God who speaks: He is its principal subject. The clearest proof for this thesis is to be found in St. Paul: "Therefore we too give thanks to God without ceasing, because when you heard and received from us the word of God, you welcomed it not as the word of men, but, as it truly is, the word of God, who works in you who have believed" (1 Thess. 2:13). For the opposite to make sense it is necessary to oppose to the word spoken by men the word spoken by God. When "Word of God" means the word about God, "word of men" should have the same meaning. This would have an absurd connotation in the Pauline texts. The Apostle would be thus giving thanks to God because the Thessalonians received as word about God what really was the word about men.

Another proof can be found in Romans 10:14: "How then are they to call upon him whom they have not believed? But how are they to believe him whom they have not heard ?" God is the one who speaks and is heard in preaching.

A nearly identical text is found in the Epistle to the Hebrews: "See that you do not refuse him who speaks. For if they did not escape who rejected him who spoke upon earth, much more shall we not escape who turn away from him who speaks to us from heaven. His voice then shook the earth; but now he promises thus, 'Yet once, and I will shake not the earth only but heaven also!' " (Heb. 12:25–27).[3] He who speaks here is God; it is His word which is heard in the preaching. The author of the letter warns us not to reject it.

Likewise, it seems that we must interpret the passage of 2 Corinthians 2:17 in the same subjective sense: "We, at least, are not, as many others, adultering the word of God; but with sincerity, as coming from God, we preach in Christ in God's presence." There is no doubt that in this text "Word of God" means word coming forth from God, uttered by God.

God really operates in the Apostle to achieve the conversion of the Gentiles "by word and deed, with mighty signs and wonders, by the power of the Holy Spirit" (Rom. 15:18–19). What this working of Christ in the Apostle's word means is explained by St. Paul in 2 Corinthians 13:3: "Do you seek a proof of the Christ who speaks in me, who is not weak in your regard, nay, is powerful in you?" Therefore, it is Christ who speaks in the words

[2] *Ibid.*, p. 14.
[3] Schlier calls this text "bemerkenswert"; *ibid.*

of the Apostle. Thus, St. Paul can say that the precepts and instructions he has given his listeners have been given to them "by the Lord Jesus" (1 Thess. 4:2), and he can beseech them "by the meekness and gentleness of Christ" (2 Cor. 10:1) or entreat them "through our Lord Jesus Christ" (Rom. 15:30). Through the Apostle it is Christ Himself who commands and exhorts (2 Cor. 5:20) and disseminates knowledge of Himself (2 Cor. 2:14).[4]

Jesus could rightly say, "He who hears you hears me; and he who rejects you, rejects me; and he who rejects me, rejects him who sent me" (Luke 10:16). God or Christ is the principal subject of preaching: it is He who speaks through the mouths of His emissaries; when someone accepts the word preached by the Apostles, it is Christ in whom that person believes, because it is not the Apostles' word that is preached, but the Word of God.

The contrary opinion

Not everybody, as we have said, agrees with the interpretation that the genitive "of God" or "of Christ" has subjective value.

In his comments on the Epistle to the Romans, Cornely[5] interpreted the passage wherein the Apostle preaches "the gospel of his Son" (Rom. 1:9) in the objective sense. For Cornely the genitive means "Gospel regarding His Son." The same author compares 2 Corinthians 9:13 with Colossians 2:5. In the former the Apostle speaks of the profession of faith in the Gospel of Christ. This could easily be interpreted in a subjective sense; the faith is in the Gospel proclaimed by Christ, whereas the Epistle to the Colossians speaks only of "faith in Christ." The attempt to explain the former by the latter shows that Cornely attributes to it an objective sense.[6]

Lagrange, too, interprets Romans 1:9 in an objective sense,[7] and he does the same with the expression "pervert the gospel of Christ" in Galatians 1:7.[8] In an even more general sense Massie writes that "after the Death and Resurrection of Christ, the Gospel is 'about Christ' and not 'by Christ.' "[9]

---

[4] *Ibid.*, p. 15.
[5] Cornely, *Cursus Scripturae Sacrae* (Parisiis, 1896), p. 57.
[6] Cornely, *Commentarium in 2 ad Cor.* (Parisiis, 1909), p. 82.
[7] M. Lagrange, *Épitre aux Romains* (Paris, 1950), p. 13.
[8] M. Lagrange, *Épitre aux Galates* (Paris, 1918), p. 6.
[9] *Sub voce* 'gospel' in *Dictionary of the Bible*, p. 23.

This difference can be explained when one reflects that God or Christ are not only the subjects of preaching but also the objects; they are not only the ones who speak but those who are spoken about. No wonder that in some cases it is hard to decide through exegesis alone if it is a subjective or an objective genitive.[10] To us it seems that in spite of the differences among exegetes, the opinion which holds that the genitive "of God" in the expression "Word of God" has a subjective sense is well borne out by Scripture.[11]

The doctrine of St. Augustine

The doctrine of God's principal causality in preaching can also be found in tradition. Here we will quote only a few texts from St. Augustine.

In sermon 288 about St. John the Baptist—called "vox" in John 1:23—St. Augustine applies the same term to the preachers of the Word of God. The preacher is a *voice* in which resounds that of the Word which is Christ. In fact, says the Bishop of Hippo, "not only he (John) was the voice. Every man who preaches the Word is the voice of the Word. . . . How many preachers were sent who have remained close to the Father! God sent the patriarchs, the Prophets and many, many forerunners. By remaining Word, he sent the voices, and after having sent before him many voices, the Word itself came, as if in his own vehicle, his own voice, his own flesh."[12] For St. Augustine it is the Word of God which speaks

[10] See what Zerwick says on the question: *Graecitas biblica,* (Rome, 1949), n. 26.

[11] The tendency of seeing in God or Christ the principal subject of preaching in the above-mentioned sense, more or less in relation to biblical text examined by us, is more and more widespread. See for instance, P. Hitz, *L'annonce missionnaire de l'Evangile* (Paris, 1954), pp. 82–83; K. H. Schelkle, *Jüngerschaft und Apostelamt* (Freiburg, 1957), p. 65 ff.; O. Semmelroth, "Christliche Existenz und Gottes Wort," *Geist und Leben,* 31 (1958), 274, quoting Schlier; G. B. Cannizzaro, "La predicazione della Parola di Dio nel mistero cristiano," *La Parola di Dio nella communità cristiana* (Milan, 1957), pp. 394–443; E. H. Schillebeeckx, "Parole et sacrement dans l'Eglise," *Lumiere et Vie,* 46 (1960), 32.

[12] These are St. Augustine's words: "Personam gerebat Joannes in sacramento; nam non ipse solus vox erat. Omnis homo annuntiator Verbi, vox Verbi est. . . . Quantos predicatores fecit Verbum apud patrem manens! Misit Patriarchas, misit Prophetas et post multas praemissas voces, ipsum unum, Verbum venit, tanquam in vehiculo suo, in voce sua, in carne sua" (ML 38, col. 1306).

in preaching. But in order that this Word may reach our ears, a means of transporting it is required, a flesh in which it may consist, and a voice to make it resound. For this purpose the Word has first chosen the voice of the Prophets, then that of the man Christ, and now that of the preachers.

In another text St. Augustine states the same thing under a different guise. He comments on the Gospel passage wherein Jesus exhorts the Apostles not to worry about what they would reply if they were dragged before the tribunals, because "it is not you who are speaking, but the Spirit of your Fathers who speaks through you" (Matt. 10:20). The Bishop of Hippo then applies these words to the preachers: "If, therefore, the Holy Spirit speaks in those who for Christ's sake are dragged before the persecutors, why would He not also speak in those who give Christ to those who are learning?"[13]

For St. Augustine it is Christ who teaches all His members, that is, the Christians. Referring to the text in which the Apostle says that Christ speaks through him (2 Cor. 13:3), the great bishop comments in his *sermo de disciplina christiana:* "It is Christ who teaches; his pulpit is in heaven . . . and his school is on earth, and the school is his (mystical) body. The head teaches its members, the tongue speaks to its feet."[14]

This doctrine, according to St. Augustine, concerns all preachers, successors to the Apostles as well as the Apostles themselves. Commenting on the passage in John 15:22–23—in which Jesus says of the Jews, "If I had not come and spoken to them, they would have no sin"—St. Augustine touches on the problem of the pagans. Christ has not spoken to them; are they therefore without sin? And St. Augustine replies that they can be excused if they really have not heard Christ in any way. But we cannot number among the pagans here mentioned those to whom Christ has spoken indirectly, through His Apostles and their successors. Here are St. Augustine's words: "Nor do we include in this number those to whom he has come by means of his disciples, and to whom he has spoken through his disciples as he is still doing. In fact, it is through the Church that he has come to the pagans, and through the

---

[13] St. Augustine, *De doctrina christiana,* IV., 32; ML 34, col. 103.
[14] ML 40, col. 678.

Church that he speaks to them."[15] He illustrates this doctrine with the texts of Matthew 10:40, Luke 10:16 and Paul (2 Cor. 13:3).

St. Augustine makes his thinking about the pagans even clearer in his comment on 10:14 of the Gospel of John. It is true, he says, that Christ spoke only to the Jews, while He sent His disciples to speak to the pagans. But we need not draw the conclusion from this that the pagans have not heard His voice. "See, he himself (Christ) speaks through his own, and through their voice it is his which we hear."[16] And elsewhere, in the same context, we read, "He himself grazes therefore when they graze, and says: I graze because in them is his voice, his own charity."[17]

No less picturesque is another expression employed by the Bishop of Hippo to describe preachers. In his *Enarr. in Ps. 96, 8–10* he asks, regarding the words *Apparuerunt fulgura eius orbi terrae*: "From where comes the lightning? From the clouds. Which are the clouds of God? The preachers of truth. Christ has sent His Apostles, His preachers, like the clouds. Just as God sits in Heaven, thus does He sit among His Apostles, and thus does He sit among the preachers of the Gospel."[18]

Let us once more point out a remark of St. Augustine's made in passing and without reference to biblical texts, but which is important to us because of the question of the causality of God in preaching. Speaking in *De catechizandis rudibus* of the necessity of putting beginners on guard against the scandals of the Church, the great bishop finishes his exposition in this way: "Here are the consequences to which one must point in particular: he who listens to us, or rather, more exactly, he who through us listens to God. . ."[19] This correction in the middle of a statement is characteristic. It is not man who is heard in preaching, even though all appearances point to it, but God himself who speaks through the preachers.

If we seek to understand why St. Augustine states so clearly that God Himself, or Christ, speaks through the mouths of preachers,

[15] "Sed non in eo sunt numero hi ad quos in discipulis suis venit, et quibus per discipulos est locutus, quod et nunc facit; nam per Ecclesiam suam venit ad gentes, et per Ecclesiam loquitur gentibus." (*Tract. in Joannis Ev.*, c. 15; ML 35, col. 1857).

[16] *Ibid.*, c. 10.

[17] St. Augustine, *Sermo* 46, c. 13; ML 38, col. 287.

[18] ML 37, col. 1242–1243.

[19] "Hinc enim fiet, quod maxime commendadum est, ut cum ille qui nos audit, imo per nos audit Deum . . ." (ML 40, col. 318).

we confront the doctrine of the Mystical Body. Christ and the Church form a unity: one cannot be separated from the other. Between Christ and the Church exists a union so intimate that it can be compared with marriage. Augustine writes: "We recommend to you, and do not mind repeating it because it is useful to you, that Christ often speaks by Himself, that is in His person because He is our head; at other times He speaks in the person of His body, that is in us and His Church; but this is done so that (the words) sound as if they came from the mouth of one man only, to make us understand that the head and the body form one and the same and cannot be separated *tanquam conjugium illud, de quo dictum est: Erunt duo in carne una* (Gen. 2:24; Eph. 5:31). *Si ergo agnoscimus duo in carne una, agnoscamus duo in voce una.*"[20] The intimate union between Christ and the Church is such that when one speaks, the other must speak. And this applies to Christ when speaking of that which pertains to Himself alone as well as when He speaks of that which pertains to the body. If, indeed, Christ speaks in the Church and the Church in Christ, there is perfect unity between the two, two in one single voice. "Fit ergo tanquam ex duobus una quaedam persona, ex capite et corpore ex sponso et sponsa. . . ." And applying this to preaching, he continues: "Si duo in carne una, cur non duo in voce una? Loquatur ergo Christus quia in Christo loquitur Ecclesia, et in Ecclesia loquitur Christus, et corpus in capite et caput in corpore."[21] Therefore, when the Church preaches, Christ does not keep silent but speaks: "Cum enim nos loquimur, ille non tacet; et istae omnes voces Dei per orbem terrarum fiunt."[22]

For St. Augustine, then, there is an exterior magisterium of God Himself, or of Christ, who explains Himself through the instrumentality of the preachers. And there is likewise an inner divine magisterium which illuminates the word of the preachers and makes it fruitful and effective. It is God Himself who speaks, who announces the Word of truth and salvation, but who avails Himself of the human word in order that His Word may reach us.[23]

We would like to add another remark with regard to St. Augustine's thought. As we saw, he makes use of the voice-image to

---

[20] St. Augustine, *Enarr. in Ps. 40;* ML 36, col. 453.
[21] St. Augustine, *Enarr. in Ps. 30;* ML 36, col. 232.
[22] St. Augustine, *Enarr. in Ps. 93;* ML 37, col. 1200.
[23] See also *Sermo 102m,* c. 1; ML 38, col. 611.

express the principal causality of God and the instrumentality of man. This is a frequent image in early patristic literature with respect to biblical inspiration. Clement of Alexandria, for instance, states that "he who receives Scripture receives the voice of God because it is the Holy Spirit who has told them."[24] Tertullian also calls Scripture the "voices of God." At the same time hagiographers are described as "voices through which God speaks." For Theophile of Antioch the word of God speaks through Moses as "through an instrument" or, according to the image of Justin, "through a lyre."[25]

The analogy between inspiration and preaching seems quite clear. In spite of differences, the two realities are similar in that both are "voices of God." If one who receives Scripture receives "the voice of God," so one who receives the preacher's word receives "the voice of God."

St. Augustine's doctrines, and often also his expressions, are repeated down through the Middle Ages. Fathers Alszeghy[26] and Schneyer[27] have given us a description. Preachers are called channels through which the voice of God passes, tongues in which he speaks, cases which contain the seed he sows, or interpreters, organs, and instruments of God.

The opinion of St. Thomas

St. Thomas' opinion in this regard is not as clear as St. Augustine's. Aquinas states in general terms that God is the principal cause of preaching, while the Apostles, and preachers in general, are its instruments. "Praedicatio principaliter est a Deo, figuraliter a prophetis, executive ab apostolis."[28] But when it comes to the explanation of the principal causality of God and the instrumentality of man, his thought becomes somewhat uncertain.

Several times he teaches that in preaching God Himself speaks.

---

[24] Clement of Alexandria, *Protrep.*, 9, 82.

[25] Theophile of Antioch, *Cohortatio ad Graecos*, 8.

[26] Alszeghy, "Theologie des Wortes Gottes bei den mittelalterlichen Theologen," *Gregorianum*, 39 (1958), 685–705.

[27] J. B. Schneyer, "Die Heilsbedeutung der Predigt in der Auffassung der Katholischen Prediger," *Zeitschrift für katholische Theologie*, 84 (1962), 152–170. For St. Augustine's doctrine see also the article by D. Pirovano, "La Parola di Dio come 'Incarnazione' Del Verbo in St. Agostino," *Angustinianum*, 4 (1964), 77–104. 85 ff.

[28] St. Thomas *In Ep. I ad Thess.*, c. 2., lect. 2.

"The faithful believes in man not because he is man, but because God speaks in him, which can be deduced from certain indications. In contrast to this, the unbeliever does not believe in God who talks to him through man."[29] He is no less explicit in another passage: "Therefore the assent given to the testimony of a man or an angel would not take us infallibly to the truth if it were not for the testimony of God who speaks in them."[30] And in another passage he says, "There is a certain external expression in which God speaks through the preacher."[31] St. Thomas Aquinas expresses the same opinion in a few passages of his commentary on the letters of St. Paul. Referring to Galatians 4:14, in which the Apostle states that he was received by the Galatians like Jesus Christ Himself, Aquinas writes that this may be said quite accurately in as much as in the Apostle Christ Himself "profecto ad eos venerat et in eo loquebatur."[32]

The Angelic Doctor is, however, less clear in other passages of his works. Thus, he explains the well-known Pauline text "Ergo fides ex auditu, auditus autem per verbum Christi" (Rom. 10:17) in an objective sense. For Aquinas *verbum Christi* means "that which regards Christ, or those who have a mission from Christ."[33] And referring to the expression *qui in me loquitur Christus* (2 Cor. 13:2), he says: "You must not doubt in my power, because everything I say, either judging, or forgiving, or preaching, is said because I am moved by Christ. . . . The things man does under the impulse of the Holy Spirit are said to be done by the Holy Spirit. Thus the Apostle, speaking while inspired by Christ, attributes it to Him, saying: 'Do you seek a proof of the Christ who speaks in me. . . .' "[34] Christ speaks through his Apostle in an even wider sense, in as much as He moves him to speak.

[29] "Fidelis credit homini non quia homo, sed in quantum Deus in eo loquitur; quod ex certis indiciis colligere potest. Infidelis autem non credit Deo in homine loquenti" (III *Sent.*, dist. 23, q. 2, 2–2m.)

[30] "Unde neque hominis neque angeli testimonio assentire infallibiter in veritatem duceret, nisi in quantum in eis loquentis Dei testimonium consideratur" (*De Ver.*, q. 14, a. 8, c.).

[31] "Est quaedam locutio exterior, qua nobis Deus per praedicatorum loquitur" (*De Ver.*, q. 14, 18, a. 8c.).

[32] St. Thomas Aquinas, *In Ep. ad Gal.*, c. 4, lect. 5.

[33] "vel quia est de Christo vel a Christo habent ut mittantur" (*In Ep. ad Rom.*, c. 10, lect. 2).

[34] St. Thomas Aquinas, *In Ep. II ad Cor.*, c. 13, lect. 1.

In general, however, we may say that St. Thomas is inclined to attribute to God a principal causality in a very restricted sense. As a matter of fact, the same text from Romans 10:17 which was interpreted as objective above is elsewhere treated as subjective. St. Thomas says that faith is induced by the word of man, but is founded on the Word of God. And he continues, "Thus he induces us to believe, through the word of man, to believe not in the man who speaks but in God 'cuius verba loquitur.' "[35] The words which the preacher utters are God's. The same can be said about 2 Corinthians 13:3. In his commentary on 1 Thessalonians 2:13, *cum accepissetis a nobis verbum Dei,* he says, *Verbum auditus Dei a nobis, id est per nos.* It is God who speaks through the mouth of the Apostle. The Angelic Doctor compares these words to Psalm 84:9, *Audiam quid loquatur in me Dominus Deus,* wherein the principal causality of God is evident, and then to Romans 10:17, *Fides ex auditu, auditus autem per verbum Christi.*[36] This is additional proof that the Angelic Doctor finds a subjective sense in the Pauline text of Romans.

This tendency is also clear with respect to 2 Corinthians 3:2, in which, speaking about the Corinthians, St. Paul says, "You are our letter, written in our hearts, which is known and read by all men." St. Thomas comments, "manifestati quod estis Christi, id est a Christo informati ed inducti scilicet principaliter et auctoritative." To sustain this, he quotes Matthew 23:8, where it says that Christ "is your Master." Then, in explaining the words "written in our hearts," he adds, "sed a nobis secundario et instrumentaliter."[37]

It can be seen, then, that the Angelic Doctor is less clear and incisive than St. Augustine. If we want to know why, we can search for an explanation in the biblical texts, in which it is not always simple to decide if the genitive *of God* or *of Christ* should be taken objectively or subjectively. Or we can explain it by the conditions which prevailed in theology in St. Thomas' times. Under the influence of Aristotelian philosophy the progress of Scholasticism brought about a shift of emphasis in the concept of Revelation. Thus, Revelation was now seen from the intellectual

---

[35] St. Thomas Aquinas, *In Joannis Ev.,* c. 5, lect. 4.

[36] St. Thomas Aquinas, *In Ep. I ad Thess.,* c. 2, lect. 2.

[37] St. Thomas Aquinas, *In Ep. II ad Cor.,* c. 3, lect. 1 (see also *II ad Tim.,* c. 2, lect. 1).

angle of truth manifested by God rather than from the historical one of God's intervention in space and time for the purpose of calling man to participate in His very own nature. According to Scholasticism it was not so much God who seeks man, *Deus desiderans*, as man who seeks God, *Deus desideratus*. Logically, preaching was no longer seen in the context of God turning to man to express His love, but as a kind of discourse which tries to convince man that he should turn to God by kindling in his heart the fires of love. Hence, the definition given by Alan of Lille, "Praedicatio est oratio salutem animae persuadens."[38] It is this concept which permits not a few preachers to turn away from biblical texts at their pleasure or to use them solely as a starting point for their elocutions. After St. Thomas the principal causality of God, in the sense explained before, becomes less and less clear.[39]

The doctrine of the preachers

If the accent on the intellectual element in Revelation has made theologians minimize the concept of principal causality of God, it has remained in full force with the preachers, who are more faithful to Scripture and the Augustinian tradition. In speaking about their ministry they do not hesitate to call themselves "organs" or "instruments" of God. The conviction that God speaks through their mouth, compels man, and calls him to faith and penitence, is fundamental in them, and they express this thought especially in their sermon on the Word of God. We quote here some passages to show how vividly this fundamental datum of Christian preaching appears in them.

"When a preacher preaches the Word of God," says St. Vincent Ferrer in his sermon for the Thursday of the second week after Trinity Sunday, "and is not concerned with poets . . . or how to flatter the listeners with sonorous phrases . . . but preaches only the Word revealed by God, it is not he who preaches, but the Holy Spirit in him, or Christ Himself . . . and the preacher is noth-

[38] Alszeghy, *art. cit.*, p. 698 with notes.
[39] How far the tendency has gone to consider preaching as the human word can be seen in the text of Laynez in the Council of Trent. In a rebuttal to the Protestant opinion that the spiritual sacrifice consists in preaching, he says: "Neque de praedicatione potest intelligi, quia praedicatio non est sacrificium et quia non est munda, cum proveniat a nobis quorum opera sunt immunda" (*Acta Con. Trid.*, vol. VII, p. 385).

ing but a sounding instrument. Just as, when a musician plays an instrument, we do not say that the melody belongs to the instrument but to him who plays it, so in a preacher who lives a saintly life the word is a simple sound. But the real preacher is Christ Himself who fires his will to love, his intelligence to comprehend . . . Non enim vos estis qui loquimini sed Spiritus Patris vestris qui loquitur in vobis" (Matt. 10:20). This is why St. Paul states, "Cum accepissetis a nobis . . . (1 Thess. 2:13). Therefore, we must honor not the orator, but Christ.[40] It is interesting to observe that St. Vincent Ferrer establishes his doctrine of the principal causality of God on biblical texts which we have already examined. How closely he reasons can be seen from the example of the musical instrument which the Fathers use to indicate the causality of God in inspiration.

The same conviction holds true for preachers of the period after the Council of Trent, when theology was occupied with the polemic of the Reformers. To us the three great French orators of the seventeenth century appear most characteristic: Bossuet, Bourdaloue and Massillon.

Bossuet dedicated two of his Lenten sermons to the Word of God, and in both of them he speaks of the principal causality of God in no uncertain terms. Commenting on the words "Non in solo pane vivit homo, sed in omni verbo quod procedit de ore Dei" (Matt. 4:4), the great orator asserts: "Before ascending his tribunal to condemn the guilty (Jesus Christ) speaks from the pulpits to call them back to the right way with charitable exhortations."[41] Then he addresses the Savior, "Appear, oh holy truth, censure in public the bad customs, illuminate with your presence this dark and shadowy century, shine into the eyes of your faithful so that those who do not know you listen, and those who do not think of you turn their glance toward you, and those who do not love you, embrace you."[42] Bossuet speaks of the Holy Spirit, "who acts through the organ of his ministers" and exhorts his auditors

---

[40] Rev. Joseph Anta Jares has written a doctoral thesis which is wholly given over to the idea of preaching as seen in the thought of this great preacher, who was also a theologian, The thesis, entitled "La predicacion cristiana en la doctrina de San Vincente Ferrer," includes a few chapters which he has published (Astagora, 1962). The text cited here can be found on page 23.

[41] Bossuet, *Oeuvres complètes de Bossuet*, ed. by Lachat, vol. 9, p. 40.

[42] *Ibid.*, p. 41.

"to listen to Jesus Christ who comes to disturb our false peace and puts his hand into our wounds."[43]

He speaks even more clearly in the sermon for the Second Sunday of Lent. The Gospel of the Transfiguration, especially the words "ipsum audite," lend themselves admirably to stating the characteristics of Christian preaching. "It is the Word of the Son which is heard in evangelical pulpits everywhere. We are no longer seated on Moses' platform but on Christ's, whence echoes His voice and His Gospel. Come and learn not in what spirit you have to listen to our voice, but rather to hear the voice of the Son of Man."[44] Further, he says that in the Word the Son of God is incarnate and present just as in the Eucharist. This is why we can adore Christ in the Word as well as under the Eucharistic species. "Let us adore Jesus Christ who speaks to us, let us contemplate in silence and respectfully the divine Word on the altar, before we start teaching from this pulpit."[45] Hence, the preacher must be "a mirror in which Christ appears in His reality, a channel from which come the waters of His Gospel—or if one wants something livelier, a faithful interpreter who never wavers, never imitates, vitiates or weakens the sacred word."[46] The preacher is he "who makes Jesus speak."[47] He must therefore be careful not to "falsify the eternal truth."[48] From this Bossuet concludes that the preacher must adhere faithfully to the Bible, in which the Word of Christ is contained. It is the very Word which Christ utters with His lips: to say something, then, that is not in the Bible, means to make Christ say something which is not His.

Bourdaloue is no less determined. "It is God," he says, "who speaks through the mouth of the preachers, and it is His word which they preach. From the moment that they have their legitimate mission from the Church, you must not listen any more to them as men: they are only the organs, the voices, the interpreters of God and His Holy Spirit."[49] As proof of this doctrine, he cites Matthew 10:20, "For it is not you who are speaking, but the

---

[43] *Ibid.*, p. 51.
[44] *Ibid.*, p. 114.
[45] *Ibid.*, p. 133.
[46] *Ibid.*, p. 121.
[47] *Ibid.*
[48] *Ibid.*
[49] Bourdaloue, "Sermon pour le Dimanche de la sexagesime. Sur la parole de Dieu," *Sermons du Père Bourdaloue*, vol. I (Paris, 1726), p. 386.

Spirit of your Father who speaks through you." As a consequence, we must listen to the preachers as if to God Himself, "because God, speaking as God, wants to be heard as God; and because He speaks through the organ and the ministry of men, He wants to be heard as such in their persons."[50] The orator notes how much strength this thought gives his listeners: "This thought that God calls me through the mouth of His ministry, that it is He who gives me His divine teaching, reveals His mystery to me, lays bare His ways for me, shows me His will, explains to me His Gospel and His sacred oracles: this memory alone, brethren, will excite your will and awaken all your ardor."[51]

Finally, let us examine a text of Massillon. "The word which we preach is not our word but the Word of Him who sent us. From the moment that He has placed us into the ministry by His call, He wants you to regard us as sent to speak His Word, those who do nothing but lend our voice to the Divine Word."[52] He exhorts the faithful to listen "to the sacred maxims addressed to the multitude as addressed only to you: to consider yourselves before God who speaks to you through our mouth and who probably sends us here only for you."[53] At the end of the sermon he complains that "people come to the sermon looking for the human qualities of the preacher where God alone speaks and acts."[54]

In more recent times the same statement can be found in Zocchi: "Without doubt all preachers, who have a legitimate calling, may tell the people who listen to them in the words of St. Paul: *'pro Christo legatione fungimur tanquam Deo exhortante per nos'* (2 Cor. 5:20). On behalf of Christ, therefore, we are acting as ambassadors, God, as it were, appealing through us. We exhort you, for Christ's sake, be reconciled to God."[55]

The presence of which these preachers speak is that of God in the word of the preacher, clear and distinct from internal grace, the word of the invisible Master who is present in the heart of every man and makes the word fruitful. Bossuet makes a very fine distinction. He says, "You hear from the outside the truth of his

[50] *Ibid.*, p. 394.

[51] *Ibid.*, pp. 404–405.

[52] Massillon, "Sur la Parole de Dieu," *Oeuvres complètes de Massillon* (Paris, 1825), vol. 2, p. 199.

[53] *Ibid.*, p. 207.

[54] *Ibid.*, p. 220.

[55] Zocchi, *La predicazione. Vizi e rimedi* (Siena, 1907), p. 17.

word, you hear from the inside his interior preaching."[56] It is the case of two words in preaching, the external and the internal. But both are Christ's. With the second, Christ calls attention to the first and helps to penetrate its meaning.

When we ask why preachers have remained faithful to a doctrine which has been so obscured by theologians, we may answer that it resulted from greater contact with Scripture and less preoccupation with polemics.

As for all preachers, contact with Scripture was essential for these orators; preaching must spread the Word of God and this Word is to be found above all in Scripture. As we have seen, Scripture teaches that God Himself, or Christ, or the Holy Spirit speaks through their envoys. It was not difficult, then, for preachers to apply these words to themselves and to see in Christian preaching a continuation and prolongation of the Word of God addressed to man. Unless we say that this voice was stilled when Revelation was accomplished, unless we are satisfied with a purely passive kind of assistance to insure the transmission of the Word—then we must admit that the voice continues to be heard in preachers. Just as God spoke in His Prophets, in Jesus Christ and in the Apostles, so He has spoken in the preachers who succeeded them.

Their doctrine is based on biblical texts which we have already examined (Matt. 4:4, 10:20, 17:5; Luke 8:11, 10:16; 1 Thess. 2:13). The meaning of these texts is clear, and the preachers are inclined to interpret them literally in order to put the greatest value on their ministry. Nor has polemics diverted them as it did the theologians, because preachers have not directly been involved in anti-Protestant polemics. Because it has been necessary to defend the doctrine of the sacraments—that is, their validity and effectiveness—against adversaries who tended to overestimate preaching in order to downgrade the sacraments, theologians have been very careful to distinguish between the two. It was easy for them to make a neat distinction, because the principal cause in preaching is man, whereas in the sacraments it is God: in the former there is no conferring of grace, while in the latter it does take place.

Let us now conclude that in spite of all the gaps in theology and all the abuse perpetrated by preachers, the Catholic Church

[56] *Ibid.*, p. 116.

has never lost the vision of the phenomenon of preaching, which is the principal means for spreading the Gospel according to the will of God. We shall see below, in the works of some of the greatest of theologians, how this doctrine has remained faithful to the best biblical and patristic tradition.

Theological reasons

Some theological considerations which we consider valid reach the same conclusion concerning God's prime causality in preaching.

Let us first consider the aim of preaching, which is faith. As St. Paul says, "Faith then depends on hearing, and hearing on the word of Christ" (Rom. 10:17). For the listener to derive faith from preaching, God must be present and He must speak through His envoys and that in their words men listen to the Word of God. By its very nature faith is an encounter with God, a cleaving to Him and, consequently, to what He says and, even if not immediately evident, the beginning of a dialogue which is fated to become ever deeper. This encounter happens first in the word and then in the sacraments. Now it is not clear how this can happen, since the word that is heard in preaching is the word of man even though originating from the deposit of faith and concerning God. The word *about* God is not the word *of* God. It is possible, however, to establish a close causal connection between faith and preaching, in as much as the word of preaching which generates faith is the word spoken *by* God Himself and not only *about* God. To meet man, God has to call him, to show him His will. A word about God could only excite man to seek God. This reasoning becomes more evident if we consider that faith is a vocation of love. By taking the initiative himself, God shows clearly that it is an invitation extended for reasons of love, perfectly gratuitous. "When we consider," writes Schillebeeckx, "what influence a glance or a human smile may have on our life, how it can transform us so that starting with an unexpected gift of love freely offered, we begin a new life and possess strength which we did not have before, we can well understand how the smile of God on the face of the man Jesus, a glance of the God-Man fixed on us, can transform our life. This is what the sacraments are: an expres-

sion of the love of the God-Man with all its attendant consequences."[57]

But the glance of God can fall upon us all in the sacraments
only if it has fallen upon us in preaching. God meets man in the
sacraments and sanctifies him by uniting him in grace to Himself.
But this encounter presupposes that man has permitted himself to
be sanctified, that he has already met the eye of God and suc-
cumbed to the contagion of love which emanates from it. In
order to produce its effect, the sacrament presupposes faith, and
therefore the preaching from which faith comes. The real encounter is in faith; in a certain sense the sacrament is a consequence
of faith, the seal of a meeting that has already occurred. All this
acquires special significance when we consider that God is present and speaks through the word of His envoys. The dialogue
begins in preaching; in fact, one of the most frequently used
expressions in Scripture is "to believe in the word." "But many of
those who had heard the word believed, and the number of the
men came to be five thousand" (Acts 4:4), says the Bible after
the discourse of Peter following the healing of the lame man.
Simon believes in the words of Phillip (Acts 8:13); the pagans of
Antioch listened and believed (Acts 13:14); a multitude of Jews
and Greeks in Iconium heard and believed (Acts 14:1), like those
who believed the word of St. Paul in Thessalonia (17:4) and in
Athens (17:34). Let us also note the equivalent expressions in the
Acts concerning the origin of faith: that faith comes from the
reception of the Word (Acts 2:41) or from the glorification of the
Word (Acts 13:14).

The Johannine expression "to come to Christ" is no less incisive.
Jesus says, "He who comes to me shall not hunger, and he who
believes in me shall never thirst" (John 6:35). And further we
read, ". . . him who comes to me I will not cast out" (John 6:37).
Again, "No one can come to me unless the Father who sent me
draw him . . ." (John 6:44). Note also the expression "No one
comes to the Father, but through me" (John 14:6). All these
quotations illustrate that faith is the personal encounter with
God in Christ and that this encounter takes place in the very
Word of Christ Himself, who calls and invites all to come to Him.

[57] E. Schillebeeckx, *Christ the Sacrament of the Encounter with God*
(New York, 1963), p. 78.

Little does it matter, as we shall see later, that His Word comes forth in human tones.[58]

The sacramentality of preaching

The presence of God in the word preached attests to yet another quality about which we shall later speak at length, namely, its effectiveness, or as we are wont to say, its sacramentality.

This effect of the Word of God presents no difficulty once one grants that God Himself is present and active in the word preached. God is the author of grace, truth and salvation. Nothing, then, is easier to understand than that preaching by its very nature can be as effective as the sacraments. This efficacy would be difficult to grasp if preaching were just a word of man about God.

In this context of the prime causality of God in preaching, the unique magisterium of Christ affirmed in the Gospel assumes its full significance. "But do not you be called 'Rabbi'; for one is your Master, and all you are brothers" (Matt. 23:8). This statement of the divine Master is matched by St. Paul's doctrine: "Let a man so account us, as servants of Christ and stewards of the mysteries of God" (1 Cor. 4:1). These texts defining the role of God and of man in the ministry of the apostolate acquire a special significance when one realizes that God Himself speaks through the mouth of the preachers. Undoubtedly, Christ is more pre-eminently the master if His magisterium is not limited to the action of internal grace, but embraces also that of external grace, or preaching. Nor does the role of man remain submerged. Just as the principal causality of God in inspiration detracts nothing from man, whom God employs to reveal His thought to humanity, so the role which man plays in preaching does not suffer from the fact that he is limited to being only an instrument.

The assistance of Jesus

The principal causality of God in preaching makes it possible for us to understand correctly the help Jesus promised His Apostles when He sent them forth to preach the Gospel (Matt. 28:18–20). Theologians, in general, think that it is an example of

[58] The doctrine of the presence of Christ in the word of the Church is also clear in Suarez, who is a typical representative of the post-tridentine theology. Cf. *De Fide Disp.* III, sect. X, n. 8.

passive assistance. In His assistance to the preachers of the Gospel, Christ limits Himself to helping them interpret and proclaim His message with fidelity. This is true, so far as it goes. However, we do not believe that Christ's assistance is limited to this one negative function. The assistance would be much more complete and effective if Christ Himself were speaking through His preachers.[59]

This opinion is usually opposed on the grounds that Revelation closed with the death of the Apostles. Therefore, while according to this argument one may speak of active assistance for the Apostles in their roles as instruments of Revelation, the same assistance cannot be claimed for their successors.[60]

We do not agree that this line of reasoning is beyond dispute. Revelation, to be sure, was terminated with the death of the Apostles; and the preachers who followed them, whether popes or bishops, are not organs of Revelation. On the other hand, it does not seem fair that the presence of God or Christ in the words of the successors of the Apostles should necessarily be considered as a revelation of new truths.

Let us compare this with inspiration. Nobody doubts that God is the principal author of the sacred books, nor that He spoke through the mouth of the hagiographers. But this does not mean that speaking through their mouths, He revealed facts and truths unknown to them. The Evangelists, for instance, could have known, by direct or indirect experience, the facts which form the content of their narration without the necessity of a special revelation. St. Luke tells us that he carefully gathered information from those who had been eyewitnesses from the very beginning (Luke 1:3). In his first letter, which is considered by some a preview of the Fourth Gospel, John speaks about the message, ". . . what we have seen with our eyes, what we have looked upon and our hands have handled: of the Word of Life" (1 John 1:1). The same may be said for other writings in the Old and the New Testaments. Modern research has demonstrated how deeply the hagiographers drank from the sources that were available to them.

[59] Günthör also links the presence of God in preaching with the help of Jesus promised to the Apostles (*Die Predigt*, p. 19).

[60] E. Haensli, "Neusteste Versuche einer Theologie der Predigt in kritischer Sicht," *Theologie und Predigt* (Würzburg, 1958), pp. 272–303, especially p. 281 ff.

Yet we say God has spoken through these hagiographers and not that He limited Himself to assisting them in the choice and elaboration of the material. Why should we not say the same thing for preaching? Why limit the assistance of Christ to a purely passive function?

Some may fear that following such a line of reasoning could falsely elevate mere opinions, or even the errors, of preachers to the status of equality with the Word of God. This fear is well founded, but we must answer that one must not mistake for preaching what often is nothing more than elocutions or opinions of the preachers. If the expression "God speaks" is to be taken seriously or literally, the secondary causality and instrumentality of man has to be taken likewise. God speaks, but through the mouth of those He has sent, of those on whom He and His Church have bestowed full authority to preach His word. From these stewards we expect fidelity to the task assigned them (1 Cor. 4:2).

If this fidelity fails, preaching itself fails. If instead of preaching the Word of God according to the mandate received, one were to preach his own word—that is, his opinions or fantasies—he could not be called a preacher.

In sermon 46 St. Augustine maintains that a preacher should never be permitted to assist his listeners in their failings by letting them do what they want. "Avoid us when we tell you: live as you like, be assured that God will not condemn anybody as long as you are faithful to Christian faith, for God will not abandon those whom he has saved through his own blood." And he ends, "If we do so, *non verba Dei non verba Christi dicentes sed nostra; erimus pastores nosmetipsos pascentes, non oves.*"[61] Whoever preaches not the law as established by Christ but his own opinion destroys the very concept of preaching, which consists in the proclamation of the Word of God. He preaches not *verba Christi, sed propria.*

St. Vincent Ferrer says this even more explicitly in the text mentioned above. In order that God may speak through the mouth of a preacher, the latter must preach the Word of God as found in Holy Scripture and not in the poets.[62] St. Alphonsus Liguori agrees: "It is the same not to preach the Word of God at all as to preach it distortedly in elegant style, because it will not produce the same fruit that it would if it were given simply

[61] ML 38, col. 274.
[62] See note 40.

and clearly."[63] Herein, it seems to us, is the precise difference between the presence of God in inspiration and in preaching. In the former God pledges infallibly what the hagiographers express; this is not so, however, in preaching. In preaching, infallibility is dependent on certain conditions, that is, on the unanimous magisterium of the bishops in councils and in the dioceses and on the *ex cathedra* teachings of the Pope. In other cases preaching is infallible when it is in union with the Church and with the mind of the Church.

In this light Christ's promise of assistance to His Apostles "to the end of the earth" assumes a quite different proportion. God is really the principal agent of salvation, and man is the secondary and instrumental agent.

The presence of Christ

When we speak of the presence of God in preaching, we intend to speak of all three of the Divine Persons: as *actio ad extra* it belongs to all the Trinity. However, we can still speak of the presence of Christ and of the Holy Spirit in a special way.

As Eternal Word of the Father, Christ is the one in whom the Father speaks. He is the Word which the Father speaks in Himself and through which He communicates His message to humanity. The Word of God, we said, is Christ, and that is true not only because God speaks *of* Him, for God also speaks through Him. If there were no danger of misunderstanding, we would say that the Word is the instrument through which the Father speaks.

When He became flesh, God spoke in Him as the real instrument, but this is under a special title. If indeed, as St. Augustine says, every preacher is the "voice of the Word," it is much more appropriate when applied to the humanity of Christ, which is substantially united to divinity. In the humanity of Christ, God, who had already spoken through the mouth of the Prophets by allying Himself to them in an accidental way, spoke in such close union as had never happened before or would ever happen again. If every preacher loans God his mouth and his tongue so that He can speak to man, Christ alone has been the mouth and the

[63] *Lettera apologetica ad un religioso amico intorno al modo di predicare colla semplicità evangelica, evitando lo stile alto e fiorito* (Naples, 1868), p. 39.

tongue of God Himself. Never was it so true as in Him that God has spoken to us (Heb. 1:2).

Christ is therefore the prototype and the exemplary cause of all preaching. In Him God has demonstrated perfectly the extent to which He is present in, the manner in which He speaks through the mouth of His ministers, and to what extent the union wrought between Him and those who help to spread His message may grow. If the expression which Christ applies to Himself, that the Father has not left Him alone (John 8:29), applies to all preachers, it has certainly attained its highest degree in Christ. He is the model for the preachers of all times. In Him is clearly exemplified what it means to be "servants of Christ and stewards of the mysteries of God" (1 Cor. 4:1). Preaching fulfills its definition the more perfectly the more it resembles Christ's own, the more the preacher is united with Christ as Christ is with the Father.[64]

But Christ is present in the prophetic preaching of the Old Testament as well as in that of the Apostles and their successors, albeit under another guise. As Redeemer of the human race, He it is who has won for us the grace which preaching imparts. Christ's humanity is the source of grace. Through His merits, through His Death and Resurrection, grace surges up and inundates the soul. Christ the Man is therefore constantly present in the word of preachers as meritorious cause of the grace which it confers.

The role of the Holy Spirit

Next to the role of Christ is also that of the Holy Spirit. In his Epistle to the Ephesians, when St. Paul is speaking about the mystery, the divine plan of salvation, he says, "Now it has been revealed to his holy apostles and prophets in the Spirit" (Eph. 3:5). Revelation takes place in the Holy Spirit; thus, He too is an agent of Revelation. The Spirit is at the very font of Revelation, because He represents the profundity of God (1 Cor. 2:10). It is in Him that God knows Himself. Nevertheless, if Revelation happens in the Spirit, its proclamation to the world also happens in the Spirit. St. Paul continues: "But to us God has revealed them through his Spirit. For the Spirit searches all things, even the deep things of God. . . . Now we have received not the spirit of the

[64] See Cannizzaro, *op. cit.,* p. 40.

world, but the Spirit that is from God, that we may know the things that have been given us by God. These things we also speak, not in words taught by human wisdom, but in the learning of the Spirit, combining spiritual with spiritual. . . . But we have the mind of Christ" (1 Cor. 2:10–16). The Holy Spirit, then, is present in the preacher; He keeps within Himself the Word received, He makes its sense known, and He presides at its dissemination. Therefore, Jesus promised the Apostles to send Him to them, to remain in them forever, in order to leave with them the knowledge of the truth (John 14:16, 26).

Thus all three Divine Persons are present and active in the word of the preacher. The Father is the source of the Word, He who pronounces it; the Son is the Word which the Father speaks; and this Word communicates the mysteries explored and penetrated by the Holy Spirit.

Christ—subject and object of preaching

In this way the Word of God, the Word made flesh, is at the same time the subject and object of preaching. It is He who speaks and is likewise the object of His speech. And of whom could God speak, after all, if not of Himself? Jesus tells the world only what He learned from His Father (John 8:26, 15:15).

Writing about Mary Magdalene, who seated herself at Christ's feet to listen to His words, St. Augustine says: "What pleased Mary so much when she listened. What did she eat, what drink? Do you know what she ate, what she drank? Let us ask the Master who is preparing the table for His own: 'Blessed are they who hunger and thirst for justice, for they shall be satisfied' (Matt. 5:6). Mary who sat at the Master's feet nourished herself on some crumbs of this granary of justice, of a few drops from this fountain. Of what did Mary rejoice? What streamed so full from the faucets of her heart? Justice and truth. She delighted in truth, listened to truth, breathed truth, sighed the truth; hungry, she ate truth; thirsting, she drank truth; she had her fill and what nourished her never diminished. What delighted Mary? What did she eat? I dwell on it because it moves me: I dare to say that she ate what she heard. If she really ate truth, did He not say: 'I am the truth?' "[65]

[65] St. Augustine, *Sermo 179;* ML 38, col. 968 ff.

God becomes man to talk to man, to show him His design of love, to start with him a dialog between father and son, between friends. And in so speaking, He tells him who He is, what man is, what He has done for him—all in order to love him and lead him to accept His plan of salvation.

Thus the problem of preaching is further clarified. It is not enough to transmit the knowledge of a person. One must listen to the person who calls and invites; one must distinguish and accept his voice in that of the man in whom he hides.

CHAPTER III

Mediation of the Human Word

In PREACHING there is not only a principal subject, a word pronounced by God, but also a secondary subject, the word pronounced by man.

God enters into contact with man, speaks to him, tells him about His plan of salvation by means of mediation. At the very moment in which He reveals Himself in time, He conceals Himself behind a sign, the human word.

Preaching and mystery

St. Paul says in his first letter to the Corinthians, "For since, in God's wisdom, the world did not come to know God by 'wisdom,' it pleased God, by the foolishness of our preaching, to save those who believe" (1 Cor. 1:21). Between God, the principal protagonist of salvation, and man, its secondary protagonist and beneficiary, there is a mediation, preaching. This mediation the Apostle calls foolish, not only because it preaches an object, Christ crucified, which is folly for the pagans (1 Cor. 1:23), but also because it seems an inadequate means for obtaining the desired result. What the sages of this world were not able to do with all the resources of eloquence, God succeeds in doing with an apparently fragile and inept instrument.

But salvation was conceived by God in mystery, that is, in a plan prepared from all eternity for revelation in the fullness of time. Preaching is the means for this revelation, as St. Paul bears

47

out: "Paul, a servant of God and apostle of Jesus Christ, in accordance with the faith of God's elect and the full knowledge of the truth which is according to piety, in the hope of life everlasting which God, who does not lie, promised before the ages began—he has in due times manifested his word through the preaching committed to my trust by the command of God our Savior . . ." (Titus 1:1–4). In the framework of salvation, preaching has its role to play in the revelation of "piety," or the mystery. It is part of the salvific plan of God.

The relationship between mystery and preaching is made even clearer in the Epistle to the Ephesians. On the Apostle has been bestowed the privilege of "enlighten[ing] all men as to what is the dispensation of the mystery which has been hidden from eternity in God, who created all things" (Eph. 3:9; cf. Rom. 16:25–26). Through the words of the Apostles the Gentiles are learning what God has prepared for them from the beginning of time. To the Colossians St. Paul says that he "has become a minister of the Church in virtue of the office that God has given me in your regard. For I am to preach the word of God fully—the mystery which has been hidden for ages and generations . . ." (Col. 1:25–26). Preaching, therefore, forms a part of the economy of the mystery: it is the means God has devised to communicate His plan of salvation to man. To enter into contact with man and call him to salvation, He uses mediators, the preachers. It is always He who calls, but He does it "by our preaching" (2 Thess. 2:14), "by [means of] the gospel," of which the Apostles have been appointed heralds and masters (2 Tim. 1:10–11).

Preaching—a phase of sacred history

But there is more. Preaching is not only a means of effecting the encounter between God and man, an integral part of the story of salvation, but it is also a phase of history, or rather the last phase, which extends from the Ascension of Christ to His Second Coming. Cullmann says, "The missionary duty of the Church imparts to the time between Resurrection and parousia its significance for the history of salvation in relation to the actual sovereignty of Christ."[1] The present period of sacred history is the period of preaching, when the Christian message is proclaimed

[1] O. Cullmann, *Le Christ et le temps* (Neuchatel-Paris, 1947), p. 111. See also the English translation, *Christ and Time* (Philadelphia, 1950).

in all the world. It has only one aim: to make known to all men, regardless of origin, the salvific plan of God. The parousia will not come until this message "is preached to all the nations" (Mark 13:10; Matt. 24:14).

Cullmann thus interprets a disputed text in the Second Epistle to the Thessalonians: "You know well the present obstacle (κατέχον), by which the adversary cannot reveal himself except at the time appointed to him. The conspiracy of revolt is already at work; only he who checks it now will be able to check it (κατέχων) until he is removed from the enemy's path" (2 Thess. 2:6–7). Many exegetes believe that the power of which the Apostle speaks was the Roman Empire, which could have halted the outbreak of anti-Christian activity. However, basing his stand on a tradition which goes back as far as Theodore of Mopsvestia and Theodoret, Cullmann thinks that the obstacle is the missionary preaching of the Church. If the parousia, as Christ says, cannot take place until the Gospel of the Kingdom has been preached over all the world (Matt. 24:14, Mark 13:10), that which frustrates the goal is the missionary preaching (κατέχον). And the individual who frustrates it (κατέχων) is the Apostle himself, who was called to the preaching of the Gospel.[2]

In this connection Cullmann also explains the meaning of the knight on the white horse of which the Apocalypse speaks (Apoc. 6:1–9). Joining this text with Apocalypse 19:11, in which the knight on the white horse is "The Word of God," he states that the aforementioned text must also refer to the preaching of the Gospel. Preaching is thus the last phase of world history and, therefore, a harbinger of the Antichrist.[3]

Therefore, preaching is the protagonist of that phase of history, the means which God is given to make history. On the plane of universal history, preaching does what the Word of God to the Prophets did in the history of the Chosen People.[4] Preaching is the great reality of the last days (ἔσκατα), the reality in which everybody is interested and about which all are called to take a position. Compared to it, even the sacraments assume a secondary position, since they presuppose the acceptance of the word. Preaching is the one great reality of this phase of history: all the

[2] *Ibid.*, p. 117.
[3] *Ibid.*, p. 114 s.
[4] E. Jacob, *Théologie de l'A.T.* (Neuchatel-Paris, 1955), p. 109.

rest either depends on it or relates to it. If after the Resurrection, as Cullmann says, the sacraments "take the place of the miracles of Christ from the time of His Incarnation,"[5] we must hold that preaching takes the place of Jesus Himself, who speaks and invites us to enter His Kingdom. It is the continuation and the prolongation of the Word of Christ. Summing up this characteristic of preaching Schnackenburg calls it "an eschatological event of cosmic importance."[6]

Preaching as a means of grace

Preaching is not only the vehicle through which God makes man aware of His plan of salvation but also a means of grace, a salvific act. It not only announces salvation; it confers it as well. Its function is not limited to the intelligence, but extends also to the will. It is a *virtus Dei in salutem omni credenti* (Rom. 1:16).

In the well-known passage of the First Epistle to the Thessalonians St. Paul says: "Therefore we too give thanks to God without ceasing because when you heard and received from us the word of God, you welcomed it not as the word of men, but, as it truly is, the word of God, who works in you who have believed" (1 Thess. 2:13). It is not a case of a simple human word without efficacy, but the Word of God which announces a mystery which is made present in the soul of those who receive it in faith. In the Epistle to the Romans the Apostle defines more precisely of what this force consists: "But I have written to you rather boldly here and there, brethren—as it were to refresh your memory—because of the grace that has been given me by God, that I should be a minister of Christ Jesus to the Gentiles; sanctifying the gospel of God, that the offering up of the Gentiles may become acceptable, being sanctified by the Holy Spirit" (Rom. 15:15–16). The preaching of the Gospel makes of the Gentiles an offering worthy of acceptance.

But what effect has the Word of God on the one who receives, whereby he is transformed into an offering worthy of God? Above all, faith, which is the premise of the supernatural order, without which "it is impossible to please God" (Heb. 11:6). The aim of the grace of apostleship is to call to the Faith those who hear it (Rom. 1:5). A person is an apostle, a preacher of the Word, for the faith "of God's elect" (Titus 1:1), and preaching is the instru-

[5] O. Cullmann, *Les sacrements dans l'evangile joannique*, p. 83.
[6] R. Schnackenburg, *Die Kirche im N.T.* (Freiburg, 1961), p. 35.

ment through which faith is transmitted. St. Paul points this out in a famous text in the Epistle to the Romans: "For whoever calls upon the name of the Lord shall be saved. How then are they to call upon him in whom they have not believed? But how are they to believe him whom they have not heard? And how are they to hear, if no one preaches? And how are men to preach unless they be sent? . . . Faith then depends on hearing, and hearing on the word of Christ" (Rom. 10:13–17). Preaching is therefore the vehicle of faith; it forms a bridge between God and man, establishes the first contact between Creator and creature, between God who calls and man who must reply.[7] If it is His will that all men shall be saved and be led to recognize the truth (1 Tim. 2:4), it is His will that all shall listen to preaching, which is the instrument of faith.

By imparting faith, preaching also imparts eternal life, the consequence of faith. "Amen, amen, I say to you, he who hears my word, and believes him who sent me, has life everlasting, and does not come to judgment, but has passed from death to life" (John 5:24). And immediately after that the Apostle says, "Amen, amen, I say to you the hour is coming, and now is here, when the dead shall hear the voice of the Son of God, and those who hear shall live" (5:25). The Word of God is so potent and effective that whoever receives it in faith will possess eternal life; it will transport the receiver from death to life and will work so radical a transformation in him that it will make of him a son of God. "But to as many as received him, he gave the power of becoming sons of God" (John 1:12). The Word of God is "the spirit that gives life" (6:64) because it is the source of life. "He who believes in me, as the Scripture says, 'From within him there shall flow rivers of living water' " (7:38).

To bestow eternal life, the Word of God must first purify from sin. And it has this power: "You are already clean because of the word that I have spoken to you" (John 15:3), as Jesus said to His disciples on the evening of the Last Supper. And once purified, the word sanctifies in truth, because the Word of Jesus, which the Father pronounces in Him, is truth (John 17:17). St. James teaches, "Of his own will he has begotten us by the word of truth, that we might be, as it were, the first-fruits of his creatures"

---

[7] "Prima coniunctio hominis ad Deum est per fidem," says the Angelic Doctor (*IV Sent.*, dist. 39, a. 6, ad 2m).

(James 1:18). And he exhorts Christians to cast aside "all uncleanness and abundance of malice" and to "receive the ingrafted word, which is able to save your souls" (1:21).[8]

The Church Fathers often speak about doctrine in scriptural terms. For them the Word of God is omnipotent,[9] a sword that cuts stone,[10] a sword with which one slays his enemies and which brings division in the family,[11] bread that nourishes without ever diminishing,[12] a seed that generates divine life,[13] the vehicle of faith,[14] a force which liberates us from the forces of evil and evil living,[15] a medicine[16] for every sickness,[17] which brings peace,[18] immortality,[19] health and strength against the great torments of life, fear and pain.[20] And so, St. Bonaventure, in summing up the doctrine contained in biblical texts, states that the Word of God purifies the soul from guilt, saves it from wrath, liberates it from impurity, vivifies it by procuring, conserving and developing grace within it, prepares it for faith, strengthens it in the profession of faith, helps it to instruct others, inflames it with love, inspires it to devotion and consoles it with the prospect of eternity.[21]

This efficacy is inherent in the very Word of God and is its characteristic. In the Word, God Himself is present, and His pres-

---

[8] The tendency to interpret these biblical expressions objectively is becoming ever more frequent with contemporary scholars. Cf. Th. Soiron, *Die Verkündigung des Wortes Gottes* (Freiburg, 1943), p. 19–24; O. Semmelroth, *Das geistliche Amt* (Frankfurt, 1958), p. 189 s., and *Wirkendes Wort* (Frankfurt, 1962), pp. 167–171; K. H. Schelkle, *Jüngerschaft und Apostelamt* (Freiburg, 1957), p. 59 ss.; A. Günthör, *Die Predigt* (Freiburg, 1963), p. 47 (more quotes under note 13). See especially H. Schlier, *Wort Gottes*, p. 41 ss., to which the others often refer. R. Spiazzi retains the probable interpretation (*Verbum salutis* [Rome, 1963], p. 44).

[9] St. John Chrysostom, *In Ep. ad Eph. homil.*, 24, 1; MG 62, col. 169.

[10] St. Augustine, *De doctr. christ.*, L. IV, c. 14 n. 30; ML 34, col. 102.

[11] St. Augustine, *Enarr. in Ps. 44, 1;* ML 36, col. 500.

[12] St. Augustine, *Sermo 179, 5;* ML 38, col. 969.

[13] St. Augustine, *Contra Litt. Petil.;* ML 43, col. 249.

[14] St. Augustine, *Confessiones* I, 1; ML 32, col. 661.

[15] St. Augustine, *Enarr. in Ps. 36;* ML 36, col. 390.

[16] St. Augustine, *In Joann. Ev.*, tract. III, c. 2, 6; ML 35, col. 1399.

[17] St. Augustine, *Enarr. in Ps. 36*, 3; ML 36, col. 357.

[18] St. John Chrysostom, *In Matt. Ev. Homil.*, 32, 6; MG 57–58, col. 384.

[19] St. Augustine, *Sermo 125, 1;* ML 38, col. 687.

[20] St. Augustine, *Sermo 125, 2;* ML 38, col. 687.

[21] St. Bonaventure, *Opera Omnia* (Quaracchi, 1892), vol. VI, p. 339, note 1.

ence, His contact with man, cannot fail to be effective. "Dicere Dei," teaches St. Thomas, "est facere: Dixit et facta sunt."[22]

The New Testament can, therefore, rightly speak of preaching as the word of life (Phil. 2:16), of salvation (Acts 13:26), of grace (Acts 14:3), of reconciliation (2 Cor. 5:19) and of truth (Eph. 1:13). It is a word, then, which gives life, salvation, grace, reconciliation and truth. The word of the Apostle contains extraordinary strength; he who receives it receives the power of becoming a son of God (John 1:12).

This effectiveness, however, is operative not merely in the one direction, but in two. In God's intention preaching is the Word of life and salvation, but the ill will of man can transform it into the word of condemnation. Instead of accepting it man can frame his reply in terms of rejection. "Many of his disciples, therefore, when they heard this, said, 'This is a hard saying. Who can listen to it?' " (John 6:61). These comments followed Jesus' talk about the bread of life. To accept the Word, one has to be well disposed, to be a sheep of Christ, at least in desire (John 10:26) one must belong to God (John 8:47). In the contrary case, when the Word of life is rejected, man signs his own condemnation. Jesus says: "And if anyone hears my words, and does not keep them, it is not I who judge him. . . . He who rejects me, and does not accept my words, has one to condemn him. The word that I have spoken will condemn him on the last day" (John 12:47–48). Like one who approaches the Eucharist unworthily, he who approaches the Word of God unworthily and does not accept it in his heart also "eats and drinks judgment to himself" (1 Cor. 11:29). Thus the Word which God gives man for life becomes an instrument of death.

In either case the Word, whether accepted or rejected, is effective. Once it leaves the mouth of God, the Word does not return without first having achieved what it was sent forth to do (Isa. 55:11).

Preaching generates the Church

In producing faith and salvation, preaching also produces that society of faith and salvation which we call the Church. Just as faith arises from preaching, so the Church in turn arises from faith.

---

[22] *In II ad Cor.*, c. 1, lect. 2, n. 12.

St. Paul says, "For in Christ Jesus, through the gospel, did I beget you" (1 Cor. 4:15). The Word of God demands that its listeners make a choice, that they distinguish between those who are called to salvation and therefore constitute the community of salvation, and those that are not so called. "To you," Christ said, addressing the Apostles, "it is given to know the mystery of the kingdom of God; but to those outside, all things are treated in parables: that 'Seeing they may see, but not perceive; and hearing they may hear, but not understand; lest perhaps at any time they should be converted, and their sins be forgiven them' " (Mark 4:11–12). For St. Paul the Apostles are those through whom Christ spreads the "odor" of the knowledge of Himself among "those who are saved and those who are lost; to these an odor that leads to death, but to those an odor that leads to life" (2 Cor. 2:15–16).

Therefore, if one does not listen to the Word of God or understand its sense, it is a symptom of possession by the demon. "Why do you not understand my speech?" Jesus said to the crowds. "Because you cannot listen to my word. The father from whom you are is the devil, and the desires of your father, it is your will to do. He was a murderer from the beginning, and has not stood in the truth because there is no truth in him. When he tells a lie he speaks from his very nature, for he is a liar and the father of lies. But because I speak the truth you do not believe me" (John 8:43–45).

The accounts in the Book of Acts demonstrate graphically how the Church grew through the action of the Apostles' word. On the day of Pentecost, after Peter's sermon, the crowd of listeners thronged around the Apostles to ask to be converted, and they said, "Brethren, what shall we do?" (Acts 2:37). And Peter told them to repent and to be baptized. And he added further on, "Now they who received his word were baptized, and there were added that day about three thousand souls" (Acts 2:41). The Word of God, as announced by Peter, gave birth to the first nucleus of the emerging Church. After Peter's speech on healing the lame "many of those who had heard the word believed, and the number of the men came to be five thousand" (Acts 4:4). To increase them depended on the action of the word. "And the word of the Lord continued to spread, and the number of the disciples increased rapidly in Jerusalem; a large number also of the priests accepted the faith" (Acts 6:7). And again it is the word of Peter which provides the Church with its first core of Gentiles (Acts 10:44–48). Later on, Paul's word will gain for the Church "many people" in Corinth (Acts 18:10) and in other cities of the Roman Empire. And still later it was the word of apostolic successors which drew the Gentiles from over all the world to the Church.

In order to found the Church, Baptism was necessary; but the first step was taken through the vehicle of the word. Therefore, the Church, according to Liégé, first had to be assembled around the word before it could be assembled around the baptismal font.[23]

Preaching develops the Church

But the word generates the Church by more than merely calling on men to join; it consolidates and develops it until it is mature. Jesus likened the Church to a mustard seed that a man has taken and sowed in his ground; it grows into a tree so that all birds come and settle in its branches (Matt. 13:31–32). He also compares it to a leaven that a woman has taken and buried away in three measures of meal, enough to leaven the whole bread (Matt. 13:33). St. Paul tells his Galatians that he is "in labor again, until Christ is formed in you!" (Gal. 4:19). It was not enough, however for Paul to beget them in Jesus Christ through the Word of the Gospel (1 Cor. 4:15): he must continue to beget until the fullness of Christ is realized in them (Eph. 4:13). The faith which the preached word deposits in the heart of man is not complete from the very first moment; it is a seed which must be nourished so that it can develop and mature. To make it more intimate and profound, a deeper knowledge is necessary, that is, the Word of God which has made the first contact should remain to "dwell" in the faithful (Col. 3:16), to explain in them the "treasures of Christ" (Col. 2:3).

Therefore, St. Paul distinguishes between preaching that gives milk and preaching which offers more solid food (1 Cor. 3:1–2). The former announces the "crucified Christ" (1 Cor. 1:23); the latter brings "wisdom," that is, the entire divine plan of salvation (1 Cor. 2:2–6). The former is directed to the "carnals,"—that is, the Gentiles still immersed in sin—the latter to the "spirituals," that is, the Christian already illuminated by Christ. Together with the missionary kind of preaching there is the catechetical and litur-

[23] "Le catechumenat dans l'édification de l'Eglise," in *Parole et Mission*, 1 (1958), 31 ss.

gical type, which serves to strengthen the former.[24] In another text the Apostle compares the Church to an edifice whose architect is the preacher. In the work of construction the preacher first lays the foundations and then builds the edifice upon them. The foundations are the responsibility of the missionary's word, while the edifice itself is constructed through the word of the catechist and the liturgist (2 Cor. 3:10 ff.)[25]

It is with good reason, then, that the New Testament gives Christians the designation of the "called" ones. They have responded to a call which God has addressed to them through His heralds. The faithful are "also called to be Jesus Christ's . . ." (Rom. 1:6) and are "called to be saints" (1 Cor. 1:2), "to walk worthily of God" (Thess. 2:12). Christ is an object of scandal for the Jews and of folly for the Gentiles, but "to those who are called, both Jews and Greeks, Christ, the power of God and the wisdom of God" (1 Cor. 1:24–25).[26]

Christianity is thus the religion of the Word, and of that Word made visible which is the sacrament. It is, of course, this feature which clearly distinguishes Christianity from Judaism and paganism. ". . . and the Greeks look for 'wisdom'; but we, for our part, preach a crucified Christ" (1 Cor. 1:22–23).[27]

Preaching: Ways of the encounter with God

The logical consequence of all we have said is that preaching is the vehicle for communication between God and man. Side by side with the causality of God, of the Word which God utters, is an instrumental causality, the word uttered by man. Preaching—whether that of the Prophets of the Old Testament, that of Christ the Word Incarnate, or that of the Church—is the vehicle through which the Word of God to man passes. He who speaks is God, but to make His voice heard He uses a human instrument, the Church in its preachers.

Thus, preaching, from the Ascension to the parousia, serves as

[24] For the function of preaching in the early Church, see also P. Hitz, *L'annonce missionnaire de l'Evangile*, p. 124 ss.

[25] K. H. Schelkle, *Jüngerschaft und Apostelamt*, p. 59, Chap. 3 of this work may be considered a synthesis of all biblical data concerning preaching.

[26] Hitz, *op. cit.*, p. 124 ss.

[27] Schelkle, *op. cit.*, p. 59.

both the means and the place for the encounter between God and man. Acceptance or refusal of the word of the Church constitutes acceptance or refusal of God Himself (Luke 10:16). Christ is present in that Church which preaches the Gospel until the consummation of the world (Matt. 28:16–20). As nobody can come to the Father except through Christ (John 14:6), so nobody can come to Christ except through the Church (Luke 10:16; Matt. 28:16–20). Hence the New Testament can attribute to the Apostles—that is, to the Church of which they are the foundation— that which it attributes to Christ. If Christ is "the light of the world" (John 8:12), so are the Apostles (Matt. 5:14); if Christ "enlightens every man who comes into the world" (John 1:9), so do the Apostles (Matt. 5:16); if Christ is a sign "destined for the fall and for the rise of many" (Luke 2:34), the Apostles are likewise "an odor that leads to death," as they are "an odor that leads to life" (2 Cor. 2:16); if Christ is persecuted, so the Apostles will be (John 15:20); if men wish to observe the Word of Christ, they will pay equal attention to the word of the Apostles (John 15:20). In fact "nobody can have God for a Father who does not have the Church for a mother."[28] Christ and the Church are inseparable.[29]

The human word

Preaching is thus not only the Word of God but also the word of man. Thus it is that we find in the New Testament such expressions as "Word of God," "Gospel of God," "Word of Christ," and "Gospel of Christ" side by side with "word of men," or, as St. Paul calls it, "my gospel." The Apostle speaks of "my preaching and my message," of "our gospel" (1 Cor. 2:4 and 2 Cor. 4:3) and of "my gospel" (Rom. 2:6). And in the Epistle to the Thessalonians the two expressions are alongside one another: "Therefore, we too give thanks to God without ceasing, because when you heard and received from us the word of God, you welcomed it not as the word of men, but, as it truly is, the word of God, who works in you who have believed" (Thess. 2:13). The Word of God is so hidden in the word of man that when listening to the

[28] Cyprianus, *De unitate Ecclesiae*, 3, 1.
[29] See also G. Hasenhüttl, "Der Glaubensvollzug, Eine Begegnung mit Rudolf Bultmann aus katholischem Glaubensverständnis," *Koinonia* (Essen, 1963), pp. 85–108.

human voice of the Apostle, one might think that it comes from men and not from God, as it truly does. This is why St. Paul gives thanks to God that the Thessalonians have not committed a similar error. Only faith can help us recognize the divine in the human. Schlier completes this doctrine by saying, "God and Christ speak in, with, and under the word of man. . . . Man speaks the Word of Christ and of God."[30]

The event of preaching

We must state, therefore, that preaching is not primarily communication of a doctrine, or an intellectual content, but of an event. The encounter with God is the most decisive event in the life of man, a fact which radically alters his situation on earth. With this encounter every man's real history begins. Until God enters into man's life and forces him to make a choice, to take a position, there is no real history. The history of every man is the history of salvation, in synthesis, and therein everything is subordinate to Christ. All that precedes the encounter with Christ is directed towards its preparation; everything that follows is determined by it. The encounter between Christ and man takes place in the preaching of the Church even before it takes place in the sacraments. Preaching is the *now* (*hodie*) of God. God spoke through the Prophets in the Old Testament, through Christ and the Apostles in the New Testament. But the voice is not stilled: it continues to resound in the successors of the Apostles; it continues to question man and to call him to the Kingdom of God. "*Hodie si vocem eius audieritis nolite obdurare corda vestra,*" says Psalm 94:4. It is still God's voice which reaches man through His heralds, even when this voice, in contrast to the Prophets, to Christ, and to the Apostles, reveals nothing new, but only actualizes Revelation already imparted.

Sacred history did not end with the death of the Apostles but continues in the history of the Church. "Revelation," says Father Latourelle, "as a series of facts in which were proposed and accepted the chosen witnesses has come to an end. But this 'once' of the facts of salvation does not exclude the 'nunc,' the 'hodie,' of the act of God which invites our faith and our love. The call of God echoes constantly, just as present and living as it was at the

[30] H. Schlier, *Wort Gottes,* p. 17.

time of Christ and the Apostles. It remains in its truth and effect. The word has been confided to Scripture and preached by the Church in order to reach human generations, and God continuously calls us through the voice of His bride."[31]

To express the reality of this happening, the New Testament uses different terms whose meaning has been richly illustrated by modern dictionaries.[32] The most important among them are: κηρύσσειν, εὐαγγελίζειν. Κηρύσσω, μαρτυρεῖν with the nouns κῆρυξ and κήρυγμα is the verb which best expresses the nature of the event inherent in preaching. Κῆρυξ in Greek means herald, messenger, he who in the name of the king and by his command announces in public places an event that is important to the nation. What he proclaims is called the κήρυγμα, the message. The event proclaimed in preaching is God's will for salvation, made manifest in the central fact of history, in the Death and Resurrection of Christ. Like the Prophets of the Old Testament, and later St. John the Baptist and the Apostles, the Christian preacher proclaims, at the top of his voice, the fact destined to give a new direction to world history and to the history of every single man. Εὐαγγελίζειν completes κηρύσσειν by circumscribing it. What the herald announces is an event of salvation and, therefore, a Gospel, the Good Tidings, since no news could be better than that which is destined to bring salvation to those who need and seek it. Every herald can say, like the angel who appeared to the shepherds at Christ's birth, ". . . for behold, I bring you good news of great joy which shall be to all the people; for today . . . a Savior has been born . . ." (Luke 2:10). To this announcement man responds with conversion, or metanoia, a total change of mentality and moral conduct.

Μαρτυρεῖν finally, introduces the nature of preaching. It is the proclamation not only of some good news but also of a Good News which the herald has already experienced in his own life. What he proclaims is not merely a fact which he has been commanded to proclaim in his most forceful voice; it is a fact which he has lived and experienced intimately with the very person who has ordered him to proclaim it so that all people may share in it. John the Evangelist writes in his First Epistle: "I write of what

---

[31] Latourelle, *Théologie de la révélation*, p. 477.

[32] See the analysis of these terms in Kittel's *Dictionary*. We took note of them.

was from the beginning, what we have heard, what we have seen with our eyes, what we have looked upon and our hands have handled: of the Word of Life. And the Life was made known and we have seen, and now testify and announce to you, the Life Eternal which was with the Father and has appeared to us" (1 John 1:1–2). The verb μαρτυρεῖν helps us recognize that preaching, by the very fact that it presupposes a special mission, also requires a life which will be a testimonial to truth and to the message proclaimed. In this way preaching can obtain its effect and make the "Tidings" which it announces appear to be "Good." Preaching must not only bring a message but must also provoke a "communion among those who receive it and those who bring it." The preacher is not only a herald or messenger but also a witness.[33]

The dynamic dimension of preaching

In preaching there are two dimensions corresponding to the two dimensions of the Word of God. Besides the intellectual content, the object of belief, there is a dynamic element, an internal virtue which acts upon the one who listens, inducing him to reply to the God who claims him as His own.

This dynamic dimension is a fact which present-day Protestant theology especially stresses, and Catholic theology, in turn, is blamed for having completely neglected it.[34] This is correct as far as it goes. Doubtless, the desire of the theologian to distinguish between preaching and the sacraments was what led them to allow such an incontrovertible biblical and patristic fact to be overshadowed. It would not be exact, however, to say that they have completely ignored it, or that they have failed to see anything else in preaching than the intellectual content.

It suffices to note Suarez' comment in this regard. Suarez was probably the most important of post-Tridentine theologians, and he was the exponent of an era entirely directed to defense against the attacks of Protestantism. As far as Suarez was concerned, the dynamic dimension of preaching was a well-known fact.

[33] See also what Söhngen says about preaching as event: "Denn Verkündigung, falls sie wirklich als solche statt hat, ist mehr als ein *Reden über* (italics in text) oder ein Berichten über Geschehenes oder ein Ermahnen: Verkündigung ist gegenwärtiges Zeugnis" (*Symbol und Wirklichkeit im Kultmysterium* [Bonn, 1937] p. 23).

[34] Already cited is K. Barth, *Dogmatique,* vol. I, t. I, p. 64. See below.

Speaking about the grace that is necessary for belief, he says that the means generally used by God to impart grace is "the external word of preaching."[35] This is an external grace which would not be sufficient by itself to produce salutary works "if the spirit of grace did not penetrate them and use this means to produce an even greater stimulus to the mind."[36] This grace which God confers by means of preaching endows man with a new heart and disposes him toward faith. It is joined intimately with the word just as divine help is joined intimately with the ability to act.[37] Using Scholastic terminology, we might say that preaching is the subject in which grace is contained and through which it touches the human heart. The external and internal graces of preaching form a single cause that produces the common effect we know as faith.[38]

A change of perspective

It is really a pity that such a clear concept, based on the Bible and the Fathers, could not maintain itself. Some time along the way it was abandoned by the theologians. Apparently, it seems this was Ripalda's fault.

As is well known, Ripalda could not bring himself to admit that an external object can confer on man an enlightenment or movements of the will that are not natural. In this case he would have had to alter the interpretation of biblical and patristic doctrine, which speaks of preaching as the vehicle of grace. As a reality outside man, according to Ripalda preaching can confer only intellectual enlightenment and motions of the will which are naturally good. The fact that Scripture and the Fathers describe preaching as an organ of grace meant to Ripalda that preaching furnishes God with "an opportunity to enlighten the intellect and to move the will and so make naturally good acts supernatural and wholesome."[39] Thus does Ripalda reduce preaching to a simple external grace incapable of producing supernatural acts in men. Preoccupied with a pet theory, he tried to adduce arguments in its favor without paying heed to biblical or patristic

[35] Suarez, *De gratia*, L. IV, c. 10, n. 8, in *Opera Omnia*, vol. 8, p. 309.
[36] *Ibid.*, n. 6, p. 308.
[37] *Ibid.*
[38] *Ibid.*, L. III, c. 27, n. 4.
[39] Ripalda, *De ente supernaturali*, t. I, Disp. XX, n. 41.

texts in their most obvious meaning. He wanted to see in preaching only an outside magisterium, a work of men even though they were men charged with a divine mission, and not the presence of God, who through preaching comes into contact with the men whom He calls to faith.

It is difficult to say what influence Ripalda's opinion has had on the development of a theology of preaching. It is a fact, however, that at a certain point theologians generally lose the notion of preaching as a means of grace.[40] They have conceived it as a simple external grace which adds nothing to the soul,[41] and they add that, properly speaking, it should not even be called a grace.[42] The ones who have continued in the biblical and patristic tradition are the preachers.[43]

In general, the development of a theology of preaching in a negative sense can be explained in terms of a response to the anti-Protestant spirit which characterized theology after the Council of Trent.[44] We think this is beyond doubt. As a consequence, theologians have not given to preaching the attention which such a subject merited. In order to demolish the theses of their adversaries, theologians have concentrated on the most disputed points in theology, and they have left aside those points not in dispute, such as preaching. Protestant reaction forced theologians into controversy and bolstered the development of "extrinsicism," one of the greatest faults of post-Tridentine theology and the one on which the loss of the concept of preaching as a means of grace may be blamed.

The pre-eminence of preaching

Preaching is therefore the vehicle of grace, in particular, of the fundamental grace which is faith.

It is precisely this close relation between faith and preaching

[40] Cfr. J. Kuhn, "Zur Lehre von dem Worte Gottes und den Sakramenten," *Theologische Quartalscrift,* 37 (1855), p. 14.

[41] Cfr. Palmieri, *Tractatus de gratia divina actuali,* t. I (Galopiae, 1885), p. 14.

[42] Cfr. Garrigou-Lagrange, *De gratia* (Turin, 1946), pp. 6 and 122.

[43] Cfr. Bossuet, *Oeuvres complètes de Bossuet,* ed. by Lachat, vol. 9, p. 52. Before the Council of Trent cfr. Bernardino of Siena, *Sermo IX* in *Opera Omnia,* t. III, p. 147.

[44] F. X. Arnold, *Wort des Heils als Wort in der Zeit* (Trier, 1961), p. 21.

which explains its pre-eminence among the ministries of the Church. Above all, preaching is more important than works of charity. When the Apostles were confronted with the necessity of dedicating more time to charitable works than to preaching—at least it seemed necessary as the Christian community grew—they did not hesitate. "It is not desirable that we should forsake the word of God and serve at tables" (Acts 6:2). Thus they elected seven deacons whom they put in charge of this detail, while they devoted themselves to "prayer and to the ministry of the word" (Acts 6:4).

Besides, for St. Paul the gifts showered upon preaching hold the first place among those which the Spirit bestows on the faithful. "To one through the Spirit is given the utterance of wisdom; and to another the utterance of knowledge, according to the same Spirit . . ." (1 Cor. 12:8). Only after this gift come the others, among them the powers of healing, of miracles, of languages (1 Cor. 12:9–11). For this reason, when exhorting his Christians to aspire to the gifts of the Spirit, the Apostle puts the gift of "prophecy" above all others (1 Cor. 14:1). This is for social reasons: he who speaks in foreign tongues is talking to God, not to men, whereas "he who prophesies speaks to men for edification, and encouragement and consolation" (1 Cor. 14:3). And St. Paul adds that he would gladly see all the faithful have the gift of tongues, but even more, of prophecy: "Now I should like you all to speak in tongues, but still more to prophesy" (1 Cor. 14:5). Among presbyters deserving of double consideration, the first place should go to "those who labor in the word and in teaching" (1 Tim. 5:17).

Finally, preaching is more important than administering the sacraments, including Baptism. Even during the public life of Christ, who was conscious of the fact that the Father had sent Him to preach (Luke 4:43), he left the administering of Baptism and Penance to the Apostles. The fact is expressly noted in John 4:2. St. Paul did the same. In order to justify his practice, he appeals directly to Christ's mandate: "For Christ did not send me to baptize, but to preach the gospel . . ." (1 Cor. 1:17). The fact that the bishops of the early centuries reserved to themselves the ministry of the Word, and only much later let simple priests preach, is probably derived from the examples of Christ and St.

Paul. At least in Africa the first presbyter permitted to preach was St. Augustine,[45] and the event was so novel that Pope Celestine wrote the Italian bishops warning them against the bad example.[46]

The importance of preaching is also attested to by the great variety of terms which describe it in the New Testament.[47] It is an indication of the richness of this phenomenon, so important for the life of the Church.

Consequently, in the actual order of providence, wherein God has willed faith to result from the announcement of His Word, preaching has justly assumed the same importance and the same necessity as faith. If it is impossible to please God without faith (Heb. 11:6), faith itself is unattainable without preaching (Rom. 10:17). The two realities are on the same plane. Since it is a question of God's positive law, in case of necessity preaching can be substituted for by other means. A state of necessity may arise from the fact that preaching cannot reach men scattered over all the world in a short interval of time. Faith is spread progressively, as Jesus Himself demonstrated when He ordered the Apostles to preach the Gospel first in Jerusalem, then in Judea, Samaria, and, finally, to the ends of the earth (Acts 1:8). Even today the voice of preachers has not reached all men.

Preaching is thus the ordinary and normal way of faith. This means that faith can come to persons of good will who do what they can to live according to the natural law by other ways which the theologians call "extranormal," as, for instance, by inner inspiration.[48] In the plan of God these ways are destined to disappear, because the preaching of the Church must be the vehicle of faith for all.

The necessity for preaching

The necessity of preaching for faith explains why St. Paul is willing to permit it to be done for motives not wholly noble. "Some indeed preach Christ even out of envy and contentiousness,

---

[45] Van der Meer, *Augustine the Bishop* (New York, 1961), p. 9.

[46] *Ibid.,* p. 32.

[47] K. H. Schelkle, *op. cit.,* according to Kittel's *Dictionary,* p. 57.

[48] Questions referring to internal inspiration and its function for the faith are discussed in depth by Santos Hernandez in *Salvación y Paganismo* (Santander, 1960), pp. 555–520.

but some also out of good will. Some proclaim Christ out of love since they know I am appointed for the defense of the gospel; but some out of contentiousness, not sincerety, thinking to stir up affliction for me in my chains" (Phil. 1:15–17). Better to preach by factiousness or hypocrisy than not to preach at all; what counts is that Christ be proclaimed.

To have a good conscience, the Apostle must be able to say that he has neglected nothing in carrying out his task. On the eve of his departure for Jerusalem, thinking of persecutions and of the possible death which awaited him in that city, St. Paul is quiet, because his conscience tells him that he has fulfilled the gravest task of his life, that of preaching. As he told the presbyters of Ephesus: ". . . I have kept back nothing that was for your good, but have declared it to you and taught you in public and from house to house, urging Jews and Gentiles to turn to God in repentance to believe in our Lord Jesus Christ" (Acts 20:20–21). And now going to Jerusalem and not knowing what is in store for him, he has no fear for his life: "But I fear none of these, nor do I count my life more precious than myself, if only I may accomplish my course and the ministry that I have received from the Lord Jesus, to be as witness to the gospel of the grace of God" (Acts 20:24). In prison at Rome, about to appear before his eternal judge to give an account of his stewardship, he experiences the same sentiment of tranquility. "But the Lord stood by me and strengthened me, that through me the preaching of the gospel might be completed, and that all the Gentiles might hear . . . (2 Tim. 4:17). And in his last will he adjures his much beloved disciple to "preach the word" (2 Tim. 4:2).

According to their own definition, the Apostles are "eyewitnesses and ministers of the word" (Luke 1:1), "ministers" of the Gospel (Eph. 3:7; Col. 1:23). Preaching may cost them persecution and incarceration; it does not matter. When Peter and John, dragged before the Council, hear a sentence imposed that forbids them to preach the name of Christ, they declare that they cannot obey, "For we cannot but speak of what we have seen and heard" (Acts 4:20). The responsibility of the Apostles and the preachers who succeeded them was indeed enormous. On their word hinged that faith without which salvation is impossible, on their word depended the imparting of grace, the insertion of man in Christ. Rightly did St. Paul say that proclaiming the Gospel was for him a necessity of conscience, so great that ". . . woe to me if I do not preach the gospel!" and thus fulfill his duty (1 Cor. 9:17).

The duty to preach

Echoing the doctrine of Holy Scripture, the Fathers and the theologians have pointed out the seriousness of the obligation to preach. For St. John Chrysostom preaching was the only medicine to heal the sickness of the Mystical Body: "In our case (of the sickness of the Mystical Body) there is one vital medicine, that is, the ministry of the divine Word. It is the instrument, the food, the temperature, the perfect climate; it takes the place of medicine, of cauterization, of the scalpel; if it is necessary to burn and cut, then we have to use this means, and if this does not help, there is no other remedy."[49] Discussing preaching in his second apologetic sermon, St. Gregory of Nazianzus appears to excuse himself for having relegated to a secondary place "what is the first duty of all of us,"[50] that is, of the bishops. For St. Gregory the Great whoever refuses to preach when able, even if humility is the motive, is guilty of "fratricide" "no less than the surgeon who refuses to operate on a wounded man, thus causing his death."[51] If the souls in his care are lost to God through the absence of God's salvific word, the preacher is responsible for their death, the murderer of all those lost because of his silence.[52]

St. Thomas calls preaching "principalissimum munus episcoporum,"[53] while in Suarez' eyes it occupies the first place in the ministry of the Church.[54] The Council of Trent adopted the patristic line when it taught that preaching is "praecipuum munus episcoporum."[55] The same doctrine was recently proclaimed by the Second Vatican Council in the "Constitution on the Church."[56]

---

[49] St. John Chrysostom, De sacerdotio, L. IV, c. 3, MG 48, col. 668.

[50] St. Gregory Nazianzus, Oratio II apologetica, MG 35, col. 441 s.

[51] St. Gregory the Great, Reg. Past., L. III, c. 25, ML 77, col. 96.

[52] St. Gregory the Great, Homil. in Ez., L. I Homil. 11, n. 9, ML 76, col. 909–910.

[53] St. Thomas Aquinas, In Ep. ad Eph.

[54] Suarez, De virtute religionis, tract. IX, lib. IX, c. 1, n.l.

[55] Council of Trent, Sessio V, de ref. c. II.

[56] This doctrine is often quoted by preachers and theologians to inculcate the necessity of listening to the Word of God. Suarez also alludes to it in De Virtute et statu religionis, tract. IX, L. IX, c. 1, n. 1.

The duty of listening to preaching

Along with the duty to preach is the duty to listen to preaching. There is a famous passage attributed to St. Augustine, but really of Caesarius of Arles, where the bishop puts on the same level failure to listen to preaching and dropping the Body of Christ.[57] Bourdaloue observes that if God imposes on him the duty to preach, He also imposes on his auditors the duty to listen and to put into practice what he tells them. Bourdaloue then observes that this duty is not observed at all. "Of all the sins of which we must beware, Oh Christians, is there one of which we are less afraid, about which we have less scruples? We do not accuse ourselves of this before God, not even in confession: some make it a habit never to listen to preachers of the Gospel and say so openly. Others listen, it may seem, quite regularly without showing any sign that they have heard. Ask them if they think themselves responsible for the neglected word before God, or for having dissipated it.[58] He exhorts them to reflect on their duty so that they do not become "criminals in the eyes of God."[59] For Bossuet listening to sacred sermons is "one of the most important duties of Christian piety."[60] In S. Bernardino of Siena's eyes it is preferable to neglect the Mass and listen to the sermon when it is impossible to do both."[61]

There are several reasons for fulfilling the duty of preaching. First of all, the apostle is obliged to proclaim the Word of God by reason of his faithfulness to the mandate received (1 Cor. 4:1–2). It is a mandate which was given him by God Himself, by the Lord of the universe, whose slightest sign must be obeyed. How much more true is this, then, if he receives so important a task as that of spreading the Faith in the world? As a creature, every man has the obligation to render God the worship which is due to Him as supreme Lord and Redeemer of the human race. There is no means more appropriate or acceptable to God than to proclaim throughout the world His "mirabilia" for man, that is, the sending of His Son to earth so that in Him we would have life (John

[57] The speech is of Caesarius of Arles and is found in Migne, ML 39, col. 2319.
[58] Bourdaloue, *Sermons du Père Bourdaloue*, vol. I, p. 423.
[59] *Ibid.*, p. 426.
[60] Bossuet, *op. cit.*, vol. 9, p. 41.
[61] St. Bernardino of Siena, *Opera Omnia*, vol. 3, p. 188.

10:10). Among God's works this is the most admirable. Could there be, then, any other form of worship superior to preaching, which has for its precise aims the proclamation of the divine plan for salvation and the influencing of man to accept it? Then there is charity towards our neighbor. Jesus has set love for one's neighbor as the second commandment of the New Law, equal to the first one about love for God (Matt. 22:36–38), and He has urged His disciples to love one another (John 13:35). If this is the case, then no greater love for neighbor is possible than to show him the way to salvation, to lead him to the knowledge of truth.

Listeners, in their turn, have reasons for listening to the Word of God that are no less compelling. Thus the worship of God, to which the natural law obliges man, demands that man render to God due homage in the manner He deserves. In the order of providence acceptance of the call to divine life is the best and the only worship that man can render to God, the one form of worship which pleases Him. Any other form, unless it is derived from this one, has no value for Him. The man who wants to live according to God must therefore listen to God's Word wherever He signifies His will and proclaims the means necessary to translate it into practice. Acceptance of faith is the most welcome worship for God. And this holds not only for missionary preaching, for the first encounter with God, but for preaching in all its forms. If man wants to please God he must not only encounter Him but live "by every word that comes forth from the mouth of God" (Matt. 4:4). Man must listen continually to what God tells him through the mouth of His heralds. Listening to preaching is therefore the best form of worship that man can render to God.

Then there is charity towards ourselves. If every man is forced to provide for his own good, he owes it to himself to listen to the Word of God. From it stems the faith which is the beginning, the foundation, and the root of justification for the greatest good which man can attain on earth, a pawn and a warranty of eternal salvation. The same argument tells us that man has an obligation to instruct himself about all that concerns his own end and destiny. Preaching is the means which God employs to tell him what is the most essential part of life.

CHAPTER IV

The Mystery of Preaching

THE HUMAN word in preaching becomes the vehicle for the Word of God: the preacher lends God his voice so that God may use it to call men and offer them salvation.

The mystery of preaching

A real mystery surrounds preaching, because, hidden behind outward and sensible signs like the human voice, God Himself is the one who speaks and acts. This is a fact that pervades the entire economy of salvation. It is the law of the Incarnation, and, as such, is typical of all Christianity: the divine is communicated to men through visible signs to which an omnipotent God has attached special significance. To recognize in these signs the divine presence and activity, one must have faith.[1]

This law of the Incarnation is nothing else but the continuation and prolongation of the central fact of salvation economy. To speak to man in order to communicate to him His plan for salvation, the Word has assumed human nature and lived among us. Outwardly He appeared a man like any other: the son of Joseph the carpenter. In order to discern in Him the presence of the divine, a Revelation by the Father was necessary (Matt. 11:25, 16:17). The humanity of Christ was the organ through which the Word acted and permitted grace to flow (John 1:16).

[1] C. Vagaggini, *Il senso teologico della liturgia,* 2nd ed. (Rome, 1958), p. 231.

But this fact was not fated to flash like a meteor and then disappear; it was to continue long after the Word Incarnate was no longer visible. Salvation was held forth not only for those who lived at the time of Christ but also for those of all times and all places. To reach all men, Christ instituted the Church in the variety of its mediations; in the hierarchy, in the sacraments, and in the liturgy Christ was through His humanity to continue fulfilling the same functions He had in life. In the Church and through the Church Christ would have contact with each and every individual. Preaching is one of these mediations, actually one of the most important because it is basic to all the others. Through the word of the Church it is Christ Himself who continues to preach the Good News of salvation and to invite men to enter His Kingdom.

Here we confront a real mystery: a visible sign has been made the vehicle of suprasensible and divine reality. The visible sign consists in the word of the preacher, and God uses the word with a view to inducing man either to accept the message presented or else to renew promises already generated.[2]

Preaching is a mystery not only of faith but also of humility. The visible vehicle in which God communicates with us, the matter in which He clothes His thought, not only is as fragile and weak as a word can be but it even lacks the sublimity that some weaknesses manage to retain. St. Paul in his First Epistle to the Corinthians states that he "did not come with pretentious speech or wisdom" (1 Cor. 2:1), because their faith had to rest "not on the wisdom of men, but on the power of God" (1 Cor. 2:1–4).

Following St. Bonaventure, Soiron shows how in all this the mystery of the Incarnation is continued.[3] The Word took on not only human nature but also decadent and corruptible nature that He might redeem us by sharing in our condition. He does the same thing in preaching. St. Bonaventure tells us that in this ministry the "humilitas in sermone" is joined to the "profunditas sententiae."[4] Taking this image a little further, somebody even went so far as to say that the Word of God is clad in "rags."[5]

[2] *Ibid.*, p. 667.

[3] Soiron, *Die Verkündigung des Wortes Gottes* (Freiburg, 1943), pp. 24–32.

[4] St. Bonaventure, *Breviloquium, Prol.* 4 (*Opera Omnia*), vol. V., p. 206.

[5] The expression is by J. G. Hamann and is quoted by Schreiner: *Die Verkündigung des Wortes Gottes,* 5th ed. (Hamburg, 1949), p. 19.

Without pursuing the argument too far,[6] we may note that in the Bible humility of style arises from the end it is to serve. If God, by His own power, must communicate a message and evoke faith, He must necessarily use a language accessible to everybody. However, this does not exclude the mystery of humility. The fact remains that God communicates Himself to man in simple and popular form and not in a style consciously literary, such as men are accustomed to attempt.

Preaching and Eucharist

What takes place in preaching also takes place in the sacraments. In them, too, Christ is present and acts; these, too, He uses as visible instruments to impart to man His invisible action and to bring him supernatural life. In the second part of this study we shall speak of the analogy between sacraments and preaching.

Nevertheless, it is interesting to note that of all the sacraments the one most closely analogous to preaching—at least in the judgment of some Fathers of the Church—is the Eucharist. In a speech by Caesarius of Arles already cited, the good bishop asked his faithful whether they thought the Word or the Body of Christ had greater dignity. And then he answered his own question: "If you want to tell the truth you will doubtless say that the word of Jesus Christ appears no less estimable than His Body."[7]

In a discourse we have mentioned several times previously, Bossuet has revealed and developed the analogy between preaching and the Eucharist. Since Jesus, in His visible Body, had to leave this earth even though He wanted to remain with us, "He has taken a sort of second body, that is, the Word of the Gospel, which is like a body vested in His truth; by means of this new body, He still lives and talks among us, acts and operates for our salvation, preaches and imparts teachings of eternal life each day and renews all His mysteries before our eyes."[8] The Body of Christ is present in the sacrament of the Holy Eucharist no more truly than is the truth of Jesus present in the words of the Gospel.

---

[6] St. Augustine is convinced that the sacred authors also wrote with eloquence (*De doctrina christiana*, L. IV, 6, 9).

[7] The sermon is found in St. Augustine's works (ML 39, col. 2319). Before Caesarius the same concept was expressed by Origen (*In Exod. Homil.* 13, 3; MG 12, col. 391).

[8] Bossuet, *Oeuvres complètes de Bossuet,* ed. by Lachat, vol. IX, p. 118.

"In the mystery of the Eucharist, the species which you see are the signs, but what is enclosed in it is the true Body of Christ. In sacred speeches the words which you hear are signs; but the thought which produces the mind that it brings to your spirit, is the very doctrine of the Son of God."[9]

In preaching, just as in the Eucharist, there is an element which strikes the senses, an object of experience, and a suprasensible element, which is not seen but believed. What man listens to in preaching is the human word, but faith tells him that this word which calls him is the Word of God and that it demands an answer. It is the same with the Eucharist: one sees the bread and the wine, and one believes that under these visible forms there is the Body and the Blood of Christ.

This is a paradox which, basically, is the paradox of Christianity. At the very moment that God enters time and speaks to man, He hides behind the visible sign of the human word. God is present, in front of man, and He calls him; but He places an instrument between Himself and man. To perceive in it the presence of God demands an effort and a particularly acute eye we call the eye of faith. This is why St. Paul could render thanks to God that when he delivered the divine message to the Thessalonians, they "welcomed it not as the word of men, but, as it truly is, the word of God" (1 Thess. 2:13). Externally the word of the Apostle appeared as a word of man, but in reality it was the Word of God. The Thessalonians received it as such. It was a gift from God, and the Apostle gives thanks for it to the giver of all good.

The missio canonica

At the very root of this mystery, of this union between the divine and human word, there is a positive act of God, who wanted His Word to be communicated by means of the human word. After His Resurrection but before His Ascension, Jesus, recalling the mission entrusted to Him by the Father, bade His Apostles to preach the Gospel to the whole world. He said: "All power in heaven and on earth has been given to me. Go, therefore, and make disciples of all nations, baptizing them in the name of the Father, and of the Son, and of the Holy Spirit, teaching them to observe all that I have commanded you; and behold, I am with you all days even unto the consummation of the world" (Matt. 28:18–20; cf. Mark 16:15–16 and Acts 1:8).

[9] *Ibid.*, p. 119.

Because of this mandate handed down by the Redeemer, the Apostles and their successors were given the obligation to preach the Gospel to all men, since in their word echoes the Word of Christ Himself. It is Christ who has joined His voice to the voice of His Church. If listening to and believing the word of the Apostles is listening to and believing the Word of Christ and of the Father, it is because he willed it so (Luke 10:16).

The Apostles are well aware of this in their ministry. Peter said before Cornelius, "And he charged us to preach to the people and to testify that he it is who has been appointed by God to be judge of the living and of the dead" (Acts 10:42). Because the Apostles received this mandate from Christ Himself, no human authority like that of the Council, however legitimate, could impose silence upon them. "We strictly charged you not to teach in this name . . ." (Acts 5:28). And Peter answered the Council, "We must obey God rather than men" (Acts 5:30).

St. Paul, in particular, refers to this in his Epistles. He says (Gal. 2:7) that to him "was committed the gospel," that he has "received the grace of apostleship" (Rom. 1:5, Eph. 3:8), that Christ sent him not to baptize, "but to preach the gospel" (1 Cor. 1:17), and that, therefore, in preaching he acted "under constraint" (1 Cor. 9:16). Referring to this commission while arguing with those who considered him only a second-rate apostle because he had never seen the earthly Christ, he states that God chose him, and set him apart from the day of his birth, . . . so that he could preach the Gospel to the Gentiles (Gal. 1:15). He had every right to claim to be a real apostle like the Twelve, and in some respects he had even more right than they (2 Cor. 11:22). And when he was forced to reproach the Corinthians because they discussed which particular preacher baptized them, the Apostle was glad not to have baptized anyone except Gaius and Crispus. In that way nobody could say the same of him (1 Cor. 1:14–15).[10] To justify his habit of leaving baptizing to others while reserving to himself the preaching chores he recalled the express wish of Christ, who sent him forth to preach the Gospel, not to baptize (1 Cor. 1:17).

Accordingly, one must say that preaching is not only *of* Christ, insofar as in it one can perceive the voice of Christ, but also *by* Christ because it is done in His name and in virtue of a mission received from Him. The preacher is not only a messenger of Christ

[10] See also St. Thomas' commentary (*In Ep. I ad Cor. in h.l.*).

but also, in a stricter sense, an ambassador of Christ, who speaks in His name and through whom Christ appeals to men (2 Cor. 5:20). Hence arises the obligation of preachers to be faithful to Him from whom they received the mandate to speak: "Let a man so account us, as servants of Christ and stewards of the mysteries of God. Now here it is required in stewards that a man be found trustworthy" (1 Cor. 4:1–2).

Thus, preaching is a function of the Church, the office of the apostolate, instituted by Jesus Christ for the proclamation of His message to the world,[11] and destined to be transmitted and continued in the successors of the Apostles. This apostolate will remain with the Church so long as there are men to be converted to the Faith. It is a permanent and essential office of the Church.

So that this ministry could faithfully be exercised according to His mandate, Christ promised His Apostles His assistance (Matt. 28:20) and that of the Holy Spirit (John 16:13), to whom the work of sanctification is attributed in particular. Jesus promised this during the night of His Passion and again on the day of His Ascension. ". . . but you shall receive power when the Holy Spirit comes upon you, and you shall be witnesses for me in Jerusalem and in all Judea and Samaria and even to the very ends of the earth" (Acts 1:8). The Spirit will be with them forever (John 14:16) and will bring them to the knowledge of all truth (John 16:13).

Mission makes a tradition of preaching. The preacher did not discover, through his own mental activity, what is preached, but it has been communicated to him by others, especially by Christ through His Apostles. Hence the necessity for the legitimacy of the mission, a concept which encounters much difficulty with Protestants because of their negation of the apostolic succession. There can be no legitimate mission unless there has been a true investiture by Christ or His Apostles to whom He entrusted His word so that it might be preached to the end of time. Nobody, therefore, can preach without being in communion with the successors of the Apostles and without having received a mandate from them.[12]

---

[11] A. Seumois, *Apostolat* (Rome, 1961), c. 2, spec. p. 76.

[12] For the "missio canonica" of laymen see the article by J. Cadet: "La mission canonique des laics, d'apres le Code et les documents récents," *Catéchèse*, 8 (1962), 297–312.

Preaching and priesthood

We may ask when the power of preaching is conferred. As far as bishops are concerned, this faculty is undoubtedly imparted with their episcopal consecration. Since in this moment they receive the fullness of the Holy Spirit, they must at the same time receive the faculty of preaching, which, as may be seen from the text of the Acts (1:8) cited above, is an effect of the Holy Spirit. The connection between the Holy Spirit and preaching implies that the faculty of preaching is conferred at least by the time one has received the Holy Spirit in its fullness.

The problem, however, is to know if the power of ordinary priests to preach is derived from their own priestly ordination, through which they participate in the priesthood of Christ, or by delegation from the bishop.

This question of the right of religious to preach was very much alive in the Middle Ages. It was denied them by the diocesan clergy, who said that they were monks, of whom prayer and meditation alone were expected. The argument of mediaeval theologians in favor of preaching by religious consists in the statement that this right is conferred on them through ordination. The very fact that one is a priest gives one the faculty of preaching the Gospel. There should be no differentiation between religious and diocesan priests in this respect: all have received the same sacrament, and therefore the rights are inherent, among them that of preaching. If at some point monks could not preach, it was because they were not priests. Concluding his study of the question, Peauchmaurd sums it up as follows: "In the atmosphere of the twelfth century which we have examined, the reflection on the *officium praedicationis* has brought with it a *potestas praedicandi* conferred by ordination. It is the sacrament which makes one apt to serve the altar as well as the Word."[13] The *officium sacerdotale* conferred by ordination makes the priest a minister of the Word as well, though the exercise of this faculty depends on the bishop.

---

[13] "Le prêtre ministre de la parole dans la théologie du XII siècle," in *Récherches de théologie ancienne et médiévale*, 29 (1962), 69. See also the conclusion on pp. 75–76. The same author has continued the treatment in the article "Mission canonique et prédication. Le prêtre ministre de la parole dans la querelle entre Mendiants et Séculiers au XIII siècle," *Rev. cit.*, 30 (1963), 122–144.

The same argument is raised by St. Thomas in his defense of the right of religious to preach. To him the faculties of orders and preaching are one and the same. "Preaching and hearing confessions are at one and the same time faculties of jurisdiction and of orders. But those faculties which are of this type can be entrusted at least to those who are in orders."[14]

The question was also treated at the Council of Trent in 1552 and 1562 and earlier in the session held at Bologna in 1547. The discussion was influenced by the necessity for making a clear distinction between preaching and priesthood, and thus for answering effectively the Protestant doctrine which confused the two things. Finally, Seripando's formula was accepted, according to which "while it has always been certain and undisputed that the ministry of the Word also belongs to the priesthood, it does not follow that it should cease being such if priests do not exercise such an office."[15]

From the discussions at the Council, we may assume that the Council Fathers intended only to react to the doctrine of the Reformers, which reduced the priesthood to preaching alone. In making the distinction between the faculties of orders and of preaching, the Council Fathers did not intend to deny the strong relationship between them.

But what is the nature of this relationship? Can we really say that preaching is an essential function of the Catholic priesthood and also of simple presbyters?

According to some, by the words of consecration the priest, as "cooperator ordinis nostris," is a participant in the faculties of a bishop, and therefore possesses the faculty of preaching by the very fact of his ordination. This opinion readily explains why *potestas praedicandi* is connected with ordination, and why it can be exercised alone with the permission of the bishop.

For Dillenschneider, whose opinion is supported by Masure and Thils, the power of preaching is derived directly from ordination, since in ordination the priesthood of Christ in its entire function of mediation for the Church is included. Therefore, the

---

[14] St. Thomas Aquinas, *Contra impugnantes Dei cultum et religionem,* c. 18.

[15] "Et quamvis certum semper et indubitatum fuerit, ministerium quoque verbi sacerdotibus convenire, sacerdotes tamen esse non desinunt, tametsi hoc munus iusto impedimento non execerant" (Vol. IX, p. 41).

function of the preacher of the Good News[16] is also included. But when during consecration, the bishop says, "sacerdotem oportet praedicare," he confirms a fact that is intrinsic to the very nature of the priesthood.

We believe that this conclusion can be reached from another side, that is, from the very nature of the priesthood. To participate in the priesthood of Christ means, basically, to share in his power to sanctify, as exercised in the sacraments in general, and in Baptism and the Eucharist in particular. The sacraments, however, cannot be effective without faith. Therefore, it is essential that he who has the power to sanctify should also possess the power to preach, because preaching is necessary to faith (Rom. 10:17). Preaching and sacrament are, therefore, two realities intimately linked to each other.[17] It is impossible to be a minister of the sacraments without also being a minister of the Word. In this regard it is indicative that the deacon, the minister of Baptism, is also the minister of preaching. This fact serves as additional evidence of the unity between the two faculties.

Once this unity is admitted, it is easier to understand why St. Paul insisted so strongly that the candidate for the episcopate should be outstanding in his speech. In addition to moral virtues he demands that the bishop be "a teacher" (1 Tim. 3:2), not to quarrel, "but to be gentle towards all, ready to teach, patient, gently admonishing those who resist" (2 Tim. 2:24–25), and, therefore, to encourage "the faithful word which is in accordance with the teaching" (Titus 1:9). Like Timothy, he has an obligation to warn against teaching "novel doctrines" (1 Tim. 1:3) and against studying "fables and endless genealogies which beget controversies rather than godly edification, which is in the faith" (1 Tim. 1:3–4). Against all these temptations the bishop must fight ceaselessly, refusing to condone error while preserving the faith of his faithful. The Apostle foresees times when those who have embraced truth will turn to "fables" (2 Tim. 4:4).[18]

The Fathers of the Church echo the teachings of St. Paul. St.

[16] Dillenschneider, *Le Christ l'unique prêtre et nous ses prêtres* (Paris, 1960), vol. 1, p. 153. See also the preceding pages where the author explains the doctrine of the Fathers of the Council of Trent.

[17] The Fathers of the Church continually point out the unity between preaching and sacrament. We shall speak of this in Chapter VII.

[18] See also Spicq, *Spiritualità sacerdotale in San Paolo*, (Rome, 1952), c. 6.

John Chrysostom requires as the first qualification of a bishop that he be able to speak: "Do not you see how many things a bishop needs? He must be sufficient and adapted to teach, patient with the bad, tenacious and faithful in the doctrine." In his dialog with priests he emphasizes that the priest must excel in the ministry of the Word, because it is necessary to confound the enemies, internal and external, of the Church, and to answer the questions which may arise from the faithful; he stresses especially that to lead a saintly life is not sufficient.[19]

On the other hand, we have already seen that the Bible and Tradition insist on the pre-eminence of preaching over all the other ministries of the Church. This would be incomprehensible if the faculty of preaching were not considered essential to the Christian priesthood. Preaching could never be termed the first duty of bishops, who represent the fullness of the priesthood, if this faculty were not so intimately linked with the priestly duty of sanctifying through the sacraments, the Holy Eucharist included. This becomes clear when we reflect that the sacraments are not effective without the faith which comes from preaching. It would thus be useless to administer the sacraments if there were no means available for disposing the faithful to receive the sacramental effects.

The reason for the Law of Incarnation

At the very root of the union of God's Word with the word of man is a positive divine act, which, in order to continue the mission of the Word Incarnate in the world, requires the cooperation of the Church's legitimate ministers.

But why, we may ask ourselves, has God wanted to speak through the human voice of the Church?

In replying to this question, on the one hand, we find ourselves confronted by a fundamental need of human nature, and, on the other, by an upsetting fact which has constantly created problems for our formal logic.

The fundamental need of human nature, universally experienced, is man's desire to understand, within human limits, who God is and in what His contact with man consists. God is pure spirit; as such He can not be seen, or heard, or touched by man, who, as spirit enclosed in matter, can know the divine only by

[19] St. John Chrysostom, *De sacerdotio*, L. IV, c. 11.

means of sensible things. And God adapts Himself to this intrinsic deficiency in order to help man understand, at least in some degree, all that transpires in the supernatural order. In the call to divine life He confers this life upon man by means of sensible things that bear a certain analogy to supernatural reality. By bestowing sanctifying grace through the waters of Baptism God gives man some knowledge of the nature of grace, here conferred for the first time. The same goes for the other sacraments. It is through the natural element that man rises to the knowledge of the supernatural.

In theology this reasoning is classic, and it is explicitly put forth by St. Thomas in regard to the sacraments.[20] Basically, the law of Incarnation corresponds to the desire of man to see and touch God, a desire we find developed to greater or lesser degree in so many religions.[21] St. Paul hints at it in his discourse at Athens, when he says "that they should seek God, and perhaps grope after him and find him, though he is not far from any one of us" (Acts 17:27). This fundamental need of man has found its deepest satisfaction in Christianity. In the Old Testament the fact that God was always near His people was pointed out as a particular characteristic of the Hebrew religion. "For what great nation is there that has gods so close to it as the Lord, our God, is to us whenever we call upon him?" (Deut. 4:7). And yet, the Old Testament presence was only the forerunner of the much more real presence which characterized the New Testament, when the Word, the Son of God, was made man. In Jesus Christ, God Himself has become flesh and dwelt among us (John 1:14). In his First Epistle John the Apostle could truly say that he announces what he had heard, what his eyes had seen, and what his hands had touched of the Word of life (1 John 1:1). In Christ is embodied the whole plenitude of the Deity (Col. 2:9). He is the true likeness of God (Col. 1:15), the radiance of his Father's splendor (Heb. 1:3). To see him is to see the Father (John 14:9). In the Church, His Mystical Body, in preaching and in the sacraments, Christ continues to let Himself be seen, touched, and heard.

[20] St. Thomas Aquinas, *Summa Theologica*, III, q. 61, a.1, c. *Contra Gentes* III, 119.

[21] A. Durand, "Incarnation et Christocentrisme" in *Nouvelle Revue Théologique*, 69 (1947), pp. 474–485.

Divine discretion

There is still another reason for God's speaking through men, and it is the divine discretion, or His respect for human liberty.

If God had wanted to call each man, directly and individually, to divine salvation, He could have done so by showing Himself to each man as He is, in His very nature, just as He does in the intuitive vision. Or He could have made man aware of His presence by means of an internal or external miracle, such as He performed for several of the Old Testament Prophets. It is clear that in the first case man would not have remained free to accept or reject the divine offer. There is no freedom where infinite good is concerned. In the second case, however, where God Himself is not seen but His divinity is reflected in some extraordinary fact, freedom would not have entirely been eliminated. However, it would perhaps have been attenuated.

In several episodes in Scripture the upsetting character of the miracle is described most graphically. In the Old Testament the people beg Moses that God should not speak to them directly, because this could bring about death. "When the people witnessed the thunder and lightning, the trumpet blast and the mountain smoking, they all feared and trembled. So they took up a position much farther away and said to Moses, 'You speak to us and we will listen; but let not God speak to us, or we shall die' " (Exod. 20:18–19). The presence of God in extraordinary circumstances causes fear in men. We see the same sort of reaction to a miracle, though in milder form, in the New Testament. After the miraculous catch of fish Peter and his companions are so stupefied that they ask Jesus to leave: "But when Simon Peter saw this, he fell down at Jesus' knees, saying, 'Depart from me, for I am a sinful man, O Lord.' For he and all who were with him were amazed at the catch of fish they had made . . ." (Luke 5:8–9). Even here, although the miracle is not spectacular, it induces fear in those confronting it. In more recent times Alexis Carrell has described his impressions on seeing a miracle occur at Lourdes: he says that he felt he was going mad.

The profound impression which a miracle is capable of producing certainly does not negate freedom. Proof for this is to be found in the fact that many who witness miracles, like the Pharisees of the Gospel, still do not believe. It seems to us, though, that we can rightfully say that miracles generally so disturb man that he is no longer master of himself. Therefore, in Holy Scripture we see a sort of degradation of the miracle: in general we may say that the miracles of the Old Testament are more grandiose and more spectacular than those of the New Testament. The Pharisees found them so modest that even after having seen a number of them, they asked to see a sign of Christ (Matt. 12:38). This indicates that Jesus sought to impress His listeners with miracles as little as possible so that He might leave them the full power of decision.

This also explains another fact: even though Jesus had promised that miracles as proofs of divine assistance would form a part of the Apostles' preaching (Mark 16:17), from a certain moment on they became more and more rare. The reason for this is that physical miracles were gradually replaced by the moral miracle of the Church, an extraordinary fact, no doubt, and an equally strong motive for the credibility of miracles, but less conspicuous and therefore leaving complete freedom.

While God has chosen the way of mediation to reveal Himself to man, He has tampered with man's freedom as little as possible. Only a very few receive Revelation directly in order that they may serve as mediators with other men.

The scandal of Incarnation

The reasons so far examined, which make the law of Incarnation comprehensible and necessary, do not remove an aspect which we may term "a scandal." If, on the one hand, the law of Incarnation fulfills a need of human nature, on the other, it finds in it an overwhelming obstacle.

In Incarnation we have the union and cooperation of two elements: the finite and the infinite, the divine and the human, which our mind finds difficult to understand. According to our mode of viewing, the divine and the human are two distinct entities, separated one from the other. There is no possibility of a union or cooperation between them.

Philosophy takes great pains to understand the coexistence of God and the world, of the infinite and the finite. It has always been inclined to have one absorb the other. Hence the eternal quarrel between pantheism and transcendence, between monism and dualism. The quarrel has often been resolved by the elimination of one or the other term. It is said either that all reality is divine (pantheism) or that it is material (materialism). The difficulty lies in reaching a synthesis: the infinite and the finite each exists in its own reality and, in spite of their distinction and diversity, are in communication with each other. Both are beings, but in an analogous way. Even Aristotle, who succeeded in conceiving the coexistence of the infinite and the finite by means of the concept of analogy, did not succeed in understanding their union. "God does not concern himself with us," he said. Providence was outside His perspective. That is why he denied creation but admitted eternal matter.

In Christianity the problem of the relationship between God and man, or religion, has been made a great deal easier because it has believed in union and cooperation. On the other hand, the problem has indeed grown more difficult because the union and cooperation of God and man constantly forces the intelligence to consider as united and cooperating two beings which it instinctively conceives as separate, if not incommunicable. While Aristotle found it impossible to believe that God should be concerned with man, Christianity believes that He is concerned to the point that He permits man to share His intimacy.

To accept Christianity, the mind has to overcome this apparent *absurdum*. He can do it only by believing that God is love and that love can overcome distance. Outside this perspective a God who becomes man is impossible to conceive.

In the Gospel Jesus Himself is aware of this "scandal" which His person arouses. "And blessed is he who is not scandalized in me" (Matt. 11:6), He says to the disciples of John. The Pharisees, who lived in the tradition of the Old Testament, considered God too lofty to be able to reveal Himself in the simple and friendly human features of Jesus, and they were especially susceptible to this "scandal." They could not bring themselves to admit that the Almighty, who had created heaven and earth, could have assumed such weakness or that the Infinite would have degraded Himself to the form of a man limited in time and space. And like the Pharisees, the heretics of all times would be scandalized. Basically, heresy occurs in two ways: in an attempt to eliminate the "scandal" of the Incarnation by conceiving Christ either solely as man (Nestorianism) or solely as God (Menophysism); or else in an attempt to eliminate the cooperation between man and God, which seems either to reduce God to the level of man, or to raise man to the height of God.

Through the Incarnation, Christianity is an object of contradiction. There are those who accept the scandal and those who reject it. As we said, preaching is a concrete example of the union and cooperation between God and man.

The word

There remains a final question, Why is the word the visible sign which God employs to talk to us? Could not God choose another means?

It so happens that the word is the means of communication between persons, the means by which one person transmits his thoughts to another in order to get an answer. In his well-known work, *Sprachtheorie*, Buhler distinguishes three aspects of the word: the content, or what is to be communicated to another; interrogation, that which causes one to turn to another to get an answer; and the opening of the self to another. In summing up these three aspects Latourelle defines the word as follows: "The action through which one person addresses himself and expresses himself to another person in view of a communication."[22] Even though modern scientific thinking has objectivized the word, reducing it to the communication of an impersonal concept, it has not made us forget that in this very communication of a concept man manifests something of himself, more or less profound according to the degree of communication. At the same time that the word causes one subject to communicate with another, it leads the other to respond and to open himself to the first subject with confidence.

In the word there is an *I* which turns towards a *Thou* to begin a dialogue with him. It originates in his knowledge that he is not enough by himself, that he is insufficient unto himself, and that he has to look outside to complement himself. Therefore, we often speak to others not in order to communicate, but to break the silence which surrounds our life, to relate to others, to emerge from our solitude. This is the significant meaning of certain apparently useless and insipid talks, such as speaking about the weather, the heavy traffic, the view from a train window. Man cannot support solitude and tries to escape it at all costs. Man is a social being, and only in society, in contact with others, can he find the completion of himself, the fullness of life which he does not find in himself. That is why he speaks, turning to

[22] Latourelle, *Théologie de la révélation* (Paris, 1963), p. 336.

whoever is near him and trying to draw the other to himself, to associate him with his own life.

But if man's word includes an effort to get out of himself in order to initiate a dialogue with another, the Word of God has other needs. God does not *need* anybody; He is self-sufficient. In the communication of divine nature in the Trinity there already exists the most perfect communication possible. And so, if God decides to turn to another outside of Himself, it can only happen because of love for the one who is not self-sufficient and who is always searching for a dialogue partner who can give him the sense of life. But in this turning to man God wants to remain hidden. Therefore, He chooses a vehicle through which He can communicate His action, which is the human word. God speaks through man and employs the human word to communicate His intentions and His design for salvation. The human word is the best means of obtaining the aim which God has set Himself. We shall see that this vehicle is not sufficient, but the word is fundamental. What is missing in the word can be completed and clarified by what surrounds it: but the word itself knows no substitute.

If faith is the encounter between God and man in the intimate sense, as we shall later see more clearly, the best means for such an encounter is the word, which expresses the total person.[23] In the Old Testament God used the word of the Prophets, who were instruments morally united to Him; in the New Testament He uses the humanity of Christ, an instrument substantially united to His divinity. After the Ascension He uses the word of the Church as phrased by its legitimate ministers, who are instruments as truly as the Prophets, separated from his divinity even though morally united to it.

The cooperation between man and God

Preaching, consequently, means cooperation between two causes: the principal one being God; the instrumental one, man. Since we are speaking of two free causes, it must be said that man is not a mute and inert instrument. He has his part to play, even though it is subordinate. It is a case of cooperation between two intelligent and free causes.

[23] See also the excellent small volume of Gusdorf, *La Parole* (Paris, 1956), in which these concepts are amply illustrated.

To understand this cooperation we think it best to refer to biblical inspiration as a frame of reference. As it has been proved, inspiration with regard to hagiographers does not necessarily mean Revelation. The object of inspiration may be constituted by natural facts, or truth and supernatural facts, already known to hagiography from other sources. The Evangelists did not need a Revelation to recount the life of Jesus to which they had been eye-witnesses or knew from accounts of eyewitnesses. In these cases the causality of God was limited to guiding the hagiographer in the choice and the faithful rendition of what he already knew.

We think that the same can be said about preaching. The facts of the message are already known from the sources of Revelation; by means of His influence on the preacher's will and intellect, God makes certain that these facts and truths are compressed, developed, and applied to the concrete facts of human and Christian life. The influence of the principal cause does not free the preacher from the effort required to study and comprehend the Revelation which is the object of preaching, just as the influence of God on the hagiographers did not free them from the responsibility of informing themselves about everything (see Luke 1:3). The study of Revelation and the norms of expression are required by a theological principle.

CHAPTER V

Man's Response: Faith

E VERY CALL demands a reply, and the proclamation of a message demands that he who receives it take a stand. God's call, addressed to man through the preaching of the Church, demands the reply of faith. Here is another important aspect of our research.

The impoverishment of faith

Faith is one of the most widely studied themes of contemporary theology,[1] and the way in which it is understood has vast repercussions for pastoral theology. Spurred on by biblical and patristic research,[2] the concept of faith is reacquiring more and more of those elements which anti-Protestant polemics had pushed into the background. Professor Arnold, in his book *Glaubensaverkündigung und Glaubensgemeinschaft*,[3] has given over a chapter to

[1] R. Aubert, "Questioni attuali intorno all'atto di fede," *Problemi e orientamenti di teologia dommatica* (Como, 1957) vol. II, pp. 655–708.

[2] There are many studies in this matter. See, among others, J. Aduriz, "El objeto del Pisteuein cristiano en las epistolas paulinas," *Ciencia y Fe,* 14 (1958), 195–210; O. Kuss, "Der Glaube nach den Paulinischen Hauptbriefen," *Theologie und Glaube,* 48 (1956), 3–17; A. Decourtray, "La conception joannique de la foi," *Nouvelle Revue Théologique,* 81 (1959), 561–76; A. Liégé, "Foi," *Catholicisme,* VI, col. 1370–1397: *Lumière et Vie* has two issues given over to the problem of faith, no. 22 (1955) on biblical data and no. 23 (1955) on the theology of faith. See also the mimeographed paper of J. Alfaro, *Fides, spes caritas* (2 vol.) (Rome, 1963) with bibliography. By the same author: "Fides in terminologia biblica," *Gregorianum,* 42 (1961), 463–505.

[3] (Düsseldorf, 1955), c. 2 (si veda anche il c. 1).

this subject. In it he shows that in reaction to Protestant thinking which reduced faith to a pure act of confidence, Catholic theology and preaching accentuated the intellectual aspect, the upholding of God's revealed truth. In this way Catholic theologians upset the balance which the Council Fathers of Trent had established when they taught that faith is "the beginning, the foundation and the root of every justification without which it is impossible to please God."[4]

In this definition the two components of faith are plainly stated; God's Revelation is accepted as true and at the same time man adheres to God by an act of confidence. Both elements are equally necessary; one cannot believe in what God says, in His eschatological promises, if one does not have confidence in Him, if one does not believe that He will be faithful to His promises. The *fides quae creditur* is impossible without the *fides qua creditur*. One is inseparable from the other.[5]

Faith as encounter between persons

Faith thus becomes an act of the whole person—not only of the intelligence—an act of the whole man, an abandoning of the creature to God. In a word, it is the response of one person to another, an encounter between persons, between God in Christ and man.

The Fourth Gospel in particular underlines this personalistic aspect of faith. For St. John faith is essentially to "believe" in Jesus (John 3:15; 6:35; 6:45; 11:25–26; 12:44; 14:12; etc.), to "receive" Jesus (1:12; 5:43), to "glorify" His name (12:28), to "bear witness to Jesus" (3:11, 32), to "follow" Jesus (8:12), to "come" to Him (5:40), to "abide" in Him (15:4–5). In all these cases faith invariably stresses a rapport between persons, between him who calls and him who responds, between him who invites to follow and him who follows and remains with him and with his love.[6]

St. Thomas has expressed this personalistic aspect of faith in a text which J. Mouroux takes as a guide for a small volume dedicated to this argument.[7] "Every believer," says the Angelic

---

[4] *Denz. Sch.* 1532.
[5] Arnold, *op. cit.*, French translation (Brussels, 1957), pp. 12–18.
[6] D. Mollat, "La foi dans le quatrième Evangile," *Lumière et Vie*, 22 (1955), 91–107, spec. 92.
[7] J. Mouroux, *Je crois en toi. Structure personelle de la foi* (Paris, 1948).

Doctor, "follows the word of some one. Therefore, what appears as the principle and, in some way, as the end of every act of faith, is *the person to whose words one gives* assent. As to the details of the truth confirmed in this wish, one has to adhere to somebody, it is a secondary matter."[8] In this perspective faith is indeed the contact between God and man, the *initium visionis intuitivae*. In faith man is already in touch with God, and carries on a dialogue with Him; but between him and God hangs a veil which does not permit the two participants in the dialogue to see each other face to face. One day this veil will lift, and the dialogue will take place in full clarity.

We do not want to discuss here the differences among theologians about the act of faith.[9] It will suffice to list the elements which seem important to us in understanding the role preaching plays in the origin and development of faith.

The drama of faith

If we ask why God should call man to participate in His divine nature, why He should want to establish a communion of life with him, thus enabling man to become a member of the Body of which Christ is the Head, we find ourselves confronted with a reply which leaves no room for doubt, mysterious though that reply may seem. God calls for love. Both the Old and New Testaments are filled with this love.[10] It is the ultimate reason for the whole plan of salvation. "For God so loved the world that he gave up his only-begotten Son" (John 3:16), says Jesus, thus summarizing all Revelation.

What interests us here, however, is the reaction of man to the call of God. Upon hearing God who calls him, man, at first, is inclined to accept the invitation. In this acceptance he sees the solution to his life's problem. Man is not sufficient unto himself, and God in Christ appears to him as the one who can supply this sufficiency, by the very fact that He assures man of eternal life. Christ, in whom God reveals Himself, is everything man can

[8] St. Thomas Aquinas, *Summa Theologica, II, II,* q. IX, a. 1.

[9] See R. Aubert, *Le problème de l'acte de foi. Données traditionelles et controverses récentes,* 2nd ed. (Louvain, 1950) and the article cited in note 1.

[10] J. Kahmann, "Die Offenbarung der Liebe Gottes im Alten Testament," *Cor Jesu,* (Rome, 1959), vol. I, pp. 347–409.

desire: He is truth, goodness, justice, everlasting life. In Him is sated man's thirst for happiness.

At the same time, however, this positive reaction is balanced by a negative one. If the object of faith were nothing but a complex of values—if it were only truth, goodness, life, and so on—man would have no difficulties about accepting. Intelligence and will take their orientation spontaneously from them. The difficulty arises from the fact that these values are in part supernatural—beyond human intelligence, which is formed in such a way that it assents to a fact on the basis of intrinsic evidence—and in part identified with a person, who must be accepted as a guarantee of their existence. Guardini writes: "To accept a law which has been proved just—be it a law of nature, of thought, or of morality—is not difficult for the person. It averts to the fact that under such a law it still continues to be itself; or even, that the recognition of such general laws can easily be translated into personal action. But man opposes with elemental vitality the requirement to recognize another person as supreme law of the whole sphere of religious life and with it of one's own existence, and one understands what it means to request renunciation of the proper soul."[11]

To accept a person as the norm of one's existence means that for us nothing really exists in the world except this person, and that everything else has value only in reference to him. It means losing one's independence and autonomy, giving up one's own thoughts, abandoning one's will and love, and instead following the thought, the will and the love of another. In the concrete case of faith it means that for us Jesus is "the way, and the truth, and the life" (John 14:6), "the light of the world" (8:12), the person who must be loved more than parents, brothers, or sisters (Matt. 10:34–35), even more than one's own life (Matt. 10:39). This entails such a close identification with Christ that the Christian can say with St. Paul that his life is Christ (Phil. 1:21), that it is no longer he who lives but Christ who lives in him (Gal. 2:20). To arrive at this identification, such a profound transformation is necessary that the Gospel likens it to a second birth (John 3:3), and St. Paul, to death and resurrection (Rom. 6:3 ff.) In a word, one must give up his life to obtain what Christ promises.

There is more: the goodness and truth represented in faith are identical not only with a person but also with a crucified per-

[11] R. Guardini, *L'essenza del Cristianesimo*, pp. 12–13.

son. It is a question of truth and goodness found existing in a state of deep humiliation; in itself such humiliation has nothing to attract us, but it is rather of a nature to arouse the most vivid opposition. Jesus invites us to come to Him in order to possess life, but He bears on His shoulders a cross which has nothing attractive about it.

To believe, to listen to the voice of Christ, to come to Him, is anything but easy. To human wisdom this is folly, a paradox: in order to live one must die. Confronted with the invitation of Christ, man cannot help but be assailed by the most terrible of conflicts. It is the drama of faith which St. Augustine has described in his *Confessions* and which we find more or less vividly experienced in all conversions.[12] This drama could not occur, of course, if instead of revealing Himself to us behind the cloak of sensible signs God showed Himself to us in the intuitive vision. In the latter case man would understand that God is his ultimate goal, in whom his desire for happiness can be fulfilled and toward whom his life verges as toward a final end. But until the intuitive vision is a beatific reality, man will see the negative aspects in Christ's invitation to follow Him, the sacrifices which He imposes upon his pride. In faith we see what has to be sacrificed, what has to be renounced to adhere to God, but we do not see what is to be acquired. There is a choice between two fascinations: that of the world which can be seen and touched and that of God which cannot be seen or touched. On the one hand lies everything which attracts the senses and fascinates them; on the other there is Christ with His cross—which can be seen—and the hope of Resurrection—which cannot be seen. Man is asked to renounce what he has for what he does not have but hopes to have.

How can this conflict be resolved? Will man accept or reject the invitation which God tenders him through the mouth of His heralds?

The interior Master

Man is not alone in striving to find a solution to this conflict. With him there is a supernatural reality, an interior Master who tries to help him in his difficult choice, to smooth out the difficulties, and to show him that in accepting God's invitation he does

[12] We have treated this topic in a series of articles dedicated to the problems of conversion. See "Il fenomeno delle conversioni, oggi," *La Civiltà Cattolica,* I, (1953) 489–502 and following issues.

not renounce himself, even though everything indicates that he does, but that he is actually attaining the greatest perfection to which he may aspire. The cross which Jesus carries on His shoulders, heavy as it may be, is in reality light when carried with Jesus (Matt. 11:30). It is not a disgrace, but a symbol of love that attains the dimensions of total sacrifice, that gives everything of itself in order to attract him who is far distant from the true life and cannot find it by himself. Through the intimate teachings of this Master, man's eye becomes sharpened, and he is enabled to perceive the true significance of the cross of Christ and its full attraction. In this way the natural fascination of the world, which impresses the senses, is confronted by the supernatural fascination of Christ, who puts man in the position of choosing between the two.

Sacred Scripture speaks of this interior Master in diverse forms. Jesus said: "I praise thee, Father, Lord of heaven and earth, that thou didst hide these things from the wise and prudent, and didst reveal them to little ones. Yes, Father, for such was thy good pleasure" (Matt. 11:25– 26). Jesus here contrasts the knowledge of divine things possessed by simple people and children to that possessed by the proud. The former receive their knowledge from God, while the latter find it in their own resources. The effect can be understood: while the intimate nature of God is revealed to the former, it remains hidden from the latter. And yet it may happen that both kinds of people listen to the voice of God coming from the outside. Both receive exterior revelation, both hear God speak; but while the simple ones perceive the true meaning of God's words and believe, the proud think they understand and in reality do not. These latter ones do not enjoy an interior revelation, without which they cannot accept the exterior word. Among divine things the divinity of Christ holds the chief place. Nobody knows this but the Son of God, the Word made flesh, and those to whom it is the Son's good pleasure to reveal Himself (Matt. 11:27).

Among the simple people who received the revelation was Peter. At Caesarea Philippi Peter answered Christ, "Thou art the Christ, the Son of the living God" (Matt. 16:16). Many had heard the external word of Jesus, His protestations that He was the Messiah and the Son of God, but only Peter could penetrate the mystery of His word, because the Father had revealed it to him. "Flesh and blood" could not accomplish this. A direct intervention of the Heavenly Father was necessary in order that Jesus' words, which either were overlooked or else gave scandal, might be understood (Matt. 11:6). God did the same for Lydia, the purple seller from the city of Thyatira, whose heart He opened in order to make her attentive to Paul's preaching (Acts 16:14).

St. John speaks of testimony. The Father bears witness to the Son not only through the miracles He performed to authenticate His divinity (John 5:36), not only through the Scripture He inspired (5:45–47), but also through an intimate testimony which takes place in the heart of every man. "Who is there that overcomes the world if not he who believes that Jesus is the Son of God . . . And it is the Spirit that bears witness that Christ is the truth" (1 John 5:5–6). In this case, too, we have an internal testimony which takes place through an action of the Spirit in the heart of every man. It is the Spirit who impels us to recognize Jesus, whom preaching proclaims, as the Son of God.

Nor is St. Paul any less explicit. If to some, as the Apostle says, our Gospel remains a mystery, it is to those who are on the road to perdition: "In their case, the God of this world has blinded their unbelieving minds, that they should not see the light of the gospel of the glory of Christ, who is the image of God. For we preach not ourselves, but Jesus Christ as Lord, and ourselves merely as your servants in Jesus. For God, who commanded light to shine out of darkness, has shone in our hearts, to give enlightenment concerning the knowledge of the glory of God, shining on the fact of Jesus Christ" (2 Cor 4:4–6). St. Paul explains why the Gospel, as preached by him and the other Apostles, remains veiled for some, who fail to perceive its meaning. This occurs because God Himself has "blinded" their senses. If, however, the faithful of Corinth have believed, it is because God's light "has shone" in their hearts. Faith is thus due to an illumination by God. If this is lacking, faith cannot exist. The light of the Gospel needs interior illumination in order to be perceived, and this God gives to those who believe. Without it the "light of the gospel" remains hidden. Somewhere else the Apostle uses another illustration. "Now it is God who is warrant for us and for you in Christ, who has annointed us, who has also stamped us with his seal and has given us the Spirit as a pledge in our hearts" (2 Cor. 1:21–22). It is God, therefore, who through His anointing leads us to believe.

Father Latourelle sums up the doctrine contained in these Bible passages as follows: "In all the passages examined there jointly takes place an internal action with the external word. This action is described as an attraction, an illumination, a testimony, a teaching, a revelation, an anointing. In us there is someone who acts first, a sovereign initiative which invites us to believe in the words of Christ which are addressed to us from the outside. The reply is free but grafted on this divine initiative. In the attraction of grace the return movement—that is, man's reply to the Word of God—is already started. All Christian life begins with this first approach, with this first passivity. The Word does not come alone, but with the breath of the Spirit, which tends to transfix the Word and make it intimate."[13]

St. Augustine expresses this doctrine in famous texts[14] which the other Fathers often consider verbally. After him the Council of Orange sanctioned the doctrine. It teaches that nobody can give consent to evangelical preaching "without the illumination and the inspiration of the Holy Spirit who gives to everybody the sweetness of consenting and believing in the truth."[15] In the Middle Ages St. Thomas clarified the doctrine of his predecessors and expressed it in terms like "lumen fidei" and "interior instinctus Dei invitantis," which have become classic in theology. The "lumen fidei," as recently demonstrated by Father Alfaro, is the habitus of faith, which renders human intelligence capable of tending towards a supernatural object. Under the influence of the habitus of faith man comprehends that it is fitting and necessary for him to believe and to accept the invitation of God. But while preaching presents to the intelligence the object to be believed in order for this capacity to become action, God must move the will from the inside so that the intellect will accept what is proposed to it. The Angelic Doctor speaks of this *interior instinctus* as something that induces faith "movendo et instigando interius corda," that "interius illuminat et docet," that "trahit inspirando interius." Man could not believe without this thrust, this vocation, this interior teaching. Following the invitation of the interior Master, man perceives that it is good and obligatory for him to believe.[16]

---

[13] Latourelle, *Théologie de la révélation*, p. 407.

[14] St. Augustine, *In Ep. Joan. ad Parthos.*, tract. III, 13; ML 35, col. 2004.

[15] *Denz. Sch.* 377. For the doctrine of the Council of Trent see n. 1525; for that of the First Vatican Council, n. 3014.

[16] For the doctrine of *lumen fidei* see the long article by P. Alfaro, "Supernatualitas actus fidei iuxta Sanctum Thomam," *Gregorianum*, 44 (1963), 501–542, 731–787. The texts quoted are on p. 753.

The three solutions

The interior magisterium does not rob man of his freedom; it does not strip external things of their attractiveness, or does it heal the corruption of human nature. Man remains free, and his passions continue to dominate him. The attraction of the interior Master does not lessen the conflict of faith; it indicates the way to be followed and it smoothes the obstacles that dot its path. But the conflict remains. How to resolve it?

Three solutions are possible, and all three are to be found in the concrete situations in which man lives and operates.

There are those who in the face of the moral and intellectual claims of faith refuse to take up their cross and follow Christ. Obeying the natural instinct, they refuse to yield to a solution to the problem of life which costs so dearly and destroys all that they hold as their very own. They do not feel like "losing their own life," which they see, in order to obtain another, which they do not see. To their way of thinking, such people are not renouncing the search for the true meaning of life, but they believe they can achieve this aim in another way, by means of their own strength. Such people speak of science with a capital "S," of reason, progress, the arts, sociology. They think that these values suffice to fill their life without any need of recourse to Christ and His message. These approaches represent the different forms of humanism, the most violent and decisive of which is today represented by atheistic communism. It is the reply of human pride, which does not accept any norm of truth other than that indicated by their own reason.

This attitude was widespread among men during the age of illuminism and rationalism in the last century. They really believed they could do without God.[17] Today it is rather rare among intellectuals, whereas it is common among people who are galvanized by propaganda and technical progress. They are sure that once they have succeeded in securing everything technical progress

[17] Even though aware of the paradox of his statements, George Tyrrell writes: "Truth compels me to say I would rather risk hell on my own lines than secure heaven on those; that I would rather share in the palpitating life of the sinful majority than enjoy the peace of the saintly few" (*Autobiography and Life of George Tyrrell* [London, 1912], vol. 1, p. 263). In the case of Tyrrell, see our study, "La conversione e l'apostasia di Giorgio Tyrrell," *Gregorianum,* 38 (1957), 446–480), 593–629.

can offer, they will be happy and will not need God at all. The man in the street today thinks that science has taken the place of God.[18]

It is clear that the rejection of God is not made with the coolness and lucidity with which we have described it. Pride is very seldom self-conscious. The man who is not disposed to follow the call of God will do everything possible to convince himself that such a call does not really exist. Not satisfied with the proof that God gives him, with the signs of credibility with which Jesus and His Apostles have been accredited, man presents God with his conditions: he will believe if God will give him proof in the manner he demands.

St. Augustine tells us that before his conversion he wanted to have the same proof for the things he did not see (as things of faith are) as for the mathematical proposition that seven and three make ten.[19] Tyrrell cannot understand how God, with omnipotence at His disposal, could have tolerated "ignorance, sin and pain."[20] Camus cannot believe in a God who lets children suffer.[21] In Christianity there is a zone of light and a zone of shadow. When one does not want to believe, one sees only the latter.

The second solution, which may be found mainly in certain circles of existentialist culture, cloaks itself in an attitude of skepticism and incredulity. The solution for the problem of life, as projected by faith, seems to them too good to be true. Is it possible, they ask, that God takes an interest in man? What is man that he can arouse God's interest? What is there so lovable about man that should move God to concern for his happiness?

In so far as this attitude is not inspired by a pride so refined that it parades under the pretext of humility and modesty, it is the result of a state of mind in which a profound knowledge of one's own misery is mingled with the morbid outlook which gives perverse pleasures to some modern men. It is a mixture of humility and morbid introspection, typical of an era like ours, born of the deluded thinking and experiences of two world wars, in which

[18] See also the well-known book of Huizinga, *La crisi della civiltà* (Turin, 1938), in which this attitude is well illustrated.

[19] St. Augustine, *Confessions*, VI, c. 4.

[20] *Il Papa e il modernismo,* (Rome, 1912), p. 141.
1912), p. 141.

[21] Cf. Albert Camus, *The Plague* (New York, 1954).

man has given a bad account of himself. Thus man finds it strange and cannot understand why God should take an interest in him.

In a passage of his *De Trinitate* St. Augustine has described this state of mind, which in its basic elements is to be found in all times. Asking why God, who could have redeemed man in many other ways, had chosen the most painful way of all, the Death of His Son on the cross, the great doctor answers that it was "very fitting." If God had worked out the Redemption in an ordinary way, man would not have believed Him. Man is so miserable he could never have imagined that God would make him the object of His love. One believes only when one sees the Son of the Almighty hanging from the cross. How can anyone doubt the love of God when He gave up His only begotten Son for the world? (John 3:16).[22]

Men in this second category fail to see in the cross the symbol of the love of God. The universe has two dimensions for them. There is doubtless something pathological in this difficulty, which is why we speak about modern man as of a man in crisis.

In the two categories of men just examined the attraction of the interior Master bears no fruit whatsoever. God tries to insert Himself into the soul of man, to illuminate his intelligence and move his will, but He finds there such obstacles that His action is neutralized.

Faith and love

But there is also a third category of men, those who accept the invitation of God: these are the faithful.

But did we not say that this acceptance is a folly, a paradox so far as human logic is concerned? Certainly. How, then, can a man decide to commit it? There is only one answer: this folly is only possible when one recognizes that there has been another folly on the part of God. If renunciation of oneself to take on God as the norm of existence seems to be folly, it was a much greater folly for God to renounce the splendor of His divinity for man, to assume human nature, and die on the cross for him (Phil. 2:5–8). It is in the face of such enormous love which goes to the point of folly that man gives an answer of love which seems also to be folly.

In the perspective of love everything becomes possible and understandable. *Omnia vincit amor*. Love overcomes all obsta-

---

[22] *De Trinitate*, L. XIII, c. 40.

cles. It is love which helps God overcome the obstacles which lie between Him and the encounter with man, between Him and the Redemption, when the call to divine life in Paradise was rejected for the first time. He who knows what love means understands everything quite easily. Guardini says, "In the experience of a great love all the world is grouped around the I-Thou relationship, and everything which happens becomes related to it. . . . All is true and has resonance between that I and that Thou."[23] In faith we respond to the love of Him who has first loved us. One approaches Christ, as St. Augustine says, not "motu corporis, sed voluntate cordis."[24] Faith comes from the heart. Hence, "love is the portal of faith."[25] In summing up the Fourth Gospel's observations on this theme, Mollat says that faith is "an encounter for which God has taken the initiative. . . . In its most essential foundation, faith is an encounter of love."[26]

If one conceives of faith as an encounter of love between man and God, the whole history of salvation, all divine teaching, is easily understood. God has first loved us and demonstrated this love by His works, including the greatest of them all, the gift of His only-begotten Son (John 3:16). Then He has asked us to reciprocate. The invitation to the love of God from all the facts of sacred history seems to spring as St. John has expressed so happily in his first letter, "Let us therefore love, because God first loved us" (1 John 4:19).

In *De catechizandis rudibus* St. Augustine, from the action of God has set up a universal norm which we may define as the general law of love: "There is no mightier invitation to love than to anticipate in loving; and that soul is overhard which, supposing it unwilling to give love, is unwilling also to give the return of love."[27] ". . . it is evident that no greater reason is to be found why love should be either originated or enlarged than what appears in the case when one who as yet loves not at all comes to know himself to be the object of love, or when one who is already a lover either hopes that he may yet be loved in turn, or has by this time the evidence of a response to his affection."[28] This means much

[23] R. Guardini, *op. cit.*, p. 12.
[24] *In Jo. Ev. Tract.*, 26, c. 6; ML 35, col. 1608.
[25] J. Mouroux, *Je crois en toi*, p. 48.
[26] D. Mollat, *op. cit.*, p. 98.
[27] St. Augustine, *De catechizandis rudibus*, 4, 7.
[28] *Ibid.*

more when it is a superior who takes the initiative in love, because in this way it is quite clear that he does not love the inferior because he needs him, but only out of benevolence. But who is superior to God? Faith thus comes from love. In order to say Yes to Christ it is sufficient to be susceptible to love.

Only when He finds a heart which is susceptible to love can the interior Master obtain His aim. Through the reverberations of love the attachment to God in Christ, the losing of one's life for Him, ceases to be folly and discloses its true nature. In renouncing himself, man no longer considers his action a paradox, but a fully rational and personal step, indeed the most rational and personal step that he can take.

The communication of love

But how does this exchange of love between God and man come about? This is the problem we must solve if we want to understand how faith is spread.

First, we must state that the exchange does not arise as the consequence of a syllogism or of a series of syllogisms: reason can prepare us for the encounter with God, can dispose us toward it, can show that man needs God to obtain eternal life, that God has really spoken, but it cannot provoke love. All the reasoning in the world may leave us indifferent.[29] It has been said that apologetics have never effected a conversion. Perhaps such a judgment is too sweeping, and it is likewise true that the objective of apologetics is not to effect conversions but to demonstrate the credibility of Revelation. There is, however, a kernel of truth in this remark: reasoning may convince but it cannot produce faith. As we have said, this is due to that exchange of love between God and man which reason cannot produce. As Mouroux says, "A person cannot be captured at the end of a series of abstract relations."[30]

Nor is faith the end result of a blind instinct. It is a rational act; man has many reasons to believe, to adhere to God. He needs Him, since without Him he cannot give meaning to his life. God is truth and supreme good, everlasting life. Nothing could be

---

[29] We briefly treated this in an article: "Esperienze di convertiti," *La Civiltà Cattolica*, III (1953), 263.

[30] J. Mouroux, *op. cit.*, p. 55.

more reasonable than an act of faith. No other act assures man of such certain guarantees.

There is only one explanation for this passage of love, and it is not an explanation but a statement: love has passed from God to man as a phenomenon of communion. As fire communicates heat to the bystander, so the love of God communicates love to whoever leaves himself open to it. It is a contagion, as Mouroux says.[31] But in order that love may pass, man must refrain from placing obstacles in the way; rather he must let himself be conquered. This is possible only when man already belongs to God, at least by desire. Man believes, and comes to Christ, when he belongs to Christ's fold (John 10:16, 27), when he is on the side of truth (18:37), when he is a friend of the bridegroom (3:29). But when man belongs to the Devil, the Word of Jesus is incomprehensible (8:44–45), and His attraction is without effect.

The Vocation of the Apostles

In the Gospel we have examples of this contagion, of this communion through which faith is spread. In more than one example we see how man comes to Christ, how he listens and accedes to Christ's invitation.

Jesus' method is that indicated by St. Augustine: He takes the initiative and loves first; then He asks that man respond to His offer.

The vocation of Nathanael, of whom St. John speaks in the first chapter of his Gospel, seems to us characteristic in this respect. Nathanael was a just man who respected the Law, one among the many who awaited the coming of the Messiah, about whom they had definite preconceptions. From what John says about him, he must have been a prudent man, not given to easy enthusiasm, and gifted with a certain critical sense. Hearing his friend Philip say that Jesus was the Messiah did not convince him. A native of Cana, not far from Nazareth, he was quite sure nothing good could come from a place like Nazareth, least of all the Messiah. However, being a sincere man, he consents to come and see Jesus.

As soon as Jesus sees him, He addresses him in very flattering terms: "Behold a true Israelite in whom there is no guile" (John 1:47). This was praise such as could be extended to only a handful; it was praise that was especially exceptional in a milieu as

[31] *Ibid.*, p. 67.

hypocritical as the one in which Nathanael lived. The praise immediately penetrated the heart of the future disciple. "Whence knowest thou me?" he asks Jesus. He knew that Jesus was not paying him a compliment. Transfixed by the glance of the Nazarene, Nathanael knew intuitively that Christ had read his heart, that He spoke like this because He knew him. Yet Nathanael did not understand how Jesus could have such knowledge of him. In His answer Jesus hinted at His prophetic powers, "Before Philip called thee, when thou wast under the fig tree, I saw thee" (1:48). Nathanael did not doubt the word of Jesus, or did he think that Christ might have guessed at this knowledge, or have been informed by somebody else. Overcome by the praise given him at the beginning of the conversation, Nathanael at once guesses that the words he heard constitute a sign that Jesus is really the Messiah, and he says as much to Philip. Nathanael answered Him and said, "Rabbi, thou art the Son of God, thou art King of Israel" (1:49); in a few brief moments he has traveled the road from the "nothing good can come from a place like Nazareth" to recognition of the Messiah. And yet, Nathanael was a man of the people, and he certainly did not expect anybody as simple and humble as Jesus to be the Messiah. But faced with one who hailed him as a true Israelite, he does not hesitate to free himself of his preconceptions and to accept Jesus as the one of whom the Prophets have spoken. In his case the attraction of the Father has found free play. Jesus Himself is surprised at the speed of Nathanael's transformation: "Because I said to thee that I saw thee under the fig tree, thou dost believe. Greater things than these shalt thou see" (1:50). To a man without falsehood no great proofs are necessary; the truth conquers him easily. Faith in the case of the disciple from Cana is really an encounter of love in which Jesus takes the initiative.

Jesus uses the same method to call to His side the two pairs of brothers: James and John, and Peter and Andrew. The calling of these disciples takes place in two stages. The first occurs on the banks of the river Jordan. Andrew and John are disciples of John the Baptist, and follow their master as far as their occupation as fishermen permits. They probably witnessed the baptism of Jesus and heard John's expressions of humility when He came to him. Nor can the possibility be excluded that they were spectators at the events after baptism, when the heavens opened and the Holy

26074

Spirit in the form of a dove descended while the Father pronounced the words "This is my beloved Son in whom I am well pleased" (Matt. 3:17).

When Jesus returned to the banks of the river the next day, John the Baptist addressed Him once more by saying, "Behold the lamb of God." This is enough to let Jesus' two future followers know who He is. They already know that He is an exceptional person, because otherwise there would be no explanation for the praise of the Baptist whom they know to be a prophet. Jesus, turning and seeing them following Him, asked; "What is it you seek?", thus taking the initiative for the dialogue (John 1:38). And the two, already favorably impressed that such an important person should address them first, called him "Rabbi." This is a title which shows esteem, and it is especially significant since it comes at a time when Jesus has not yet taught anything. They ask, "Rabbi (which interpreted means Master), where dwellest thou?" And Jesus invites them to follow Him. The report of the conversation ceases right there. What they talked about during the whole day the Evangelist does not tell. But many years after this conversation he still recalls the hour.

The conversation with Jesus undoubtedly made a great impression on them, because Andrew had scarcely returned home when he told his brother Simon that they had found the Messiah. Partly out of curiosity, partly because he is attracted by a person who has so aroused the enthusiasm of his brother, Simon agrees to meet Jesus. Immediately when Jesus sees him, He fixes his gaze upon him and says, "Thou art Simon, the son of John; thou shalt be called Cephas (which interpreted is Peter)" (John 1:42). Here, too, Jesus takes the initiative and speaks first; here, too, the conversation begins with praise. Jesus changes Simon's name because it had special significance for the Jews.

The second stage in the call of the four disciples takes place on Lake Genesareth. Jesus asks Peter to let Him teach the multitudes from his boat, and after His speech He asks Peter to proceed to deep water and to let down his nets for a catch. Peter tells Him about his difficulties: they have fished all night and caught nothing. But then he consents: ". . . at thy word I will let down the net" (Luke 5:5). The catch is so abundant that Peter calls for his partners' help. This impresses Peter so much that he falls down at the feet of Jesus and says, "Depart from me, for I am a sinful man,

O Lord" (Luke 5:8). But Jesus replies without hesitation: "Do not be afraid; henceforth thou shalt catch men" (5:10). And the Evangelist concludes, "And when they had brought their boats to land, they left all and followed him" (5:11).

All this happens in a few minutes, but these few minutes are enough. Face to face with a man so interested in poor fishermen that He calls them as followers, and who at the same time is so eminent a person that He has power over the fish in the lake, the four men give in; they leave parents and families and follow Him. All this has been reduced to an act of love on the part of Jesus: it was He who took the initiative, He who showed interest in them, who compensated them for their services with a sign of His power. What is more natural than to follow such a man? In the calling of the Apostles we here touch on that phenomenon of communion to which we owe the faith.

A negative case

But in the Gospel there is also an episode in which this passage of love, this contagion between Christ and man does *not* take place. It is the episode of the rich youth.

The rich youth, too, knows Jesus, His miracles and His goodness, and he is happy to address Him, "Good Master, what shall I do to gain eternal life?" (Mark 10:17). Jesus tells him to observe the Commandments and lists them. And on hearing that he has kept all these ever since he grew up, "And Jesus, looking upon him, loved him," as the Gospel describes it with rare effectiveness, "and said to him: 'One thing is lacking to thee; go, sell whatever thou hast, and give to the poor, and thou shalt have treasure in heaven; and come, follow me' " (Mark 10:21). It is easy to imagine the sincerity and strength of this gaze. Jesus tries to make His love penetrate the heart of the youth, as it had penetrated the hearts of His Apostles, so as to make him a follower, to abandon everything. But the love does not reach him, and the phenomenon of contagion does not take place. The youth goes away, sorrowing because, as the Evangelist tells us, "he had great possessions" (Mark 10:22).

Here we see the conflict of two loves, the love of Christ, who insists that we renounce all we possess to be perfect, and self-love, which inspires us to retain our possessions. Between the fascination of Christ and that of the world the youth chooses the latter. The love for Christ is missing. There was no encounter with him because there was no love, or at least no love stronger than the desire for riches.

Commitment

The term "commitment" which is so frequent in today's religious language stems, in all its reality, from the concept of faith intended as encounter of love between man and Christ. He who follows the call of God and abandons himself to Him has made a commitment.

But what is this commitment? Liégé, taking his stand on etymology, explains the term: "The commitment is action to deposit as a pledge. Above all, to deposit the pledge of objects as warranty for a loan or guarantee of a promise; we pawn jewels at the pawn shop, we pledge capital in an enterprise. In another sense, we have come to describe as a commitment any act by which a person engages himself morally or in writing, by action or word. Finally, commitment has come to designate the content itself of the deposit, of the moral promise of assuming a duty."[32]

In faith man pledges himself, gives himself as a pledge to live according to the new man for whom he is born, according to the new mode of existence to which faith has called him. He no longer belongs to himself, independent and autonomous, free to dispose of his destiny as he sees fit; he has entered an alliance with God, he has arranged a pact with Him, as a consequence of which his whole life must be with Christ and for Christ. He can no longer think independently of Christ. Christ is the only way he follows, the only truth which he believes, the only light which he permits to illuminate him. Like the Apostles, he leaves everything to follow Christ.

It is an example of such rare dedication that should the Faith man embraces prove to be false, his very existence would have no meaning. If the Faith proved false, he would have sacrificed everything for nothing. One cannot imagine a greater error. While in other fields a pledge requires no more than a renunciation of certain sectors of activity in life, leaving man free for the rest, there are no such limits to faith; in this case error would

[32] A. Liégé, "L'engagement dans l'éducation de la charité," *Nouvelle Revue Théologique*, 80 (1958), 253–254.

mean not only the collapse of an ideal but also the collapse of everything. To live, man would have to begin again. And if by chance he discovered his error when it was too late, his entire existence would have been useless.

St. Paul has best expressed the totality of the commitment and what it means. For him faith meant living in Christ, and death a prize to be won (Phil. 1:21). Christ was the meaning of everything. His faith had Christ's Resurrection as its foundation; by this miracle Jesus had shown that He was in reality the Son of God, the Lord, the Word Incarnate, the one who enlightens every soul born into the world (John 1:9), He in whom all subsists (Col. 1:17). But if this miracle had been false—that is, if Christ had not risen and His promises had consequently been proved to be baseless—Christians, of all men, would be the most to be pitied (1 Cor. 15:19) because they would have sacrificed the goods of this world for the sake of goods that do not even exist. Therefore, we can assert that there is no greater pledge than faith.

The pledge is the consequence of love, without which faith cannot exist. Only for love can one accept a person as the norm for his life and thereby sacrifice everything.

At this point we have arrived at a most important conclusion regarding preaching: if an exchange of love between Christ and man is necessary for the faith, preaching, which is the vehicle for faith, must also be the vehicle for love.

Consequences of the property of faith

From this essentially personalistic conception of faith important consequences may be derived. Since they can help us to understand the dynamics of preaching, we must point them out in detail.

First of all, faith attains the fullness of its definition only in adults. Even if the child is capable of true acts of faith, in proportion to the knowledge he has of God at his particular age, it cannot be denied that it is only the adult, the man who has reached a certain degree of intellectual and moral development, who can assume the pledge of faith in full responsibility. However, it is difficult to say when one is truly adult.

Cardinal Billot has written some noteworthy articles in which he says that many persons, mature in their business life, remain in a state of infancy and irresponsibility in the moral and religious sphere.[33] Billot's statement is somewhat exaggerated, but it contains aspects of the truth that polemics have overshadowed. The number of individuals who, because of education, or certain psychological or sociological reasons, never grew up morally is much greater than we think. It appears that modern life, with its organization and advertising, contributes to an increase in their number.

It is possible, though, to say that normally there arrives a moment in every person's life in which he grows up and takes a position regarding his destiny, deciding either for good or for bad, either for or against God. At this moment, God enters the life of man and invites him to choose Him as the norm of his life. Sometimes the transition from childhood belief to adult belief takes place smoothly and almost unobserved; sometimes it occurs with full consciousness. This is the moment when man decides about himself. St. Thomas places this moment at the beginning of rational life,[34] while others have put it at the end of life.[35] But in either assumption the basic choice is necessary if man is to become an adult.

The option of faith, though made once and for all, is in reality undergoing constant development. There is a faith of childhood, of adolescence, of youth, of maturity, and of old age. Christ is always the same, the Word Incarnate for our salvation, but He is seen differently in the various phases of life. Faith is a voyage of discovery, as has been so accurately observed.[36] Every day one discovers new heights and new obstacles to overcome. It consists always in the dialogue with Christ, but this dialogue takes on different shadings of tone and meaning every day. Faith gives meaning to existence, and the vicissitudes of life make this meaning appear under always-changing aspects.

Thus, we may say that in a certain sense faith is in a permanent state of crisis, because it involves a choice which has to be renewed every day with growing awareness. Besides, if faith is the life of love produced by love, it is also subject to the law of

[33] Billot, "La providence divine et le nombre infini d'hommes hors de la voie normale du salut," *Etudes* (1919–1923). See also Santos Hernandez in *Salvacion y paganismo* (Santander, 1960), p. 121 ss.

[34] We hint at the Thomistic theory of *puer veniens ad usum rationis*. Santos (*op. cit.*, p. 583 ss.) treats this copiously.

[35] See also Santos, *op. cit.*, p. 603 ss.

[36] The expression is by Evelyn Waugh in *Road to Damascus*, ed. by J. A. O'Brien (Garden City, N. Y., 1949), p. 21.

PROCLAIMING GOD'S MESSAGE

love, which seems to end and begin again every day. Great loves are always torments, as the mystics teach us. Especially today, when life displays its attractions with ever-increasing vividness, faith has become a continuous battle.[37]

The personal character of faith also explains, as Guardini says, that no paths are ever trodden before and that none are alike for all.[38] Every person is a world in himself. Every one goes to God along his own path. This does not eliminate certain constants which permit us to study the phenomenon, but how many variations are there within these constants! Preaching cannot ignore this characteristic of faith. There is a way to preach to children, and another way to speak to young people and to adults.

The personalistic structure of faith also explains its obscurity and its freedom, which Mouroux has so well demonstrated.[39] Faith is obscure not only because it is contact and encounter with mystery *par excellence*, which is God, but also, and perhaps principally, because it is an encounter between persons which cannot be produced by reasoning. In faith there is a zone which remains dark and which intelligence cannot examine in all its details.

We can understand the freedom of faith. As we have repeated so often, it is indeed a product of love and love cannot be forced. St. Augustine says so well that we can be forced to enter the church, forced to go to the altar, and even forced to receive the sacraments, but we cannot be forced to believe. In order to believe we have to be free.[40] This is so because faith rises "ex radice cordis— that is, from love—which by its very nature is free. Man can pretend to believe, but he cannot be forced to believe.

We may also say that faith entails a risk and requires an act of courage. In it we abandon that which we see and possess for something vastly superior but which we do not see and only hope to possess. To every man who enters the Faith God addresses the same invitation which He once addressed to Abraham: "Leave your country, your kinsfolk, and your father's house, for the land which I will show you; I will make a great nation of you. I will bless you, and make your name great, so that you shall be a

[37] A. Liégé, "Le combat moderne du croyant," *Nouvelle Revue Théologique,* 79 (1957), 897–904.
[38] R. Guardini, *Vie de la foi* (Paris, 1951), p. 17.
[39] J. Mouroux, *op. cit.,* p. 54 ss.
[40] *In Johann. Ev.,* tract. 26, c. 6; ML 35, col. 1607.

blessing. . . . In you shall all the nations of the earth be blessed" (Gen. 12:1–3).

It is not easy to abandon one's own house and country for an unknown land; it requires an act of courage. Yes, there are the promises of God, but we cannot see them, and their fulfillment seems far away. To believe we must run a risk. But it is a risk which we take on the basis of the one word which does not deceive, the Word of God.

Conversion

Faith, the encounter with God, cannot fail to produce a change in man's life, a separation from everything in which he believed before encountering Christ, a new direction in his existence, a conversion. This is expressed in the New Testament by the term μετάνοια, to which the verbs ἐπιστρέφειν and μετανοεῖν correspond.[41]

The concept of conversion implies a twofold element: one negative, which consists in abandoning and renouncing everything which once gave direction and meaning to life; the other positive, consisting in the adherence to a new reality, that is, God, who gives to existence an altogether different direction. What is given up are the bad things (1 John 3:8), the worship of idols (1 Thess. 1:9), the darkness and the power of Satan (Acts 26:17–18). What we adhere to is "the living God" (Acts 14:14), or "the Lord" (9:35). It is not a question of a return to God of a purely external direction towards Him, but of a radical transformation of existence, of a new creation (2 Cor. 5:17), or a rebirth (John 3:5). In this rebirth we put down the old man and take up Christ, thus giving impetus to a new life in which good works which are worthy of the newly begun existence will be accomplished (Acts 26:20). And we will proceed along the new "way" which we have started to tread. Walking along it, man pleases God (1 Thess.

[41] There is a vast literature of conversion. See, among others, "La conversion," *Lumière et Vie*, 47 (1960); Y. Congar, "La conversion. Etude théologique et psychologique," *Parole et Mission*, 11 (1960) 493–523 (with bibliography); B. Häring, "La conversion," *Pastorale du péché*, (Bibliothèque de Théologie) (Paris-Tournai, 1961), pp. 65–145. See also the entries μετάνοια and μετανοεῖν in *Theol. Wörterbuch z. N.T.*, vol. IV, pp. 972–1004, and "Penitence-Conversion," *Voc. de Théologie biblique*, col. 788–796.

4:1), obeys him (Rom. 6:16), and grows in charity until he
realizes the fullness of Christ.

We thus have three dimensions in conversion: the first, a theological one, consists in faith; the second, the sacramental one, in
Baptism—which infuses the converted person's new being—and
in the other sacraments which develop him; the third, the moral
one, which consists of a new behavior, a new style of life which
conforms to the total change which has taken place in man.[42]

Thus, man proceeds toward salvation in conversion; in it man's
life becomes full and complete, and its true center of gravitation
is located and fixed. In it man sloughs off all that is negative
and false in order to arrive at the positive and at truth. This, as
St. Augustine puts it, means that before conversion man was not
"something." To be something man must convert, turn to God.
"For man to be something, he has to convert to Him who created
him."[43] Before conversion to God life did not have meaning or
aim. This meaning is given to life through conversion. Through
this, St. Augustine repeats, life "formatur atque perficitur, si
autem non convertitur informis est."[44] Before conversion life is like
matter without form. This "form" is given by God. In conversion
man leaves the darkness where he had thrashed around blindly
in search of light, and he finds light, the real light, which comes
from God.[45]

In its first phase, where man encounters God, conversion, or the
total transformation of man, is produced by missionary preaching.
It is by means of preaching that God turns to man and engages
him in a dialogue. "Faith then depends on hearing and hearing
on the word of Christ" (Rom 10:17).

Definition of preaching

At the end of this chapter wherein we have treated the goal of
preaching we are now able to supply a definition. For us, preaching is the proclamation of the mystery of salvation made by God
Himself through His legitimate representatives, with the goals in

---

[42] Congar, *art. cit.*, p. 501.
[43] St. Augustine, "Ut homo sit aliquid, convertit se ad illum a quo creatus
est" (*Enarr. in Ps. 70; ML* 36, col. 896).
[44] St. Augustine, *De Genesi ad litt.*, L. I., c. 1, 2; ML 34, col. 247.
[45] St. Augustine, *In Joann. Ev.*, tract. XX, ML 35, col. 1556.

view being those of faith and conversion and the deepening of the Christian life.

This definition seems to contain all the necessary elements. With the word *proclamation* is expressed whatever is proper to preaching and distinguishes it from any other form of teaching. It is actually not teaching, the demonstration of a thesis or a system, or a sacred discourse, but a solemn announcement of facts— the greatest facts of history. Therefore, the announcement is a proclamation, a word that indicates the solemnity and importance of the facts which are announced.

Of the mystery of salvation: this phrase indicates the object of preaching, which epitomizes Christ dead and risen. We prefer the expression *mystery of salvation* used by St. Paul to *Word of God* or *gospel,* because it seems more stringent to us. It permits the inclusion in preaching of the whole history of salvation, whereas the two other expressions do not seem quite so clear for indicating so vast an object.

Made by God Himself: these terms state that the subject of preaching is God Himself. It is He who speaks, He who proclaims His will to save man and to call him to faith.

In His legitimate representatives: in preaching we find, besides a principal subject, also a secondary subject, an instrumentality: the Word that God pronounces, the Gospel which He proclaims, is proclaimed through His qualified representatives. Thus it is stated that preaching is a function of the Church, a hierarchical act and not a gift made privately by God to anyone.

With the goals in view: the aim to which preaching is directed in God's plan is conversion to the Faith. At the same time and because of man's evil dispositions, this aim may not be achieved. Even though God, by proclaiming His will to salvation, wants man to adhere to it and save himself, man may still reject it. In this case preaching does not produce faith, even though it has the goal of faith in view.

Of conversion to faith: the aim of preaching is faith, the acceptance of the salvific plan of God, an acceptance which includes conversion. In faith man responds to God, accepts His Word of salvation and grace.

And the deepening of Christian life: This is an allusion to the other two forms of preaching. Conversion, the effect of faith, is a reality which is susceptible to deepening and progress. This can occur both on the intellectual level (through catechetics) and on the level of the will (through the homily).[46]

[46] See also the definitions by Daniélou (*Le prêtre ministre de la parole* [Paris, 1955], p. 46), by Roguet (*op. cit.*, p. 98), by Maggiolini (*La predicazione nella vita della Chiesa* [Brescia, 1961], p. 8), by Spiazzi (*Scientia salutis*, pp. 306–307), by Händler (*Die Predigt* [Berlin, 1949], p. 15). Rahner defines preaching thus: "Das Wort Gottes (auch im Munde der Kirche in ihrer Verkündigung) ist nicht zuerst und zuletzt Didache, sondern Proklamation, in der die Ankunft des Proklamierten selbst geschieht, ist das machtvolle schoepferische Dabar Gottes an den Menschen, die Weise, in der anwesend wird, in der sie aus ihrer göttlichen Verborgenheit selbst heraustritt und so allererst da ist, wo wir sind." ("Wort und Eucharistie," *Schriften zur Theologie* [Einsiedeln, 1960], vol. IV, p. 323).

CHAPTER VI

The Dimensions of Preaching

As a conclusion and synthesis of the first part of this study, we would like to discuss the dimensions of preaching. This examination will permit us to illuminate some points which have remained obscure and to develop at greater length aspects at which we have only hinted.

The sacred dimension

Above all there is a sacred dimension of preaching. In preaching, as we have said repeatedly, God uses the human word to invite man to meet him and to establish with him a community of life and love. In preaching, the eternal and the enduring flow into time and space, and lift man above himself and above his purely natural needs. Preaching has for its goal the sacred object itself and aims at a sacred ending, which is the encounter with God.[1]

It is from this sacred character that preaching derives its energy and solemnity. There is nothing more solemn than the voice of God, who through the voice of His duly authorized deputy makes known to man His will to salvation and the intellectual and moral needs accompanying it. In the Bible there is no more solemn expression than "Thus speaks the Lord." Because it is God who speaks through him, the preacher is in the fullest sense of the

[1] See the remarks by Vagaggini on preaching as *mysterium* in *Il senso teologico della liturgia* (Rome, 1958), p. 666 ss.

111

word, as St. Augustine says, "dictor rerum magnarum."[2] God speaks only of great things, such as salvation. Even apparently insignificant things are really great because preaching elevates them to a meaning which they do not naturally possess. What is there more common than a glass of water? And yet it becomes a great thing when the preacher can draw from it sparks that inflame the heart of man and prod him to do deeds of mercy worthy of eternal reward.[3]

Perhaps it is precisely this sacred character which has been so sorely lacking in the words of preachers over the course of centuries. The crisis of preaching consists in the loss of this sacrality, in the profanation of the Word of God. This profanation of the preacher's word renders it no longer a vehicle for the Word of God, but a human word. It thus transforms preaching from the *Word of God* to the *word about God* or concerning God. In this way the preacher, in the biblical sense designated as the instrument through whose voice that of God resounds, becomes a professor, the man who treats of God; and the messenger is succeeded by the orator who seeks to arouse the interest and the applause of people.

At the root of this profanation lies the scandal which the Word of God stirs in man. The very first to feel this is the preacher himself. Christ crucified, the object of preaching, is to the Jews indeed a stumbling block and to the Gentiles, foolishness" (1 Cor. 1:23), a reality of which one should be ashamed. To overcome this scandal, the preacher must firmly believe in the presence of God within him, in the validity of the mission conferred on him, and in the efficacy of the Word of God within himself and his listeners. Only in this way can the Word of God retain its power. But as quickly as these supernatural realities are forgotten, the scandal makes itself felt again. The temptation to entrust himself to the "sapientia verbi" (1 Cor. 1:17) is always latent in the preacher. It is tempting to fall back on his own natural resources and to empty the cross of Christ.

It is significant to note the frequency with which preachers themselves, who are aware of the importance and the nature of their mission, complain about the profanation of the Word of God

---

[2] St. Augustine, *De doctrina christiana*, IV, 38.
[3] *Ibid.*

as frequently heard from pulpits. To this very cause they attribute the sterility of many sermons.

For Segneri the reason for the low yield of preaching is to be found in the fact that "the divine word is no longer divine, but human, because it is so corrupted . . . profaned by a language which is all of this world."[4] Bourdeloue thinks that the reason we do not profit from preaching lies in the fact that "it is heard as the word of men, without a thought to the fact that it comes from high above, that is, from God Himself."[5] Bossuet calls it "an agreeable entertainment which just barely touches the ear with the sweetness of a passing thought."[6] Zocchi does not hesitate to label as "profanation and sacrilege"[7] the Word of God as that Word is proclaimed by so many preachers.

In this profanation Christianity, as a message of salvation destined to change the life of man and to give it new direction, is transformed into "mere philosophy,"[8] as Zocchi says, or "into a kind of religious convenience which corresponds to a philosophical and academic morality."[9] For these reasons preaching runs the risk of becoming a hybrid mixture of the human and the divine, of sacred and profane, which it is difficult to categorize. Designed to transmit the sacred, preaching runs that risk of debasement which can render it ridiculous.

The historico-biblical dimension

Besides the sacred dimension there is the historico-biblical one. As it has been mentioned, preaching's object is the approach and encounter of two privacies, that of God and that of man. This is not possible without a communication of love. Only for love can man renounce his own life and live that of Christ. Therefore God, in taking the initiative, has loved first, knowing that "there is no mightier invitation to love, than to anticipate in loving."[10] He has

[4] Segneri, *Il cristiano istruito,* in *Opere di Paolo Segneri* (Turin, 1840), p. 18.

[5] Bourdaloue, *Sermons du Père Bourdaloue,* vol. I (Paris, 1726), p. 400.

[6] Bossuet, *op. cit.,* vol. IX, p. 52.

[7] Zocchi, *La predicazione. Vizi e rimedi,* p. 11.

[8] *Ibid.,* p. 9.

[9] Anonymous, *La predicazione e la prima medicina ai nostri mali* (Monza, 1857), p. 212.

[10] St. Augustine, *De catechizandis rudibus,* 4, 7.

shown His love, first through the creation of the Universe to prepare a worthy home for man, next by elevating man to the supernatural order, then, after the Fall of Adam, in His promise of
Redemption, and finally in all the history of the Jewish people
considered as the prefiguration of God's desire for every man.
In the fullness of time God gave proof of His supreme love by
sending His Son to earth so that through His Death and Resurrection we would have eternal life (John 3:16).

These proofs of love, as they have unfolded over the ages, are
registered in Scripture, the book of the *magnalia Dei,* of the
great things which God has done for man and of what He will
do when history has concluded its cycle.

As the cause of the encounter with God in faith, preaching
must therefore be historico-biblical. It must proclaim what God has
done for man in the history of salvation and invite him to enter
this history in which God is the protagonist. The alliance which
God one day formed with Abraham, with the patriarchs and the
Chosen People, is today formed with a new people, the Church to
which He calls all men. Through preaching man must become
aware that the Bible applies to him, that it was written for him
and took place for him. St. Paul says, "For whatever things have
been written have been written for our instruction, that through
the patience and the consolation afforded by the Scripture we
may have hope" (Rom. 15:4). Holy Scripture is the book written
by God for every man, so that through it man may begin to know
himself and to live according to the plan which God has formulated for him.

The historico-biblical dimension appears in the great speeches
of the Acts, where the Apostles proclaim the Good News of the
Gospel, invite the people to accept the salvation God offers them
in Christ crucified and resurrected, and urges that they enter the
society of salvation which is the Church. They do it by proclaiming
the *magnalia Dei* (Acts 1:11); so does Peter on the day of Pentecost (Acts 2:14–39), after the healing of the lame (3:12–26) before
Cornelius (10:37–43); so does St. Paul in the synagogue of Antioch in Pisidia (Acts 13:16–41) and at Athens (17:22–31). At
the end of every speech is the invitation to do penance and to be
converted, expressed like this passage from St. John: "Let us
therefore love, because God first loved us" (1 John 4:19).

The one chiefly responsible for pointing out this dimension of preaching was St. Augustine in *De catechizandis rudibus*. Even though he speaks primarily about missionary preaching,[11] what he has to say is applicable to preaching in general. For St. Augustine preaching is the *narratio* of what God has done to show us His love. And since all sacred history is in function of this love, the *narratio* must endure from the creation of the world to the era of the Church, that is, even to the parousia and the resurrection of the dead.[12] It must comprehend the complete history of salvation, all that God has done from the moment when by His omnipotent Word He began creation to our own period when He acts in the Church in which the history of salvation is continued, to what He will do in the future until the epilogue to man's history will be written in eternal life.

This does not imply that preaching should be nothing more than a simple recounting of the history of salvation. Preaching's importance lies not in merely stating the facts, but in revealing the motivation behind them. St. Augustine says that every single case and every single fact will be accounted for by referring it to the aims of love from which neither he who speaks nor he who listens can ever lift his glance.[13] Explanations are necessary, but they should only serve to illustrate and to point out the love of God as seen in the facts. In explaining them, according to St. Augustine, one must be careful to avoid two excesses: to lead people to faith through an impressionistic exposition by empty, but dangerous, sweetness and zeal,[14] and to lose oneself in esoterics, that is, in questions of erudition and speculative reasoning.[15] The true norm to be followed in these explanations is the following: "But the simple truth of the explanation which we adduce ought to be like the gold which binds together a row of gems, and yet does not interfere with the choice symmetry of the ornament by any undue intrusion of itself."[16]

The reasons for St. Augustine's warnings are clear: preaching must lead to a love of God which is neither empty sentiment nor

---

[11] We have tried to show how this one tract by St. Augustine treats missionary preaching in "St. Augustin evangelisateur," *Parole et Mission*, 22 (1963), 357–378.

[12] St. Augustine, *De catechizandis rudibus*, 3, 5; 6, 10; 7, 11.

[13] *Ibid.*, 6, 10.

[14] *Ibid.*

[15] *Ibid.*

[16] *Ibid.*

abstraction. If the preacher, therefore, wants to secure these aims, he must not lose himself in sentimentality or in complicated questions and difficult reasonings his listeners cannot understand, and which feeds more their curiosity than their heart.[17]

The apologetic, moral and polemic elements must not be neglected, of course, but they must be subordinated to the over-all account, and they must make clear the line of sacred history. In other words, explanations should be aimed at emphasizing the significance of the facts as manifestations and symbols of the love of God.

Everybody acquainted with the history of preaching knows how these Augustinian principles have been neglected by preachers. Preaching has often served for many as a vehicle to display their dialectic power, their ability to discourse for hours about a Bible verse by abstracting from it, like a conjurer, things never expected. These are aberrations which contrast with the seriousness of the Word of God and with the manner of its proclamation by the Prophets and the Apostles.

The historico-biblical dimension first came to the fore in the preaching and catechesis of the Early Church and the Church Fathers. We have examples of it in the synthesis of faith as the symbol of the Apostles, in the catechesis of the Fathers—of Cyril of Jerusalem,[18] of St. Ambrose,[19] and of St. Augustine—which is completely centered on the history of salvation.

The Christocentric dimension

Because it is essentially historico-biblical, preaching is also basically Christocentric. The history of salvation has Christ as its center and its frame of reference. Christ is the synthesis of the plan of God for history and for man, the first and the last (Apoc. 1:17), He for whom everything comes into being (Col. 1:16–17). Early Christians were so convinced of this fact that they summed up their faith in the formula "Jesus is Lord" (1 Cor. 12:3; Rom. 10:9; Phil. 2:11).

But what does this Christocentrism mean? Above all it means that in preaching everthing is seen from the angle of the role of Christ, as part of the plenitude which He is (Col. 2:9) and from which we have all received (John 1:16). If everything has its

---

[17] *Ibid.*
[18] Paulin, *Cyrille de Jerusalem catechète* (Paris, 1959).
[19] B. Parodi, *La catechesi di Sant'Ambrogio* (Milan, 1957).

true meaning in Christ, everything discussed in preaching must be seen in the light of Christ: any other light would be false or at least incomplete. Morals, dogma, the liturgy, the Church, Scripture—all have their frame of reference in Christ.

St. Paul gives us a good example of Christocentrism; he sees all this: the Church is the mystical Body of Christ (Eph. 4:12); to believe is to receive Christ (Col. 2:5); Baptism is dying and rising in Christ (Rom. 6:3); Matrimony is a great mystery in Christ (Eph. 5:22); divisions among Christians divide the Body of Christ (1 Cor. 1:13); God is Father of our Lord Jesus Christ (2 Cor. 1:3). The expression "in Christ" occurs 164 times in his letters.[20]

We can say the same thing of this dimension that we did of the preceding one: all preaching must serve Christ, just as the thread of gold serves the gems which it holds together. Everything must contribute to making clear His function in the history of the relations between God and man.

But this dimension does not mean that we have to confine our preaching to Christology. Christocentrism demands only that everything in preaching be seen in the light of Christ, that is, in His role in the history of salvation. We have said that there is no theme which could not, or must not, be the object of preaching, precisely because everything finds its ultimate explanation in Christ. Art, politics, economics—all are realities willed by God, and every one of them plays its part in the plan of God to encounter man and to lead him to eternal life.

It will be this Christocentrism which will help preaching overcome the abstractness and moralism to which it has fallen prey today. When everything is referred to the person of Christ, it is impossible either to be abstract or to present morals as a complex of duties founded on natural law. The reference to Christ will give Christian morals that personalistic aspect which is proper to them.[21]

The ecclesial dimension

Because it is Christocentric, preaching is also ecclesial. This can be understood in various ways.

(1) Above all, preaching is ecclesial because of its subject. It

[20] F. X. Arnold, *Proclamation de foi et communauté de foi* (Brussels, 1957), pp. 43–44.

[21] J. A. Jungmann, *Glaubensverkündigung im Lichte der Frohbotschaft* (Innsbruck-Vienna-Munich, 1963), spec. c. VII.

is in the Church and through the Church that Christ speaks, because it is to the Church that He has confided His message to be proclaimed to the end of time (Matt. 28:18–20; Mark 16:15; Acts 1:8). Consequently, preaching belongs to the Church as an essentially hierarchical act, and nobody can preach unless he has received a mandate from her.

(2) Preaching is also ecclesial because only the Church can authoritatively interpret the message of Christ, given in trust to her to communicate to men of all times and all places. To her Jesus has promised His assistance (Matt. 28:18–20) and that of the Holy Spirit (John 16:13). Therefore no preaching is legitimate which is not in the sense of the Church and which does not preach in its fullness what the Church preaches, without selections and omissions. Thus it would be improper to preach Paradise and omit Hell, to stress God's mercy but leave out His justice. Nor could a kind of preaching be accepted which, in order to explain certain situations, has recourse only to historical or restricted motives, and does not state clearly enough the interpretation given them by the Word of God. Moreover, it would not be legitimate to give to dogmas interpretations which differ from those of the Church, as modernism was doing. The personal ideas of the preacher do not count in preaching; only those of the Church in whose name he is speaking count.

(3) Preaching is also ecclesial in the sense that it gives origin to the Church. This is an aspect which we have already treated: the Church emerges from preaching. From Christ's preaching came the college of the Twelve, which was the first nucleus of the Church; from that of the Twelve, the first Christian community originated in Jerusalem; from that of St. Paul, the first Christian communities among the Gentiles took their origin; from that of their successors emerged, and are still emerging, Christian communities among all the peoples of the earth. The creative aspect of preaching will continue to give children to the Church until the number of brothers of Christ will be complete (Apoc. 6:11).

(4) Preaching is also ecclesial because it develops the Church. If missionary preaching creates the Church, by calling those that are far from God to salvation, catechetical and homiletical preaching develops the Christian community by rooting the faithful ever more strongly in Christ. St. Paul recommends his converts "to God and to the word of his grace, who is able to build up and to

give the inheritance among all the sanctified" (Acts 20:32). It is the word, which, together with the sacraments, makes the Mystical Body grow and brings it to the fullness of Christ (Eph. 4:13).

(5) Preaching is ecclesial again because it forms in Christians the conscience of the Church. It must develop in the members of the Church the consciousness of belonging to a community whose dimensions are designed to embrace all humanity. An individualistic or class-structured Christianity does not make sense. St. Paul says that for Christ, "Here there is not 'Gentile and Jew! circumcised and uncircumcised,' 'Barbarian or Scythian,' 'slave and freeman' " (Col. 3:11). In Christ all differences between men disappear, and distances become shorter. One of the tasks of preaching, especially of the catechetical kind, is the formation of this consciousness of the Church by avoiding all temptations to a parochial spirit or esprit de corps.[22]

(6) Finally, preaching is ecclesial because it occurs in the Church. The Church furnishes preaching with a natural context in which to act, as well as the motives of credibility without which it cannot appear as the Word of God. We shall return to this aspect in the second part of this book.

The liturgical dimension

Preaching also has a liturgical dimension. Preaching and liturgy are closely connected: one cannot exist without the other.

To be sure, they have the same content, the history of salvation. Preaching proclaims what liturgy fulfills. The former presents the divine plan of salvation and invites man to the encounter with God; the latter is where the encounter takes place. The two realities are therefore complementary.

Vagaggini writes: "Without the ministry of the Word, the rite runs the risk of being fruitless for the faithful who do not understand its meaning and do not bring to it the necessary moral disposition. The ministry of the Word has, of course, precedence because in it God arouses the soul and disposes it; without the ministry of the rite the Word cannot save because God has willed that the encounter between Him and man should be fulfilled in

[22] On this problem see the reflections by Msgr. Renard, *Pour une évangélisation et une catéchèse d'Eglise* (Paris, 1957).

the rite, and because there is no grace without at least the desire for the sacrament."[23] Preaching prepares and disposes toward the liturgy, and is a function of it.

This is true of preaching in all its forms. Evangelization, wherein the mystery of salvation is proclaimed, contains explicitly or implicitly—as we see in the great kerygmatic discourses of the Acts—the initiation to Baptism in which man encounters Christ, takes on His form, and is born to a new life. Once man is joined to Christ by means of Baptism, preaching deepens this union by developing the life of faith in him through an explanation of its demands on the intellectual plane. This can only be accomplished by teaching the faithful to read the signs in which God has revealed Himself, among which those of the liturgy take precedence. The initiation to the Christian life, the catechesis, is fundamentally an initiation in the sacraments, in which the Christian grows in Christ by becoming similar to Him.

Even more closely connected with the liturgy is the homily. The homily takes place in the liturgy as an integral part of it. If all preaching is a call to divine life, this is especially true of the homily, which takes place during Mass. In it are joined together the two components of salvation, the call of God and the reply of man. In the first part of the Mass God proclaims His will to salvation; in the second, man replies by accepting it and offering, together with the priest, the sacrifice of Christ, the only sacrifice acceptable to God.

Preaching and liturgy, therefore, go together and cannot be separated. The moment there is a separation between them they have lost their meaning. Separated from the liturgy, preaching may give the impression of proclaiming abstract things taking place far removed from any reality. Liturgy without preaching, on the other hand, runs the risk of being transformed into a series of magic acts, of ceremonies without meaning, or of a rite destined solely for choreographic effect.

Thus, preaching pervades the entire liturgy. It produces and develops faith, without which the liturgy would not make sense.

The liturgy, on the other hand, renders an incomparable service to preaching, not only on the existential basis, because it fulfills what preaching proclaims, but also on the plane of knowledge. The liturgy expresses in visible signs what preaching expresses in

[23] C. Vagaggini, *op. cit.*, p. 682.

conceptual form. Therefore, reference to the liturgy helps preach-ing, especially the catechetical and homiletic kinds, to make understandable that which they want to teach and inculcate.

In his encyclical *Quas primas* Pius XI clearly outlined the keryg-matic function of the liturgy and the service which it can render to preaching. "To instruct the people in the divine truth and to lift them to the spiritual and interior joys, the splendors of the liturgy have more effect than the documents of the magisterium of the Church, even of the most important ones. The documents reach only educated Catholics in restricted numbers, while the liturgy touches and teaches all the faithful; the former are pub-lished only once, while the latter lift their voices, so to say, every year, regularly descending from the liturgical heaven; the first speak only to the intelligence, the others speak to the intelligence and the heart, to the entire man. We must take into account that man consists of body and soul, and is vividly impressed by beauty and variety of an exterior cult whose ceremonies penetrate the heavenly doctrine to the very foundations of the being."[24] As if commenting on these words, Blomjous says that the liturgy is faith itself concretely expressed.[25]

Without being direct preaching, the liturgy is excellent as indi-rect preaching. [26] In visible symbols it displays the truth catechesis puts before us. The best way to teach catechism, therefore, is to keep it within the liturgical framework, so that its relationship to the mysteries of the cult is made clear. The Fathers of the Church did just that.[27] Jungmann could rightly say, "Our catechesis must always, or nearly, be mistagogic catechesis."[28]

By finding once again the unity between liturgy and catechesis we can overcome that abstractness of preaching we mentioned in connection with the Christocentric dimension. By showing the liturgy's relationship to catechesis we can also show the faithful the continuity of sacred history. It can make clear how the Old Testament was only a preparation, a symbol for what was to happen in the New Testament. God today is much more present

[24] *AAS,* 17 (1925), p. 603.

[25] J. Blomjous, "Basic Links Between Liturgy and Catechesis," *Teaching All Nations* (London, 1961), p. 227.

[26] *Ibid.,* p. 391 ss.

[27] B. Parodi, *op. cit.,* esp. p. 179 ss.

[28] J. A. Jungmann, "Liturgie et histoire du salut," *Lumen Vitae,* 10 (1955), 288.

among His people than in the Old Covenant; He performs miracles of much greater impact than those of times past, even though under the veil of mystery. It is precisely the liturgy which will make modern man feel himself part and parcel of a history which endures, one can say, from eternity to eternity.

The eschatological dimension

Finally, preaching has an eschatological dimension. This may be understood in various ways.

(1) First of all, preaching is eschatological because it belongs to the *escata*, the last phase of the history of salvation, the one in which all men, without distinction of race or nationality, are invited to partake of the Kingdom of God. It is inaugurated by Christ's preaching: "The time is fulfilled, and the kingdom of God is at hand. Repent and believe in the gospel" (Mark 1:15). It is Jesus' preaching which inaugurates the Messianic epoch, wherein the symbols disappear and the Kingdom of God appears in its fullness. Preaching is therefore eschatological, pertaining to the last things. And, as we said before, it is the great, final truth, when the prophecies have been fulfilled and the Holy Spirit communicated.

In this connection Leclercq notes that according to the Scholastics the Old Testament rarely used the expression "preaching," preferring to say "proclaiming the Word of God" or to "prophecy," because preaching included knowledge of the spiritual meaning of events, which would be impossible without the outflowing of the Holy Spirit.[29]

(2) But there is an even deeper meaning which makes preaching an eschatological truth, and that is that it forces man to decide what will be his fate in view of the last judgment. Salvation and eternal damnation depend on the attitude man assumes with respect to the preaching of the Word of God.

"For the word of God is living and efficient and keener than any two-edged sword, and extending even to the division of soul and spirit" (Heb. 4:12), and is, therefore, capable of arousing in man his strongest sentiments and of obliging him to emerge from his indifference and take a stand regarding the salvation offered him. "For the doctrine of the cross is foolishness to those who perish, but to those who are saved, that is, to us, it is the power

---

[29] Leclercq, *La Maison Dieu*, 8, p. 38.

of God" (1 Cor. 1:18). The presence of Christ in the word proclaimed by the preacher is "the fragrance of Christ for God, alike
as regards those who are saved and those who are lost; to these
an odor that leads to death, but to those an odor that leads to
life" (2 Cor. 2:15–16). And St. Paul asks if he is worthy of such
a calling (2:17). It is impossible to remain indifferent with
regard to this divine reality: one must accept or reject. Christ
Himself is present in the word of the preacher for the ruin or the
salvation of many (Luke 2:34; John 3:20; 12:47 ff.; and 15:22).
Preaching is really God's judgment of man.

(3) There is a third way in which preaching is eschatological.
The Word of God imposes on man a total change, a *metanoia*;
it is a question not of details, but of a new orientation of his
whole life. Man must struggle so that Christ can become the only
reality, the norm of every action and every thought, until one
renounces everything for Him. Adhering to Christ means uprooting the human from nature and rerooting it in Christ (Eph. 3:18).
It means really exchanging death for a new life, a dying and
rising again in Christ. There is nothing more eschatological than
this.

All these dimensions can be reduced to one, the Christocentric
dimension. It is from the reality of Christ that preaching takes
on its dimensions. Christ is the object of the sacred because in
Him God Himself is revealed, the object of Scripture in which
His history is told; the object of the liturgy in which His mystery
is actualized; the Head of the Church, He who has founded it
and vivifies it with His Spirit; and finally He in whom the fate of
man is decided. It is Christ who makes the unity of the Bible,
of the Church, of the liturgy—in a word, the unity of all history.

CONCLUSION

Considered within the frame of salvation history, preaching
provides the means and the place for the encounter between God
and man, an event of cosmic significance, a reality which united
Heaven and earth. In it God Himself, using the words of Christ
and of the Church, enters into contact with a rational creature,
calls him, announces His will for salvation to him, shows him the
plan for eternity which He has conceived. And thus speaking, He
confers through the human word a force which demands of man
that he take a position concerning the salvation which He has

proclaimed. By means of grace, preaching is an effective word which proclaims salvation and confers it. It is the vehicle of faith and the instrument through which the Church is convoked and developed.

Now we must examine this efficacy itself and determine what it consists of and how it explains itself. This will be done in the second part of our examination.

CHAPTER VII

Word and Sacrament

Aᴀ Fᴛᴇʀ discussing preaching within the context of the history of salvation, we now want to consider the ministry of the Word in its very nature and no longer with regard to its relative aspects.

According to Scripture, as we have pointed out already, preaching is an effective word, a word which does what it says. We should now examine the nature of this efficacy. This is a question theologians are primarily concerned with, especially theologians in Germany.

The Efficacy of God's Word in the Old Testament

Let us examine, in greater detail than was done in Chapter Three, the fact of efficacy as it is presented in Scripture.

According to the Bible, the Word of God possesses special power and is a means of action. It is the Word of God which creates things: "God said, 'Let there be light,' and there was light" (Gen. 1:3). "Then God said, 'Let there be a firmament in the midst of the waters to divide the waters.' And so it was" (Gen 1:6). "For he spoke, and it was made; he commanded, and it stood forth" (Psalm 32(33):9). Mark the strength of the expression in Psalm 147: "He sends forth his command to the earth; swiftly runs his word! He spreads snow like wool; frost he strews like ashes. He scatters his hail like crumbs; before his cold

125

the waters freeze. He sends his word and melts them; he lets his breeze blow and the waters run" (Psalms 147–147B:15–18). Equally powerful is the description of the Word of God in Psalm 29: "The voice of the Lord is over the waters, the God of glory thunders, the Lord, over vast waters. The voice of the Lord is mighty; the voice of the Lord is majestic. The voice of the Lord breaks the cedars of Lebanon. He makes Lebanon leap like a calf and Sarion like a young wild bull. The voice of the Lord strikes fiery flames; the voice of the Lord shakes the desert, the Lord shakes the wilderness of Cades" (Psalm 28 (29): 3–8). And Jeremias has God say: "Is not my word like fire . . . like a hammer shattering rocks?" (Jer. 23:29). The best known text about the efficacy of the Word of God may be found in Isaias in the Old Testament: "For just as from the heavens the rain and snow come down and do not return there till they have watered the earth, making it fertile, and fruitful, giving seed to him who sows and bread to him who eats, so shall my word be that goes forth from my mouth; it shall not return to me void, but shall do my will, achieving the end for which I sent it" (Isa. 55:10–11).

In the New Testament

We find the same dynamic concept of the Word of God in the New Testament. As in the Old Testament usage it is full of force and power.

It is characteristic, above all, that the *Verbum,* the Second Person of the Trinity, through whom "all things were made" (John 1:3), should be called precisely the Word. Just as in the beginning, when God created heaven and earth through the Word, so in the fullness of time His Word will effect the greatest of His works, the redemption of man. The Apostle James says that the Word has generated us to divine life: "Of his own will he has begotten us by the word of truth, that we might be, as it were, the first fruits of his creatures" (James 1:18). This word implanted in us "is able to save our souls" (1:21). And Peter, in his First Epistle, can truly say that Christians must love one another because they have all "been reborn, not from corruptible seed but from incorruptible, through the word of God who lives and abides forever" (1 Pet. 1:23).

The word is "the power of God" (1 Cor. 1:18) which presents

the Gentiles as "acceptable, being sanctified by the Holy Spirit" (Rom. 15:16). It is the Word of salvation (Rom. 1:16), it is the Word of grace (Acts 14:3), of life (Phil. 2:16), of reconciliation (2 Cor. 5:19), of truth (2 Cor. 6:7). In all these cases we have the objective genitive: the Word confers grace, truth, reconciliation.

In Hebrews we find a text which is rightly connected with Isaias 55:10–11: "For the word of God is living and efficient and keener than any two-edged sword, and extending even to the division of soul and spirit, of joints also and of marrow, and a discerner of the thoughts and intentions of the heart. And there is no creature hidden from his sight, but all things are naked and open to the eyes of him to whom we have to give account" (Heb. 4:12–13).

The Word of God is so effective that Scripture can say of it that it has "continued to spread" (Acts 6:7); it is sent out and reaches people (1 Cor. 14:36); it cannot be laid in chains (2 Tim. 2:9); it runs its course triumphantly (2 Thess. 3:1). In fact, the Apostle recommends the presbyters of Ephesus to "God and to the word of his grace" (Acts 20:32).[1]

It is an efficacy, as Schlier says, which is independent from the motives which move the preacher to proclaim the Word (Phil. 1:15–18), from his probable defects, from his qualities of superiority or eloquence (1 Cor. 2:1). The word is mistress to the Apostle who is bound to serve it like a faithful steward (1 Cor. 4:1–2; Col 1:25).[2]

These texts remove all doubt. The Word of God, the Gospel which the preacher proclaims, is effective: it does what it says. Just as the omnipotent Word of God is the beginning of all things, lifting them out of nothing, so the Word of God in preaching is the beginning of God's second creation, vastly more important than the first, the call to, and the creation within us of divine life. The ultimate reason for this efficacy must be sought in the presence of God in the human word. The efficacy of preaching is the result of the action of the principal cause, God, who operates in it.

---

[1] An analysis of biblical texts with regard to efficacy was done by Aureo Torres Capellan, "Palabra y revelacion," *Burgense,* 1 (1960), 150–155.

[2] H. Schlier, *Wort Gottes,* p. 27–30.

Word and sacrament

The presence and the action of God in the word of the preacher make it possible to speak of a sacramentality of preaching. Just as God is present and acts in the sacrament, so He is present and acts in preaching. The sacraments, like preaching, are effective, and serve as vehicles of grace, and of action from God to man. The analogy between the two is incontrovertible.

Regarding this sacramentality, Betz develops a concept that is interesting in that it indicates the close link between word and sacrament. In preaching, the great events of the history of salvation (*die Heilstaten Gottes*) are proclaimed, facts whose importance lies less in themselves than in their meaning for man. Jesus Himself, on the day of His Resurrection, enlightened the Apostles' minds "that they might understand the Scriptures" (Luke 24:45). In their historical appearance, these facts are symbolic of the love and the interest God bears man. As symbols they speak, communicating with a superior being in a certain language. But this language would be incomprehensible without the word, that is, without preaching which proclaims and explains it. And Betz continues: "In this way, by its very nature, a mark of revelation is inherent in this history, a *Worthaftigkeit*.[3] In addition, the facts of sacred history not only indicate the love of God but they also contain and produce it. Through them man not only knows what God has done in the past, but what He is doing today, *hic et nunc*, to invite his participation in divine life. In them God offers His love to man seeking salvation. The analogy with the sacraments is therefore clear. They, too, are symbols of the love of God for man; they too contain and confer grace."[4]

We must also note that if preaching partakes of the nature of the sacrament, the sacrament in turn partakes of the nature of preaching, and has, as Betz puts it, a certain *Worthaftigkeit*. In fact, the sacrament too, is a symbol; as such it speaks, communicates a message, has something of the nature of the word. The word is a fundamental part of the sacrament, because this it is which renders the sacramental sign effective and capable of pro-

---

[3] J. Betz, "Wort und Sakrament. Versuch einer dogmatischen Verhältnisbestimmung," *Verkündigung und Glaube* (Freiburg, 1958), p. 88.

[4] *Ibid.*, pp. 88–90.

ducing the grace which it symbolizes. *Accedit verbum et fit sacramentum*.[5] The word is the form of the *sacrament*.[6]

Finally, the sacrament is closely linked to preaching in that it is the sacrament of faith and derives its efficacy from faith. And faith, in turn, derives from preaching (Rom. 10:17). Without preaching the practice of sacraments would be impossible.[7]

Unity between preaching and sacrament

Contemporary theology continues to discover and confirm the unity between preaching and sacrament. After centuries of unilateral development, a very natural union has been re-established.

Söhngen stresses this unity with respect to worship. "Consecration and proclamation of the Word, sacrament and word belong together and form the totality of worship which cannot exist without the effective spirituality of the word nor without the spiritual efficacy of the sacrament."[8] There is no worship that exhausts itself in the word alone, or in the sacrament alone. Word and sacrament are to each other as the formal and material element of worship.[9] For Schmaus, the Church of Christ must be "Church of the word and of the sacrament." In it has to predominate "not a unilaterality but a totality and fullness, not *l'aut aut*, but the

[5] Schillebeeckx writes: "Christ is our High Priest in his sacramental manifestation of salvation and through his preaching of the word. The spoken revelation is intrinsically required by the revelation in reality, precisely because this latter is a manifestation of something supernatural in that which is natural. In the word this saving reality is manifested as revealed and given to us" (*Christ the Sacrament of the Encounter with God*, p. 99).

[6] J. Betz, *art. cit.*, pp. 92–93. The sacramentality of preaching is commonly spoken of by modern scholars. See, among others, M. Schmaus, *Kath. Dogmatik*, Band III, I Halbband (Munich, 1958), p. 745; A. Günthör, *Die Predigt* (Freiburg, 1963), pp. 52–54 with quotes.

[7] The close relation between faith and sacrament was treated with biblical, patristic, and theological references by Yves Congar in a lengthy article: "Les deux formes du pain de vie dans l'Evangile et dans la tradition," *Parole de Dieu et sacerdoce* (Paris-Tournai-Rome-New York, 1962), pp. 2158. For the doctrine of St. Thomas see the study by Gaillard, "Les sacrements de la foi," *Revue Thomiste*, 59 (1959), pp. 5–31 and 270–309. From it is clear how far, according to St. Thomas, the efficacy of the sacrament depends on faith.

[8] Söhngen, *Symbol und Wirklichkeit im Kultmysterium* (Bonn, 1937), p. 17.

[9] *Ibid.*, p. 19.

synthesis of all revealed truths. . . . Word and sacrament are ordered to each other."[10] This applies not only to the worship action, but to all the activity of the Church. In all it does, the Church is both word and sacrament.[11]

There is nothing new in this restatement of the unity between preaching and the sacrament. The Church Fathers already knew and stated it. St. Jerome applies the biblical word to the Eucharist and describes the result as the question of two foods given by God for the soul: "If the flesh of Christ is true food and His blood true drink, we have in this life the only good, that of eating this flesh and drinking this blood, not only in the mystery of the Eucharist, but also in reading Scripture."[12] For St. Augustine the analogy between preaching and sacrament is so close that he defines the sacrament as *verbum visibile*[13] and preaching as *sacramentum audibile*.[14] For the Great Doctor, it is the same person who acts as *dispensator verbi et Sacramenti*.[15]

Contemporary Protestant theology is also coming to recognize that preaching must not be separated from the sacrament. After having defined itself as the Church of the Word, Protestantism has found today that the Church of Christ cannot do without the sacrament. Leuba points out the unfittingness of a concept which stresses one part of a reality over another. Predominance of the sacrament over preaching—as sometimes occurs in Catholicism— means that the consequence of the divine action, the participation of the creature in Revelation, is foreseen, but that the conditions accompanying that action, that is, the operation of divine initiative so as to arouse man to participate in its glory are restricted and misinterpreted. "By relegating this initiative to a subordinate position one risks forgetting that initiative is always necessary for a

[10] M. Schmaus, *op. cit.*, p. 744.

[11] Söhngen, *op. cit.*, p. 19. For K. Rahner, word and sacrament constitute the Church, "Wort und Eucharistie," *Schriften zur Theologie* (Einsieldeln, 1960), vol. IV, p. 314.

[12] St. Jerome, *In Eccl.*, c. 3; ML 23, col. 1092.

[13] St. Augustine, *In Joann. Ev.*, tract. 80, 3; ML 35, col. 1840.

[14] Sometimes we read that St. Augustine defined preaching as the audible sacrament (Sehelkle, *Jüngerschaft und Apostelamt* [Freiburg, 1957], p. 69), but we were not able to trace the text.

[15] A series of texts in this sense was collected in the volume *Etudes Augustiniennes* edited by Rondet, Le Landais, Lautas e Coutourier (Paris, 1953), p. 275. For other Fathers see Y. Congar, *art. cit.*, p. 47n.

free choice. Otherwise, the love of God is stressed, but at the expense of the divine sovereignty."[16]

On the other hand, Protestantism can fall into the opposite error of insisting almost exclusively on the conditions for the choice, while forgetting the participation of the creature in Revelation.[17]

One can avoid such lack of balance by uniting preaching and sacrament, the divine initiative and man's response and thus maintaining a link which is truly natural.[18]

The problem of efficacy

The problem now demanding consideration is the manner in which preaching and the sacrament produce grace. We know already that the sacraments act *ex opere operato*. But how does preaching act and produce grace?

It seems that any answer to this question must bear in mind the following biblical and dogmatic data:

1) *Preaching communicates grace.* This is a biblical datum which we have already sufficiently demonstrated.

2) *Faith is necessary for justification.* This is a doctrine of the Bible (Mark 16:16) clearly taught by the Council of Trent.[19]

3) *The sacrament is necessary for justification.* This we know from Scripture (John 3:5), and also from the Council of Trent, which teaches, however, that the sacrament is necessary at least *in voto*.[20]

4) *There are seven sacraments.* This is a doctrine defined by the Council of Trent.[21] Among the sacraments, however, the word is not defined. According to that Council, it is the sacrament which confers justification.[22]

---

[16] J. L. Leuba, "Signe et Symbole en théologie," *Signe et Symbole* (Neuchatel, 1946), pp. 174–175.

[17] *Ibid.* Semmelroth also warns of the danger of a liturgy which is reduced to the word only (*Das geistliche Amt,* p. 149).

[18] Von Allmen also insists on a necessary equilibrium between preaching and sacrament. See, for instance, his thesis: "The Worship of the Church is incomplete, unless the sacrament accompanies preaching, because preaching needs the sacrament as much as the sacrament needs preaching." ("La prédication," *Verbum Caro,* 9 [1954–1955], p. 137.)

[19] *Denz. Sch.* 1526.

[20] *Denz. Sch.* 1524.

[21] *Denz. Sch.* 1601.

[22] *Denz. Sch.* 1606.

5) *Faith comes from preaching.* This is a biblical doctrine (Rom. 10:17) of which the Council of Trent says that it is the beginning, the foundation, and the root of all justification, without which it is impossible to please God.[23]

Any theory seeking to determine the efficacy of preaching cannot deviate from these data. It is sufficient merely to list them in order to conclude that preaching and sacrament are two phases of the same process, that of justification. Preaching produces the faith necessary for the efficacy of the sacrament, and from this latter comes justification. The two phases are closely linked. Any separation of preaching and sacrament would, under ordinary circumstances, compromise the process of justification.

But how do these two realities act?

The opinion of St. Thomas

St. Thomas saw the problem and offered a solution. For him, what the Gospel says is absolutely true: the only Master is Christ (Matt. 23:8). This, however, does not mean that man cannot also be master, cooperating with Christ to unite men with God *dispositive et ministerialiter.*[24] The human magisterium is limited to the level of instrumental cause. Preaching, however, is *principaliter est a Deus, executive est ab apostolis.*[25]

But of what does this instrumental, regulating causality of preaching consist? The Angelic Doctor explains it by an analogy with the human magisterium. In the acquisition of knowledge the intellect of man is the true cause. It possesses certain innate general principles which it applies to the data of experience, drawing from them implicit conclusions, and then moving from one conclusion to the other. In such application man can work alone or he can employ a teacher, through whom he may arrive at the conclusions easier than by himself alone.

What does the teacher do then? Nothing but facilitate a process which the disciple could carry out by himself. He does what the physician does in curing a sickness. The cure itself is a work of nature, but the physician by the use of medicine for easier and quicker healing, helps nature along. The physician, therefore, should be called nature's collaborator, and also the disposing cause of health.[26]

[23] *Denz. Sch.* 1532.
[24] St. Thomas Aquinas, *Summa Theologica,* III, q. 26, a. 1, c.
[25] St. Thomas Aquinas, *In 2 Tim.,* 2, 1, lect. 2.
[26] St. Thomas Aquinas, *De Veritate,* q. 11, a. 1, c.

We may apply the same reasoning to the process of birth and growth in faith, with the difference, though, that in the process of acquiring knowledge, the master limits himself to facilitating work which the disciple could do by himself, while in the process of justification—where a supernatural object is to be communicated—the disciple cannot do the work alone but must receive aid from outside. This is what the preacher does. He proposes to the intellect the object to be believed, and at the same time he influences the will by showing *eius utilitatem et honestatem.*[27] Faith, however, comes from God because He it is who with His interior illumination moves the will to consent.[28] The same can be said for the will. Without internal grace, the influence of the preacher on the will could not bring about assent. In fact, "it happens that of two persons who see the same miracle or are exposed to the influence of the same preacher, one believes and the other does not."[29]

The influence of preaching on birth and growth in faith is therefore of a disposing nature: it aids the action of grace by proposing the object of faith and inducing the will to adopt it by demonstrating "its utility and honesty." The same doctrine is voiced by the Angelic Doctor in the commentary on the Epistles of St. Paul. The part of the preacher is likened to that of the farmer: he is not the principal cause of the fruits which the earth produces, but his action helps nature in its production. The same goes for the preacher. The principal cause is God, and the preacher helps his action.[30] Preaching thus does not produce grace, but paves its way for its production, which is actually accomplished in the sacrament.

It is easy to find fault with St. Thomas' theory inasmuch as it does not stick to the biblical text. In it, preaching confers no grace, either actual or sanctifying, but only disposes man for its reception in the sacrament. The way Scripture puts it, though, makes us assume that there is a real causal nexus between grace and preaching.

Scripture, as we have seen, speaks of the efficacy of preaching in terms too clear to permit its reduction to a mere disposing

---

[27] St. Thomas Aquinas, *De Veritate*, q. 22, a. 9, c.
[28] St. Thomas Aquinas, *Summa Theologica*, III, q. 69, a. 5, ad 2m.
[29] St. Thomas Aquinas, *Summa Theologica*, II, II, q. 6, a. 1, c.
[30] St. Thomas Aquinas, *In 2 Tim.*, II, 1. I, n. 46.

function. Preaching manifests its power in us (1 Thess. 2:13), it is a two-edged sword (Heb. 4:12); it empowers us to become children of God (John 1:12). These expressions presuppose an efficacy greater than mere disposing. They lead to the assumption that preaching has its own proper efficacy, that it is a means of grace.

We have already pointed out the reasons which led St. Thomas to see in preaching only a simple disposing cause.[31]

Preaching and occasion

In our day, the problem of the efficacy of preaching is the object of heated discussions among theologians.

In his excellent book, *Wie Heute Predigen* (*How to Preach Today*),[32] V. Schurr proposes an opinion which seems to him to be the only one capable of explaining the efficacy of preaching without risking exaggerations. He says that the power of the word should never be exaggerated to a point where it becomes "a sacrament or more."[33] The word does not make Christ present—not even when the Gospel is read during Mass—and it therefore cannot confer grace. The only words that could do this were those that Christ pronounced during His life on earth, or those of the forms of the sacraments. "The sermon, however, is only an external grace, on the occasion of which internal grace is offered and, in the event it is accepted, also conferred."[34] Schurr sees no other way to avoid confusion between preaching and sacrament. There is no *ex opere operato* grace conferred by preaching. Preaching confers indirectly, and only in as much as it evokes acts in man by reason of which God confers grace. When therefore Scripture or the Fathers say that preaching sanctifies, such a statement must be understood in the sense that, since preaching and grace constitute a dynamic unity, they are always united. Every time a preacher makes his voice heard, God confers internal grace on man so that he can be converted. Thus the dynamic character of the Word of God cannot be denied.

[31] Cf. Z. Alszeghy, "Die Theologie des Wortes Gottes bei den mittelalterlichen Theologen," *Gregorianum*, 39 (1958), 697–698.

[32] (Stuttgart, 1949.)

[33] *Ibid.*, p. 65.

[34] *Ibid.*

Schurr's opinion departs from the usual habit of confounding preaching with sacrament. Any theory which cannot dispel such confusion is inadmissible. The efficacy of the word, by nature directed to such personal faculties of man as his intellect, is one thing; the efficacy of a visible rite like a sacrament is another. To be effective, it must act according to the nature of a rite, and not according to the mode of the word which needs to be understood by him to whom it is addressed. It can act only when it is understood.

To us, however, it seems that Scripture attributes to the word an efficacy which is direct and not merely indirect. It is God who manifests His power in us (1 Thess. 2:13), and it is the word implanted in us which brings salvation to our souls (James 1:21). From this and from other texts cited above it appears that there is a direct connection between word and grace and not an indirect and occasional one.

Fr. Haensli would seem to be correct when, admitting as a dogmatic datum of indisputed validity the distinction between preaching and sacrament, he seeks to explain the efficacy of the word by stating that the sacrament confers grace *ex opere operato*, while preaching confers it *ex opere operantis*. Preaching confers actual grace in as much as it is aimed at illuminating the intellect and moving the will of man to accept the salvation offered him through the words of the preacher. It is, therefore, a case of true grace, which can act only if it is understood, therefore *ex opere operantis*. From this viewpoint we can understand the importance of the problem of adaptation, which is justified not only in psychology but also in theology.[35] This is also probably Schurr's opinion. He does not propose to deny to preaching the imparting of actual grace, but only the conferring of sactifying grace *ex opere operato*.[36]

[35] "Verkündigung heute aus lebendigen theologischen Einsichten," *Fragen der Theologie heute,* herausgegeben von den Professoren J. Feiner, J. Trütsch, und F. Böckle (Cologne, 1957), pp. 480–484, esp. pp. 480–1. By the same author see also "Neueste Versuche einer Theologie der Predigt in kritischer Sicht," *Theologie und Predigt* (Würzburg, 1958), pp. 272–308. The problem of efficacy is treated on p. 296 ss.
[36] See also Schurr's article: "Situation und Aufgabe der Predigt heute," *Verkündigung und Glaube* (Freiburg, 1958), pp. 185–208, spec. p. 195. Schurr seems to be of Haensli's opinion.

Preaching and sacramentals

In the article cited above, Betz has taken a step forward in determining the efficacy of preaching.[37] For him, too, Christ is present and acts in the word of the Apostles and their successors. When it then comes to the determination of this efficacy, he also is careful not to confound preaching and sacrament. In spite of their similarities, these realities are quite different from each other. Even when preaching is effective, it is not effective in the same way that the sacrament is. In addition, we know that all the sacraments—but Baptism, in particular—are essential for justification. This means that faith alone is not sufficient for justification. On the other hand, we have learned from St. Paul that preaching and faith are interdependent. This permits us to speak of justification through faith (Rom. 3:22) as well as justification through the word (2 Cor. 5:19). According to the Council of Trent, faith is necessary as the beginning, foundation and root of justification. It is, therefore, not only the presupposition for salvation but also the first phase in the process of justification. And so we must admit that while preaching does not produce sanctifying grace, it does produce actual grace, which in turn leads to sanctifying grace.

And here we have a definition of the efficacy of preaching and sacrament. The latter produces grace *ex opere operato*, that is, by reason of the sacramental action; the former produces it *ex opere operantis*, because it is aimed at arousing the personal acts of man, like faith, repentance, conversion, dedication to the Gospel—all of which may be categorized as *opus operantis*.[38]

Betz believes he can proceed even further. The faith that is necessary for justification is the dogmatic kind (*fides quae*), which can only be received through Revelation and is not producible by man. And the German theologian concludes: "Therefore, as *fides quae* faith is *opus operatum* originally operated and manifested by God, but through the medium of the word of preaching."[39] In this context, the graces necessary for justification are produced by preaching *ex opere operato*: these dispositions exert an influence on justification *ex opere operantis*. Betz concludes: "With this we come to an important conclusion: the efficacy of the word

[37] J. Betz, "Wort und Sakrament," pp. 76–99.
[38] *Ibid.*, p. 97.
[39] *Ibid.*, p. 98.

ex opere operantis is not sufficient to indicate its whole effect: it also operates *ex opere operato*. It could be said that its efficacy is halfway between the two modes, partaking of the nature of one as well as of the other."[40]

Toward the end of his article Betz asserts that preaching is not a sacrament, but a sacramental: preaching does not confer the sanctifying grace of the sacrament, but it does eliminate the obstacles hindering that grace and makes man receptive to salvation. The word, therefore, is the "ursakramentale" or the sacramental *simpliciter*.[41]

The efforts of Betz, especially his attempt to formulate a theory in harmony with biblical data and the principles of theology, deserve commendation. He seeks to attribute to preaching all possible efficacy and at the same time to avoid dangerous exaggerations through a misunderstood irenism.

For the moment let us put aside Betz's *opus operatum*, that term which describes the dogmatic faith preaching is supposed to produce in the believer, and let us instead examine the conclusion at which the German theologian arrives, that is, that preaching is a sacramental. This conclusion practically strips the *opus operatum* of all value. Preaching never can be a sacramental because it is not an ecclesiastical institution, but a divine one. Nor can it be called a sacramental because of its efficacy, since a sacramental acts *ex opere operantis Ecclesiae*, whereas preaching is in itself effective because of the presence of God in the human word. Its efficacy derives from God Himself and not from the Church. Besides, the sacramental works negatively, that is, it eliminates the obstacles which arise against justification, while preaching, as Betz himself has stated, exerts a positive influence by producing in man faith and other acts which bear directly on justification.

Father Flick makes clear in which sense preaching can be considered a sacramental and in which it cannot. He says: "The efficacy of preaching must be balanced between that of the sacraments and that of the sacramentals; preaching is similar to the sacramentals inasmuch as it confers actual grace; but it is similar also to the sacraments because it is instituted by Jesus Christ and produces its effect not only by impetration, but by the intrinsic

[40] *Ibid.*, p. 98.
[41] *Ibid.*, p. 99.

virtue which God has imparted to it."[42] Betz's theory at least clarifies the distinction between preaching and sacrament by pointing
out that while the former confers actual grace (even if only in a
certain kind of *ex opere operato* action), the second confers
sanctifying grace.

Semmelroth's theory

A courageous step toward the determination of preaching's
efficacy was taken by Semmelroth.[43]

Preaching and sacrament are for Semmleroth two inseparable
realities: they constitute unity in duplicity, a bi-polar unity. In this
unity the dialogue process, which already took place in Redemption, continues on and on. A dialogue process is indeed evident.
In the Incarnation the Father comes down to man and addresses
the Word of salvation to him, while the redemptive Death of His
Son gives man's reply to the Father. In order to participate in this
Redemption, every man must take part in the dialogue, receiving
God's Word in faith and sharing in Christ's sacrifice in the sacrament. In this process the Incarnation already possesses redemptive value, not of its own making but by virtue of Christ's Death.
Christ's Death, in turn, does not bring about salvation by itself
but only conjointly with the Incarnation. "Both form the dialogue
of salvation in which God and man together stand face to face."[44]
The conclusion is clear: sacrament and word have, respectively,
reference to Incarnation and redemptive sacrifice. Just as the
Incarnation has redemptive value because it is linked to the Death
of Christ—His Death must also include the Resurrection and the
Ascension—so the word confers grace, not by itself, but by its
relation to the sacrament. Word and sacrament are in the subjective order what Incarnation and Redemption are in the objective
one. They confer the grace of justification, not like two different
causes acting separately, or side by side, but as two causes which
are united in action and operation.

According to Semmelroth, one can reconcile Scripture, which

---

[42] M. Flick, "La predicazione e la grazia," *La Civiltà Cattolica,* I (1960),
16.

[43] Semmelroth has treated efficacy in many of his works. Here we only
quote the most recent: *Wirkendes Wort. Zur Theologie der Verkündigung*
(Frankfurt, 1962).

[44] *Ibid.,* p. 235.

attributes to the word the conveying of grace, with the doctrine of the Church, which attributes it to the sacrament. There is only one source of grace, namely, the sacrament. But preaching may be called the cause of grace, since the two are intermeshed, inasmuch as there is in preaching what the theologians call *votum sacramenti*.[45] "Only when preaching is intended as part of the sacrament or ordered by it, so that it receives from it a ray of its efficacy—only then can it have effective importance for justification."[46]

The difference between preaching and sacrament is clear: the former is the effective sign (*Wirkzeichen*) of the Incarnation of the Word, while the latter is the effective sign of the sacrifice of Christ. Since the Incarnation and the sacrifice of Christ achieve Redemption together, it can be said that man is justified both by preaching and sacrament. In preaching he receives the Word of God, in the sacrament he gives himself up to God. Justification is an action produced by two causes which act together.

Observations

One must admire Semmelroth's effort to explain the complicated theme of the efficacy of preaching so that both the biblical data and the doctrine of the Church are taken into consideration. He does an able job of explaining the roles of preaching and sacrament within the process of justification, asserting that a dialogue, in which God invites man and man replies to God, is the result.

Yet it is very difficult to agree with Semmelroth about that which forms the core of his theories, namely, that preaching has its efficacy in the sacrament insofar as the two constitute a bipolar unity. This viewpoint would seem to conflict with Holy Scripture, which is basically what the German theologian seeks to reconcile with the magisterium of the Church. The Bible attributes to preaching an efficacy all its own, independent from the sacrament. It is the Word of grace (Acts 14:3), of life (Phil. 2:16), of truth (2 Cor. 6:7), of salvation (Rom. 1:16). In all these cases there is never an indication of a direct relation with the sacrament: it is the Word which gives grace and salvation. Before attributing

[45] *Ibid.*, p. 213.
[46] *Ibid.*, p. 213–214.

to preaching an indirect efficacy, we must see if it is not possible to attribute to it a direct one.

There is a second objection which for us is decisive. For the German theologian preaching is effective only in relation to the sacrament. In reality it is effective also without the sacrament, even in the refusal of it. Semmelroth repeatedly states that preaching is the call of God which man has to answer (Wort-Antwort). The process of justification is a dialogue between God and man. That is true. We must not forget, though, that this dialogue takes place between persons who are free and that a negative answer can be given. Man can say "no" to God's invitation. If there is a reply of this nature, it occurs neither in the sacrament nor in its refusal. But even in this case preaching is effective.

We have said, of course, that preaching divides men, placing in one group those who are designated for salvation—forming, thereby, the society of salvation we call the Church—and placing in another group those who are excluded from it. St. Paul states that the Apostles' preaching manifests the knowledge of Christ to the world, "an odor that leads to death . . . an odor that leads to life" (2 Cor. 2:16). If the sacrament follows the word in the first case, it does not do so in the next. How then explain the efficacy of the word? It helps not if we consider desire for the sacrament. This desire can exercise real efficacy even when it is impossible for man to receive the sacrament, so long as the disposition to do so exists in him, as happens with the catechumen surprised by death before having been baptized, or with the Gentile who, living according to the norm of his conscience, is justified by God through faith communicated to him in internal inspiration. Therefore, even if we may legitimately speak of the process of justification as a dialogue, we must not forget that it is the case of a dialogue involving two free wills.

Furthermore, it seems dubious whether so much stress should be placed on preaching and sacrament, or that equal efficacy should be attributed to preaching as to the sacrament. As already said, the efficacy of the word is different from that of a rite because by its nature it is directed to the faculties of men. The word can act only *ex opere operantis* and only when understood by the man to whom it brings a message. Sacrament, by contrast, is a visible rite. If it can produce grace, an effect which is not consonant with its nature, it can do so only by virtue of a divine institution which has linked the conferring of grace to a determined rite. The rite, therefore, can act only *ex opere operato*. And how can we then say that the efficacy of preaching is the same as that of the sacrament? This observation makes it plain that the relationship between word and sacrament, however close we may conceive it to be, cannot be exaggerated to the point of saying that the two form a bipolar unity.

Is it then true, as Semmelroth says, that in the word God descends toward man while in the sacrament man rises toward God? The contrary seems true to us. "In attempting to determine what does prevail in preaching and in the sacrament, it seems to us rather that the causality of the sacrament is descending (the new relationship with God is due to a new heart, to a regeneration) while the efficacy of preaching seems, in general, to be ascending (he who hears the word is attracted by the Father, goes to Jesus, and therefore is justified insofar as he acts)."[47]

Concluding remarks

If we want to express a judgment on the question of the efficacy of preaching as has been discerned so far by scholars, we can make the following observations:

1) In spite of the analogies between preaching and sacrament, the two realities cannot be placed on the same level, nor can they be brought too near to each other so that the distance which separates them vanishes. The word and the rite, by their very natures, must act in different ways and pose different conditions to achieve their efficacy. Each has its proper efficacy, even though it is subordinate.

2) Therefore, the role of the minister is much more important in preaching than it is in the sacrament. In the one as well as in the other the minister is an instrumental cause, but this instrumental cause is not to be understood in one way only. In the sacrament, the part which the minister plays is reduced to making the rite possible, to helping bring it into existence. This happens when matter is applied to form and when the intention to do what the Church is doing is made. This role is so simple that not even faith or probity is required of the minister. On the part of the receiver we expect the right disposition, that he should not raise

[47] Z. Alszeghy and M. Flick, "Il problema teologico della predicazione," *Gregorianum*, 49 (1959), 741.

obstacles to grace. These dispositions can even be present when one does not understand the nature of the sacrament. In preaching, the instrumentality of the minister, that is, the preacher, is much more important and has a direct influence on the efficacy of the word: he must not only deliver the message, he must also make it understandable. Only if his message is understood can preaching provoke the crisis of conversion and bring about its deepening.

St. Thomas has observed with clarity this difference between the minister's functions in preaching and in the sacrament. Speaking of the reasons why the office of preaching is *principalissimum* among the Apostles, while that of baptizing can be exercised also by others, he assigns this motive: *"Et hoc ideo quia in baptizando nihil meritum et sapientia operatur ministri sicut in docendo. . . .*[48] In the administration of the sacrament the role of the minister is secondary, while in preaching it is truly instrumental, but more important and decisive. In the sacraments *nihil operatur meritum et sapientia ministri*; in preaching, however, *sicut in docendo*. This is the reason why Christ and the Apostles reserved preaching to themselves, while they left baptizing to their disciples. Preaching is the *officium principalissimum* of the Apostles as well as of their successors.

St. Thomas expresses the same opinion in his commentary on the Epistles to the Corinthians concerning the expression: "For Christ did not send me to baptize, but to preach the gospel . . ." (1 Cor. 1:17). Even though Christ sent the Apostles both to preach and to baptize, they baptized with the help of their disciples and reserved themselves to preaching. The reason is the same as given above: "Et hoc ideao quia *nihil operatur industria et virtus baptizantis* . . . sed in praedicatione Evangelii *multum operatur sapientia et virtus praedicantis*."[49] Here the great Doctor specifies what the *meritum* of the preacher consists in, namely, his wisdom and his virtue. These qualities have influence on the efficacy of preaching, whereas they do not have any on that of the sacraments.

Another remark of St. Thomas cannot be overlooked. In commenting on the Pauline expression, "This is my gospel" (2 Tim. 2:9), he points out the difference between the ministry of

---

[48] St. Thomas Aquinas, *Summa Theologica*, III, q. 67, a. 2, ad 1m.
[49] St. Thomas Aquinas, *In 1 ad Cor.*, c. 1 in h. 1.

preaching and that of Baptism. While the minister of Baptism cannot say "my Baptism," the minister of preaching can say, *"my Gospel."* This is because the exhortations and the solicitudes, the duties of the minister of preaching, *multum faciunt.*[50] One is a minister of the sacrament and one of preaching but in a different way: in both cases an instrumentality exists which must be understood in the sense of analogy. This merely proves that it is impossible to place these two causalities on the same level. The instrumentality of the minister of the sacraments is not the same as that of the minister of preaching. For this reason, while we can use an unknown language in the sacraments, we cannot do so in preaching.

If there are analogies between preaching and sacrament, there are also differences which do not permit the efficacy of preaching to be treated in terms of the sacraments.

3) Preaching is an external grace and can communicate only actual grace *ex opere operantis*, that is, grace acting on the faculty of intelligence and will and arousing their reaction to the offer of salvation. The sacrament, in contrast, can act only *ex opere operato*, and this, because a divine institution has linked the conferring of an effect as elevating as sanctifying grace to a rite.

4) It seems, however, that we can also attribute to preaching a certain measure of efficacy *ex opere operato*, which must be seen quite differently from the *ex opere operato* efficacy of the sacraments. We have already observed that Scripture presents the Word of God to us as a two-edged sword (Heb. 4:12), a word which diffuses among men the odor of Christ both in life and in death (2 Cor. 2:15). This means that preaching is of its own nature always effective due to the object which it proclaims, salvation, and the subject which it treats, that is, God in Christ. It contains the offer of grace and salvation to which man must react. Preaching possesses the virtue and the energy to force those who listen to emerge from their indifference and take a stand, whether positive or negative, with regard to the person of Christ, who, through the word of the preacher, offers them life. Preaching is an eschatological event, it proclaims decisive facts for the destiny of man, facts in the face of which nobody can remain indifferent. In view of these facts man must make a decision to accept or reject them. In this sense preaching is effective of its own nature,

[50] St. Thomas Aquinas, *In 2 ad Tim.*

independently of the reaction of man which can also be positive or negative.

5) Finally, in order to determine not only the mode, but what is more important, the nature of efficacy in preaching, it is necessary to determine what part the preacher plays, what his function is and in what the service of the Word consists. If preaching cannot exist without a reaction, it is necessary that the word of the preacher, to evoke such reaction, appears as the Word of God, and as such engages the life of man. We must first determine in what sense the preacher displays his *"meritum et sapientia ministri,"* his wisdom and knowledge, as St. Thomas says. Only later can we move on to the nature of preaching and the mode of its efficacy.

CHAPTER VIII

Preaching and Testimony

WHEN WE examine the missionary mandate of Christ, we see that it is expressed differently by the various Evangelists. According to St. Mark, Jesus, on sending His disciples out into the world, said: "Go into the whole world and preach the gospel to every creature. He who believes and is baptized shall be saved, but he who does not believe shall be condemned" (Mark 16: 15–16). St. Matthew uses another expression; "Go, therefore, and make disciples of all nations, baptizing them in the name of the Father, and of the Son, and of the Holy Spirit, teaching them to observe all that I have commanded you" (Matt. 28:19–20). In the Acts of the Apostles, St. Luke applies a formula which is apparently quite different: ". . . you shall be witnesses for me in Jerusalem and in all Judea and Samaria even to the very ends of the earth" (Acts 1:8).

These three expressions shed light on and explain one other. To "preach the gospel" means that preaching is the proclamation of a message, of a good tidings. To "make disciples of all nations" indicates rather the effect of preaching: a transformation so deep that it changes the whole life of man, so that he becomes a disciple of Christ, one who thinks and wills like Him. You are to be "witnesses for me" means that preaching is not solely a transmission of events that happened, but a testimonial from which springs their importance for life.

145

How closely linked these three expressions are is made clear by St. Paul, who identifies "testimony" with "gospel" and uses both expressions to indicate the object of preaching. In his Second Epistle to Timothy, the beloved disciple, he exhorts him not to "be ashamed of testimony for our Lord, nor of me . . . but enter into my sufferings for the gospel through the power of God" (2 Tim. 1–8). Just as one must not be ashamed to testify for Jesus Christ, so one must not be ashamed of the Gospel (Rom. 1:16). Both St. Paul and the Twelve proclaim the Gospel, whose object is Christ dead and resurrected (1 Cor. 15:1–11). Further on, at verse 15, the Apostle states that had Christ not risen He and the Apostles would be convicted of giving false testimony about God because they would have then "borne witness against God that he raised Christ" (1 Cor. 15:15), when this was not true.

St. Paul also likens testimony to the mystery. In saying that God has revealed His mystery in the fullness of time, the Apostle declares that he, Paul, bore "witness in his own time" (1 Tim. 2:6).

It may be this very concept of testimony which will help us determine the nature of this "service of the Word," which we have described as prerequisite to understanding the efficacy of preaching. For this reason we shall pay it special attention, even if it is necessary to repeat some of what we have already discussed in the first chapter.

The concept

The concept of testimony is found throughout Holy Scripture. Asting has devoted the last section of his heavy tome, already quoted several times, to this question. According to his conclusions, *to bear witness* means in the Old Testament, to express a will, either of the one who utters the expression or of somebody else; *witness* is the one who expresses this will, and testimony is the will which is expressed.[1] With the Greeks the concept is rationalized. To bear witness ($\mu\alpha\rho\tau\upsilon\rho\epsilon\tilde{\iota}\nu$) is to attest to a fact: the witness *par excellence* is the eyewitness, who testifies what he has seen. Even when he is not an eyewitness, his testimony demonstrates a fact, or a religious truth.[2] At the same time the

[1] R. Asting, *Die Verkündigung des Wortes im Urchistentum, dargestellt an den Begriffen "Wort Gottes," "Evangelium" und "Zeugnis"* (Stuttgart, 1939), p. 507.
[2] *Ibid.*, p. 555.

concept assumes juridical value, inasmuch as the testimony bears witness to a fact that is under discussion.

The synoptic tradition continues the Old Testament concept of testimony. St. Luke reveals the Hellenistic influence, at least in the prologue of his Gospel, wherein he speaks of eyewitnesses. For St. Paul, being a witness means being a bearer of the Revelation of God, that divine will to salvation which cannot but arouse the opposition of Satan. In his Epistles St. Paul develops the concept already present in the Synoptic Gospels: the witness must suffer, even death if necessary, because as a representative of Christ he cannot help but arouse the evil powers against him. However, the suffering of the witness is not a part of the concept of testimony, but rather a consequence of it. The same can be said of the Johannine writings. Testimony is the Revelation of God inasmuch as it enters into history and arouses Satan's opposition. The more one is united with Christ, the more one necessarily experiences persecution by His enemy.[3]

In assembling our concept of testimony as found in St. Paul and in the Synoptic Gospels (St. Luke has already been mentioned), and as it appears also in the Book of Acts, we can say that testimony confirms a fact, the veracity of which, is based on the word of the witness himself. The fact to which witness is borne is the will of God for salvation, His Revelation, and His plan to call man to participation in the divine life. To all these, man's faith is the response.

In his book *Foi au Christ et Mission*, A. Rétif[4] distinguishes three kinds of testimony: the historical, the biblical and the juridical. The first is testimony to a fact in the past, the veracity of which is guaranteed by the witness' authority. In this sense the Apostles are witnesses to the life of Christ, since they were eyewitnesses. Juridical testimony is that given in court, which will result in the convicting or freeing of somebody. Thus the Apostles were juridical witnesses of Christ's condemnation to death by the Jewish and imperial authorities. Their statements before the judges are proof of the injustice done their Master, whose innocence God authenticated by raising Him from the dead. Finally, biblical testimony is the solemn proclamation of the divine will as it concerns the future. Examples might be the testimonials of the

[3] *Ibid.*, p. 697–699.
[4] (Paris, 1953.)

Prophets, who speak in God's name and disclose His will.[5]

From this, the importance of the witness giving testimony becomes clear. The facts which he knows and to which he bears witness are believed in the same degree that he is believed. The more important and solemn the facts, the more they concern the interests and destiny of man, the more necessary is it that those who bear witness be men who can be believed.

Let us examine the testimony of the Book of Acts, which is not only the perfect example of apostolic preaching but also a norm for preaching in the Church.

The direct testimony of the Apostles

Father R. Koch has devoted his two articles[6] to the testimony in the Book of Acts, and to our mind these represent the best writing done about this theme, at least in respect to preaching. We shall draw upon these articles in our discussion.

Father Koch differentiates the direct testimony of the Apostles from the indirect testimony of the religious community in Jerusalem.

The testimony of the Twelve has a double foundation: immediate knowledge of the facts to which they bear witness, and their mission to bear witness. The Apostles were with Jesus from the beginning of His public life until the Ascension (Acts 1:21–22); they ate and drank in His Company (10:40–41), saw all He did in the country of the Jews, and in Jerusalem (10:39). In particular they were witnesses of His Resurrection, because Jesus appeared to them throughout the forty days following His Passion (1:3–4;13:13), either to one as in Peter's case (Luke 23:24), or to all together (1 Cor. 15:5). St. Paul, too, was made an object of the apparition of the Risen Christ (Acts 9; 1 Cor. 15:8).

During His last apparition, Jesus gave the Apostles the mandate to be witnesses to what they had seen and heard (Acts 1:8). It was for the sake of this mission that Jesus appeared to them (Acts 10:40–41). In this St. Paul also takes part, since his testimony can rightfully be joined to that of the Twelve (Acts 22:14–15). It is this mission which makes the Apostles qualified witnesses of Christ.

[5] Rétif, op. cit., pp. 41–44.
[6] R. Koch, "Temoignage d'après les Actes," Masses Ouvrières, 129 (April 1957) 16–30, and 131 (June 1957), 4–25.

The object of the testimony, as St. Peter said before the High Council of the Jews, is everything which the Apostles have seen and heard (Acts 4:20), that is, all the events of Christ's life, but especially His death and Resurrection. This last is so central a fact that it is often described as the sole object of the testimony (Acts 4:33). But Christ had a long prehistory: His life was announced by the Prophets; and He has a metahistory as well: He sits at the right hand of the Father and will one day return to earth to judge the living and the dead. We may say, therefore, that the object of testimony is the whole history of salvation, with Christ dead and risen as the center. In this way the object of testimony coincides with that of the Gospel, of the Word of God and the mystery already discussed.

The forms of testimony

Testimony is given in three forms. One is the word. This is clear—the witness must testify to what he has seen and heard. This is why the Apostles are called the "eyewitnesses and ministers of the word" (Luke 1:2). Without the word, testimony would be impossible. It is an example of collective testimony, given by the entire Twelve, even when only one of them, such as Peter, is speaking (Acts 3:12, ff). This is necessary in order that the testimony may have juridical value (Matt. 18:10). The Holy Spirit, whom Christ promised to send (Acts 1:8) and actually sent (Acts 2:4) intervenes to make this testimony efficacious. It is the Holy Spirit who enlightens the Apostles' minds so that they understand Scripture (Luke 24:45–48), who teaches them (Acts 10:33), who strengthens them and makes them speak (Acts 4:19–20) with confidence (4:31). Another form of testimony consists in signs. To the word of the Apostles who proclaim the Dead and Risen Christ are linked the signs which reveal His origin from God. These signs are above all the miracles (Acts 2:43; 5:12; 4:29–30; 19:11–12, etc.). To this may be added the convincing tone in which they speak, which never fails to impress those who listen to them (Acts 4:13), and their moral uprightness, which so impressed their jailer at Philippi (Acts 16:25–34).

Persecution is the third form of such testimony. The word and the signs are accompanied by persecution. Jesus had predicted it: "Remember the word that I have spoken to you: No servant is greater than his master. If they have persecuted me, they will per-

secute you also . . ." (John 15:20). But the Apostles rejoiced in
persecution (Acts 5:41), and St. Paul was ready to meet prison
and death for the name of the Lord Jesus (Acts 21:13).

The effect of testimony

The nature of the apostolic testimony cannot be understood
unless one investigates the effect it had on listeners. This seems
to have escaped Koch but we consider it of great importance.

The reaction of listeners to the apostolic word invariably
involves the taking of a position. This applies both to the testimony before the Jews and before the Gentiles. The reaction never
fails to occur and is threefold in nature.

There is above all the *positive reaction*, which consists in acceptance of the message even though its moral and doctrinal implications are not yet known. After St. Peter's discourse on the day of
Pentecost, the author of the Acts writes: "Now on hearing this
they were pierced to the heart and said to Peter and the rest of
the apostles, 'Brethren, what shall we do?' But Peter said to them,
'Repent and be baptized, every one of you, in the name of Jesus
Christ for the forgiveness of your sins; and you will receive the
gift of the Holy Spirit' " (Acts 2:37–38). The same positive reaction follows the cure of the lame (Acts 3:4), the sermon of Philip
to the Samaritans (8:12), to the Ethiopian (8:36–38), of Peter
to Cornelius (10:44–46) and of Paul at Thessalonica (17:4), and
so forth.

At other times, especially with the Jews, the reaction is *negative*. The word of Peter was rejected by the High Council, so
strongly that Peter's life and the lives of the others were endan-
gered. The Acts say, "But they, when they heard this, were cut
to the heart and wanted to slay them" (Acts 5:33), and the reaction is similar elsewhere (Acts 9:33; 9:30; 13:45; 18:6; 22:22).

Then there is a third reaction, that of *doubt*. This is the case
of the man who listens to the word of the Apostles, but does not
know what to do: on the one hand he is not drawn to accept the
message; on the other, he does not feel like rejecting it. The case
of Gamaliel is typical, who said after that discourse of St. Peter
which left the Council furious: "Men of Israel, take care what
you are about to do to these men. . . . So now I say to you, Keep
away from these men and let them alone. For if this plan or work
is of men, it will be overthrown; but if it is of God you will not

be able to overthrow it. Else perhaps you may find yourselves fighting even against God" (Acts 5:35–39). Gamaliel does not quite know what to do: he does not possess facts necessary to judge and so he remains uncertain. Similar behavior can be noted among the Jews after St. Paul's sermon in the synagogue of Pisidian Antioch. As Paul and Simon are leaving the synagogue, "the people asked to have all this said to them on the following Sabbath" (Acts 13:42). The same behavior may again be observed in Felix after the discourse of St. Paul: "But as he talked of justice and chastity and the judgement to come, Felix became alarmed and answered, 'For the present go thy way; but when I get an opportunity, I will send for thee' " (Acts 24:25).

These three attitudes *of faith, of unbelief and of doubt,* can be found together after the discourse in Athens:

"Now when they heard of a resurrection of the dead, some began to sneer (negative reaction), but others said: 'We will hear thee again on this matter' (doubious reaction), certain persons however joined him and became believers . . ." (the positive reaction) (Acts 17:32–34).

Indifference, however, is excluded. All those who listened to the words of the Apostle reacted in some definite way. All were interested and were moved to take a stand.

Facts and the meaning of facts

Here, now, is the direct testimony of the Apostles.

They proclaim events which actually happened and which they experienced in the presence of Christ, in eating and drinking with Him, both before and after the Resurrection. But these events are not merely facts of which they were occasional witnesses and to which they bear witness in virtue of a mission to which they want to remain faithful. These facts have become part of the Apostles' lives, have given them a new orientation, so new that all their thoughts are framed within this context. These facts are at the same time *values*, because they have injected new meaning into the lives of the Apostles and are proclaimed as being able to do the same for the lives of their listeners. By proclaiming them, the Twelve not only intend to right a wrong and rehabilitate a man unjustly put to death—a man whom God has raised from death—they also hope to provoke a conversion, a total change of life. These facts are important, not only and principally because they are true, nor because they are extraordinary, but because they influence human destiny. Their meaning greatly exceeds their historical truth.

Basically, the Apostles and their hearers were not interested in the fact that Christ died and rose from the dead, or that He is the Son of God, or even the Messiah—but in the fact that He is the Word of Life, "the true light that enlightens every man who comes into the world" (John 1:9).[7] If Christ, the Son of God, had become man for reasons that had nothing to do with men, the Incarnation might have stirred our respect and our admiration, because we know that God acts with wisdom. But it could have achieved nothing more. As a matter of fact, however, Christ became man, died and rose from the dead for our salvation.

It is this meaning of the Christ and of His Death and Resurrection which transformed the lives of the Apostles in such a way that they could think of nothing else except Him and the proclamation of His name. For them, Christ is the only one through whom men can obtain salvation (Acts 4:12). Therefore, they cannot be silent (Acts 4:20). To remain silent would mean more than simply failing in their mission, thus denying themselves. For them, there is no other salvation than in Christ.

Because they have understood the meaning of Christ and can apply it to their preaching, the Apostles are far more than wax records which repeat what has been cut on them. They not only state what they have heard and seen, but they solemnly maintain that in these facts lies something which transcends them, and it is precisely this "something" which gives meaning to their whole existence.

The essential part of testimony, then, is this testifying. "It is the testifying," writes Gabriel Marcel, "which is essential here. . . . In testifying I voluntarily pledge myself. . . . There is no more essential act than this. At the base of it is the recognition of a certain datum, but at the same time there is something else. When I bear witness, I declare in effect that I renounce myself, yes, that I would annihilate myself if I were to deny this fact whose reality I have witnessed."[8] Between the fact and the person who testifies to it, there is a close relationship. If the facts are separated from

---

[7] See also what Guitton has to say: *Le problème de Jésus, et les fondements du témoignage chrétien* (Paris, 1948), vol. I, spec. p. 175.

[8] Gabriel Marcel, *Being and Having* (London, 1949).

the person, they remain true, but they are stripped from significance and interest so far as life is concerned.

Here, too, St. Paul finds the right word. The Christ whom he met on the road to Damascus has so completely penetrated his existence that he can say without hesitation that for him Christ means life (Phil 1:21), and that it is Christ who lives in him (Gal. 2:20). But if, by chance, Christ had not risen, he and all Christians who believed in Him would be "the most to be pitied" (1 Cor. 15:19). This is because the Christian renounces the pleasures of this world in order to acquire the eternal ones promised by Christ. Had Christ not risen, these eternal pleasures would be mere illusions. If what the witness believes is not true or does not possess the meaning attributed to it, his whole life becomes worthless, an illusion and an absurdity.

This is why everybody reacts to the testimony of the Apostles: it poses a question of decisive reality for existence, in the face of which nobody can remain indifferent.

Testimony, therefore, is impossible without the full commitment of the person.[9] From this commitment stems the significance of the facts. From this also arises the distinction between historical science and preaching: the first transmits the facts in their truth, the second transmits them also in their meaning.

This is how faith is transmitted: through "committed" persons who have perceived the significance of the facts which they proclaim and who continue to proclaim them so that others may also perceive this significance. Testimony makes present a mystery—in a certain sense—which confronts man with the values determining his existence and which obliges him to emerge from his indifference and act. Testimony effects an upheaval in man, creates in him metaphysic and religious unrest. From this arises an attraction, a fascination, and a spiritual call which the witness has himself already experienced.

The indirect testimony of the Christian community

In addition to the direct testimony of the Apostles, the Book of Acts also recounts the indirect testimony of the community in Jerusalem. Koch treats this in his second article.[10]

[9] See A. Liégé, "L'engagement dans l'education de la charité," *Nouvelle Revue Theologique*, 80 (March, 1958), 253–263.

[10] R. Koch, *Masses Ouvrières* (June 1957), pp. 4–25.

The existence of this indirect testimony of the community is attested to by St. Peter when, speaking before the High Council, he remarks that not only the Apostles witnessed what he proclaims, namely, the Death and Resurrection of Christ, but also "the Holy Spirit, whom God has given to all who obey him" (Acts 5:32). According to this text, as Koch says, "the Holy Spirit bears witness not only with the Apostles but with all those who obey God, that is, with all who act and speak according to His direction (Acts 2:4; 4:8; 15:28). It is the Spirit who bears witness with them and through them in their lives, as well as in their preaching."[11] Thus, on the day of Pentecost, the Holy Spirit has not only descended on the Apostles but also on the disciples, even on the women who were in the Cenacle (Acts 2:4), all of whom spoke in strange languages under His influence. The Holy Spirit also descended on those inhabitants of Samaria who had accepted the word of Philip (Acts 8:12–17), on the converted Gentiles (Acts 10:44 ff), and on Stephen (Acts 6:5), who had been expressly made a witness (Acts 22:20). And Koch concludes: "The Holy Spirit, in view of its witnessing, is scattered all over the Christian community and its members."[12]

It is a testimony which finds expression in a life of joy, charity and prayer in the Christian community, and which the Book of Acts describes in expressive verses: "Now the multitude of the believers were of one heart and one soul, and not one of them said that anything he possessed was his own, but they had all things in common. And with great power the Apostles gave testimony to the resurrection of Jesus Christ our Lord; and great grace was in them all. Nor was there anyone among them in want. For those who owned lands or houses would sell them and bring the price of what they sold and lay it at the feet of the Apostles, and distribution was made to each, according as any one had need" (Acts 4:32–35; cf. Acts 2:44–46). And the sacred author explicitly says that the people were edified by the life of the Christian community, that the Christians were "in favor with all the people" (Acts 2:47), and that they were held in high honor (5:13). He also notes the influence of this testimony on the spreading of the Gospel: "And day by day the Lord added to their company such as were to be saved" (Acts 2:47). Even though they were afraid

[11] *Ibid.*, p. 9.
[12] *Ibid.*

of the priests and the High Council who persecuted the Apostles, the people were strongly attracted to the Christian life and many became converts in spite of the threats and dangers.

The indirect testimony of the community thus consists in the example of the power of the faith as shown in their lives. The life of the community ignites a strong attraction, and it stirs the admiration and sympathy of people who, even if they do not accept the Gospel, feel its fascination (Acts 5:13–14). What makes the greatest impression is the community of goods—there are no paupers among the Christians. Everyone receives what he needs regardless of what he has given to the community. It is a simple life, centered on prayer and work, in which everybody is happy. It emanates a kind of contagious joyfulness. This community life comprises the framework for the preaching of the Apostles. Within it, the listeners can see what the Faith really consists of, and what Christ means for the life of man. The joy is not disturbed by any outside event: the persecutions to which the heads of the community are subject frighten no one. The happiest of all are the Apostles themselves, who left the High Council "rejoicing that they had been counted worthy to suffer disgrace for the name of Jesus" (Acts 5:41).

It would be impossible for men so full of Christ not to feel the need to speak about Him and to attract other followers to the Church. And here we discern another form of indirect testimony: the individual kind, given by means of the word. The model for this is St. Stephen, one of the seven deacons, who, not satisfied with caring for the Apostles' table, proclaimed Christ in words also (Acts 6). It is the same with Philip in Samaria (Acts 8:5) and with the Christians scattered by persecution (8:4). In the case of Stephen the preaching is crowned by martyrdom.

The spreading of faith

This, then, is how the Faith is spread: by the word of persons who have perceived the significant personal meaning of Christ dead and risen, who have opened themselves to it, and who have pledged themselves to His service, accepting persecution for the promise of the purest joys. Their word is supported by the testimony of a community of those who have already accepted the message preached by the Apostles, and who by their lives illustrate the meaning of that message.

The two testimonies, the direct one of the Apostles and the indirect one of the community, depend on one another. One cannot exist without the other. The first proclaims the decisive facts for human existence; the second shows their meaning in the concreteness of daily life. Preaching, therefore, is not only done by the Church, but in the Church. It is the Church which demonstrates the meaning of Christ as proclaimed by the Apostles. Essentially, this is collective and not individual testimony. Even when only one person bears witness, as in the case of Stephen, the whole community is behind him.

We conclude then, that the commitment of the preacher, as well as that of the religious community in which he preaches, is fundamental for preaching. Expressed in more common terms, in the sanctity of the preacher's life consists *the service of the Word*, without which preaching's efficacy cannot be explained.

The service of the Word

According to Schlier, this commitment, this service of the Word, includes a double function on the part of the preacher, one negative and one positive.

On the negative side, the preacher is obliged to eliminate the obstacles which might keep the Word of God from being what it really is, the Word of God in the mouth of man. He must not abuse his listeners by requiring them to maintain him, even though he may rightfully do so; he must adapt to their customs and not demand that converts live in a certain way unless the Gospel compels it; in preaching he must not be moved by unworthy motives, such as a desire to please, or to flatter his listeners, or to excite their applause.

In his First Epistle to the Thessalonians, St. Paul sums up these motives: "For our exhortation was not from error, nor from impure motives, nor from guile. But as approved by God to be entrusted with the Gospel, so we speak not as pleasing men, but God, who proves our hearts. For at no time have we used words of flattery, as you know, nor any pretext for avarice. God is witness, nor have we sought glory from men, neither from you nor from others. Although as the Apostles of Christ we could have claimed a position of honor among you, still while in your midst we were as children: as if a nurse were cherishing her own children" (1 Thess. 2:3–7).

The Apostle loved his faithful so much that he desired to give them "not only the Gospel of God, but also our own souls (1 Thess. 2:8). For them he has renounced "those practices which shame conceals" (2 Cor. 4:2), and the persuasive language devised by human wisdom (1 Cor. 2:4); and he even denounces that preaching which makes high pretensions to eloquence (1 Cor. 2:1). In short, the service of the Word requires that we do not proclaim ourselves, but only Jesus Christ (2 Cor. 4:5). This is impossible without the *parresia*, that is, the boldness of the Apostle, by which St. Paul means "the liberty and courage of an existence which in itself is open to the Word of God and thus keeps itself at the disposal of God and neighbor."[13] We may say that in the negative sense the service of the Word consists in making ourselves all things for all men, to gain all for Christ (1 Cor. 9:22).

The imitation of Christ

On the positive side, the service of the Word consists of complete dedication to it. Because of this dedication, the preacher accepts his personal weakness and seeks to overcome it in the sufferings which his enemies impose on him so that he may bear witness to the sufferings of Christ, not only through the Word but through His very existence (2 Cor. 12:7 ff.).[14]

In this connection, St. Paul speaks of a "barb" in his flesh which served to remind him that favors received from God should not make him proud. He asked God to be freed from it but was not heard. "Concerning this I thrice besought the Lord that it might leave me. And he has said to me, "My grace is sufficient for thee, for strength is made perfect in weakness." Gladly therefore I will glory in my infirmities, that the strength of Christ may dwell in me. Wherefore I am satisfied, for Christ's sake, with infirmities, with insults, with hardships, with persecutions, with distresses. For when I am weak, then I am strong." (2 Cor. 12:8–10). And in 2 Cor. 4:8–11, "In all things we suffer tribulation, but we are not distressed; we are sore pressed, but we are not destitute; we endure persecution but we are not forsaken; we are cast down, but we do not perish; always bearing about in our body the dying of Jesus, so that the life also of Jesus may be made manifest in our bodily frame" (cf. 2 Cor. 6:3–10).

[13] H. Schlier, *Wort Gottes,* p. 32.
[14] *Ibid.,* p. 32.

In proclaiming the Word of salvation to the community, the apostle can speak with the force of his own experience. In short, the service of the Word consists in the imitation of Christ, in making oneself so similar to Christ as to be transformed into His image. St. Paul says to the Philippians: "And what you have learned and received and heard and plan in me, these things practice. And the God of peace will be with you" (Phil. 4:9). This pattern of Christian imitation must, in turn, be extended to others: "And you became imitators of us and of the Lord, receiving the word in great tribulation, with joy of the Holy Spirit, so that you became a pattern to all the believers in Macedonia and in Achaia" (1 Thes. 6–7).[15]

In summing up, we may say that the service of the Word consists in that sanctity of life, which on the one hand shows preaching's efficacy in overcoming the obstacles placed in its way, and which on the other hand bears witness. It is this sanctity which makes of the preacher a living commentary on the Word, "a second Word."[16] Thus is preaching's efficacy explained.

The efficacy of example

The problem which we must now examine is the nature of the relationship between the sanctity of the preacher and of the Christian community, and the efficacy of preaching. Is this relationship of a psychological nature alone, or is it also of an entological kind? Is sanctity a factor which makes preaching more efficacious but which in itself is not indispensable—or is it a factor which belongs to the very nature of preaching and thereby influences its being and efficacy?

Among those who see in the preacher's sanctity only a psychological factor is St. Augustine, who affirms that preaching could be effective without sanctity of life, though sanctity facilitates its action.[17] As proof of his opinion, he cites Philipians 1:18, and Matthew 22:2–3, where Jesus admonishes the people to practice what the Pharisees say, without, however, imitating their example.[18] The ultimate reason behind this thinking is that the true Master, the one who speaks in preaching, is Jesus and His

[15] *Ibid.*, pp. 32–33.
[16] *Ibid.*, p. 30.
[17] St. Augustine, *De doctrina christiana*, L. IV, c. 27, n. 59.
[18] "Ei ideo audiuntur utiliter, qui etiam utiliter non agunt" (ivi).

Word is always effective.[19] It does not matter that the minister be bad: what matters is that Christ be preached. We must imitate the good which the preacher does, and not the whole man.[20] Good example makes preaching more effective,[21] however, because it strips the listeners of every excuse for not doing what the preacher says. Therefore, St. Paul exhorts Timothy to be an example to his faithful (1 Tim. 4:12).

This is an intuitive fact. Today, just as in the times of the Fathers, preaching unaccompanied by sanctity in the preacher's and the community's life would have little hope of success. Contemporary man does not easily believe in authority. The vitalism which is so much a part of his psychological make-up, makes him fail to distinguish "between the preacher and the sermon, the sermon and the reality of ecclesial life."[22]

The true problem that must be solved, however, is whether the sanctity of the preacher and of the Church, beyond a psychological, has also an ontological influence on preaching by conditioning its efficacy: this is what we shall examine next.

[19] St. Augustine, *Sermo* 23, 1, ML 38, col. 155.
[20] St. Augustine, *In Joann. Ev.*, Tract. V, c. 1, 19; ML 35, col. 1424.
[21] St. Augustine, *De doctrina christiana*, L. IV, c. 27, n. 60.
[22] A. Günthör, *Die Predigt*, p. 5.

CHAPTER IX

Reasons for the Testimony

To say that sanctity is a constituent ingredient of preaching means that it is a factor without which its efficacy cannot be explained. We have already seen that bearing witness may imply even suffering and death.

In the present chapter we want to examine the reasons for such a fact so important for the understanding of the nature and efficacy of preaching.

Preaching and signs

That preaching is the proclamation of the Word of God through the word of man has already been pointed out. God Himself speaks through the preacher. To be accepted as the Word of God, it is necessary that the Word be perceived as coming from Him. To this end, as we have seen, the preaching of the Apostles, and before them, that of Christ, was accompanied by signs, especially by miracles.

Jesus clearly says (John 15:24) that those who have refused to believe His preaching in spite of the miracles He has worked are not to be excused. In the miracles the divine origin of Christ's Word becomes clear, a point which Nicodemus understood very well (John 3:2). The same may be applied to the preaching of the Apostles. In its accounts the miracles are so frequent that the shadow of Peter (Acts 5:15) or the touching of St. Paul's

(Acts 19:11–12) handkerchiefs and aprons are enough to heal the sick. The community in Jerusalem expressly asks God for these signs, because from them it becomes clear that the Apostles are proclaiming His word: "And now, Lord, take note of their threats, and grant to thy servants to speak thy word with all boldness, while thou stretchest forth thy hand to cures and signs and wonders to be wrought by the name of thy holy servant Jesus" (Acts 4:29–30). The miracles contribute to producing that atmosphere of mystery so necessary for jolting man from torpor and putting him face to face with the problem of God's call. In miracles men recognize that it is God's Word which echoes in the word of man. Miracles, therefore, are a part of preaching, a fundamental element. Without them, the Word of God would not appear as it really is.

If St. Paul could give thanks because the Thessalonians, in receiving the message, recognized it for God's Word and not that of men (1 Thess. 2:13), it was because his preaching in Thessalonica, as well as in Corinth and other places, was "not in the persuasive words of wisdom, but in the demonstration of the Spirit and of power" (1 Cor. 2:4). He showed them that he was speaking in the name of God "in miracles and wonders and by manifold powers, and by impartings of the Holy Spirit" (Heb. 2:4).

If the signs which gave the Apostles' preaching a divine aura were miracles and extraordinary gifts of the Holy Spirit, what kind of signs existed after the apostolic period, when the miracles and charismatic gifts became, essentially, a rare event? This is a problem which interested the Church Fathers from the very beginning.[1]

The doctrine of St. Augustine

St. Augustine has given a classic answer to this question. In Sermon CXVI, in which he speaks of the appearance of Christ to His disciples after the Resurrection, and of the meaning of Scripture manifested to them on that occasion, he writes: "They saw Him suffer, saw Him hanging from the cross, revive and live. What did they not see? His body, that is, the Church. They saw

---

[1] Santi Pesce, *La Chiesa cattolica perenne motivo di credibilità*, (Turin, 1960), p. 143 ss. The author reports here the opinions of the Fathers before St. Augustine.

the bridegroom, but the bride still remained hidden."[2] In speaking further of the mandate of Christ to carry the Gospel to the ends of the earth, Augustine continues: "One thing the Apostles did not see, the Church's spreading to all the people, starting from Jerusalem. They saw the head and because of the head they believed in the body. They believed in what they could not see through what they could see. We resemble them: we see something which they did not see, and we do not see something which they did. What do we not see that they did? Christ under human form. As they saw Christ and believed in His body (the Church), so we see the body and believe in the head."[3] In the case of the Apostles and in our own case as well, we see something and thereby believe in another: the Apostles saw Christ and believed in the Church, we see the Church and believe in Christ. The knowledge of Christ and of His Resurrection induced the Apostles to believe in the Church; the knowledge of the Church induces us to believe in Christ risen from the dead. In both cases the faith is linked to a miracle: the faith of the Apostles to the physical miracle of the Resurrection of Christ, our faith to the moral miracle of the Church.

Among the qualities which make the Church a moral miracle is sanctity. Augustine describes it in his *De utilitate credendi*. Speaking of the motives which should lead to belief in the Church, the Bishop of Hippo expands on this particular characteristic.

"Customs always have a great influence on the human spirit. Even when they are bad and stem from passions which seize control, we are more prone to condemn and reproach them than to abandon them and change."[4] This principle posited, Augustine puts the spectacle of Christian life before the eyes of Onoratus, the Manichean. "Just think how little humanity would have to gain when we see that not only the great thinkers who put the question, but a multitude of simple persons, among so many different peoples, believe and proclaim that we must not worship earthly bodies, or fiery bodies or visible objects, but God who can be known only by intellect; when we see that temperance is conceived of as being satisfied with a little bread and water for daily sustenance; when we see that fasting is carried on not only for a

---

[2] St. Augustine, *Sermo* 116, c. 5; ML 38, col. 659–660.
[3] *Ibid.*, col. 660.
[4] ML 42, col. 90–91.

day but for several days in succession, and that chastity goes to the limits of renouncing marriage and family; and when we see generosity, to giving up one's own goods for the poor, detachment from life, unto desire for death? Few do it, and even fewer do it with prudence: but the people approve, the people listen, the people praise all this and conclude by loving it. They cannot do otherwise, but attribute this to their weakness."[5]

This fact of sanctity cannot help but make a great impression, and it is truly present in Christianity. The Bishop of Hippo continues: "See what divine providence has realized through the medium of the oracles of the Prophets, the humanity and teaching of Christ, the journeys of the Apostles, the humiliation of the martyrs, their sufferings, their blood and death, through the admirable conduct of the saints."[6] And consequently: "When we perceive all this—such great assistance on the part of God, such progress and such results—how can we hesitate at throwing ourselves into the arms of the Church?"[7]

It is in the sanctity of its members—a moral miracle—that the Church demonstrates its divine institution. It is this miracle which makes preaching appear as the Word of God which must be received in faith. While the word of preachers proclaims the mystery of salvation, the Church's sanctity proves that this word comes from God himself. The argument of St. Augustine was later developed in detail by Savonarola in his *Triumphus crucis* and it provided the Vatican Council with its theme of proclaiming the Church as a perennial motive of credibility, *signum levatum in nationibus.*[8]

The argumentation of St. John Chrysostom

As counterproof, we would like to repeat an argument used by St. John Chrysostom, whose task it was to convert to the Faith the pagan minority that still existed in his times.

Speaking to his Christian flock, the great Doctor says (in literal terms): "Christ has left us here that we may spread the light, that we may become masters of others, a true leaven; that we may comport ourselves like angels among men, like adults among chil-

---

[5] *Ibid.*
[6] *Ibid.*
[7] *Ibid.*
[8] *Denz. Sch.,* 3014.

dren, like spiritual men among sensualists, in order to win them, to be seeds and bear abundant fruit. If we could make our life sparkle like this, there would be no need to explain the doctrine, because examples would take the place of words. There would be no more pagans if we behaved like true Christians; if we observed the commandments of Jesus, if we suffered injustice and robbery, if we blessed those who wrong us, if we returned bad with good. There is no pagan so adverse to religion that he would not embrace it if everybody behaved like that. If St. Paul, as a single individual, could attract so many to Christ, how many could we, who are so many, attract? Well, Christians are more numerous than pagans. And while in the arts one teacher is sufficient to attract many disciples, in religion, where masters are more numerous than disciples, nobody is converted. In fact, the disciples observe the virtues of the masters and when they see that the masters desire and seek the same things that they desire and seek, that is, power and honors, how can they admire Christianity? They see many of us living reprehensible lives steeped in earthly things; they see that we esteem riches as much as they, that like them we fear death, poverty and sickness, that we seek glory and public offices, that we fret over money and profit on occasion. However, could they be led to believe? Perhaps through our lives? But these are ruinous. Perhaps through love? Of this there is not even a shadow to be seen. Therefore, we must account not only for our sins, but also for the damage we have done others in these ways."[9]

In the absence of miracles, says St. Paul, a sign is necessary if pagans are to believe that Christianity is divine. This sign is our life, whereby we behave like angels among men, as spiritual beings among animals. If our lives shone in their full splendor, the pagans would be converted even in the absence of preaching. But since Christians do not differ from pagans in their behavior, no pagan feels inclined towards conversion. St. Chrysostom was not surprised at this. How could pagans believe when the Christianity they saw gave no indication of its divine origin? And continuing, St. Chrysostom asserts that it is not enough to recall the virtue of ancients like St. John and St. Paul, because pagans could recall the virtue of their own philosophers. It is necessary to show

[9] St. John Chrysostom, *In Ep. ad Tim.*, c. 3, homil. 10; MG 62, col. 551–2.

them *hic et nunc* what Christianity is. And this cannot happen so long as Christians live like pagans.

St. Gregory of Nazianzus expresses the same thought. Strangers, he says, judge the faith from the good name of those who represent it. If this is so, "how can we induce them to accept an opinion which is different from that which we have taught by our life?"[10]

A judgment of Francisco de Vittoria

In more recent times the same kind of argument can be found in the writing of the great Spanish theologian, Francisco de Vittoria.

Speaking to protect the South American Indians from the conquistadors, who alleged that since the Indians had not accepted Christianity they were falling into sin and thus deserved punishment, the Salamanca theologian demonstrates the inconsistency of this kind of reasoning. It is true, he admits, that the Indians had not become converts; but if the Indians were to be held responsible for their infidelity, the Faith should have been presented to them under signs likely to prove its divine origin.[11]

Vittoria writes: "But I have not heard speak of any kind of signs: neither miracles, nor exemplars of religious life, but, to the contrary, of numerous scandals, of horrible crimes, of much godlessness. Therefore, it does not seem that the Christian religion was preached in an adequate way so that they (the Indians) might have been drawn to embrace it. It is true that many religious and ecclesiastics have worked to this end by dint of exemplary lives and diligent preaching—with zeal and ability—but their work has been kept from fruition by those who had other concerns."[12]

In order to say that the Gospel has been preached in such a way as to induce honest conversions, it is necessary that signs indicating that preachers speak in the name of God be present. But in the evangelization of the Indians, these signs were missing. There have been no miracles, nor examples of Christian living so forceful as to demonstrate the divine value of the Christian religion. The preachers were models of zeal and sanctity, but their testimony was rendered valueless by the bad example of other

[10] St. Gregory Nazianzus, *Poem. hist.*, I, sect. I: MG 37, col. 1204 A/B.
[11] Francisco de Vittoria, *De Indis,* sect. II, n. 13, e 14.
[12] *Ibid.,* n. 14.

Christians. And how can one say that the Gospel was really preached to the Indians? Vittoria goes so far as to say that, except for the sin of infidelity, there were more vices among Christians than among the infidels.[13]

Here we find a clear example of how necessary are both the individual preacher's testimony and the collective testimony of the whole Christian community. "Then the Church offers herself for judgment, she offers herself as a whole. She is not judged solely by the clergy's preaching, but by the behavior of the clergy and of laymen as well. Every Christian is responsible for the picture of Christianity obtained by unbelievers, and every Christian, therefore, must be a positive sign for the truth of Christianity."[14]

The sanctity of both preacher and Church are thus part of preaching. Concerning the Word of God we can say that it has been proclaimed insofar as its divinity has been authenticated by physical and moral signs. Sanctity is one of these signs, perhaps the most important one. A close relationship exists between the sanctity of the Church and the word of the preacher: without the sanctity of the Church, preaching would not be received as the Word of God; but without preaching, the sanctity of the Church would be unable to explain how the Church began or why it has been so fruitful spiritually.

Thus, we can now reply to the objection that stems from St. Paul's teaching, namely, that preaching is effective even when the preacher is lacking in sanctity, and even when he is moved to preach from ignoble motives (Phil. 1:15). The efficacy of preaching is not linked to the sanctity, properly speaking, of the preacher, but to that of the Church for which, and in which, he is preaching. It is the Church and not the individual preacher who proclaims the Word of God.

Clergy and laity together, the Church forms a unity. In this unity shadows may abide, in the realm of the teaching hierarchy as well as in that of the faithful. But there must also be light. In order for the efficacy of preaching to shine through, there must be more light than shadow. In the sanctity of the Church the

[13] *Ibid.*, n. 16.
[14] L. Vereecke, "L'évangélisation chrétienne en Amérique espagnole durant la premiére moitié du XVI siècle," *Mission sans Frontières* (Paris, 1960), p. 190. Though we have consulted the original source, we have used this article in writing about Vittoria.

preacher's moral and intellectual deficiencies are absorbed, even as the light caused by the sanctity of the preacher is absorbed when the Church's shadows are too strong. In the case of St. Paul, the shadow cast by preachers who proclaimed Christ for reasons of envy or self-aggrandizement was absorbed by the sanctity of the Christian community, while in the case of the evangelization of America, the sanctity of the preachers was absorbed by the strong shadow cast by the Christian community which surrounded them. It is the sanctity of the Church, or Christian community, which counts.[15]

Christianity as message

The sanctity of the Church is not only a motive for believing, not only an external circumstance which conditions the nature and efficacy of preaching. It is necessary for more interior reasons, above all, because of the object of preaching.

As noted earlier, the object of preaching is the proclamation of a message of salvation, a complex of values, destined to give meaning to life. And values are transmitted through testimony.

If the object of preaching were a system of ideas and facts— even extraordinary ideas and facts announced through Revelation—such a system would be transmitted by teaching. As a matter of fact, science announces principles that are valid in themselves without any reference whatsoever to the teacher. When, through his own reflections, the philosopher discovers the laws governing some reality, he may teach these laws to whoever is interested in them, retracing for his listeners the rational process which led him to discover these principles. Acceptance or rejection of his teaching will depend on the strength or weakness of his argumentation. He is not engaged as a person in his teaching. It is of no importance if the professor is good or bad, more or less intelligent: it is only important that his proof is valid. For their part, the listeners should find no special difficulties in accepting a doctrine demonstrated to them as true. Science, after all, is concerned with ideas as such.

Matters take on a different hue where the spreading of a mes-

---

[15] Speaking about the preacher's sanctity, St. Vincent Ferrer says, "The crown of wisdom, which is theology, has no value without the seal of sanctity." (Sermon on the feast day of St. John the Evangelist, ed. BAC, p. 628.)

sage is at stake. Here, it is not a matter of facts and ideas that, while true in themselves, lack any close relationship to life. In the message, as we have said, "decisive realities are discovered which question our whole existence (that of the public and ours) and to which truth and sanctity bear witness."[16] Unlike teaching, it is not a case of stating how things are, of interpreting reality, but a case of pointing to a way out of a situation which has been judged impossible. To be effective, a message must arouse in the receiver the hope that the messenger's way will really solve the dilemma in which he finds himself and from which he wants to escape. This hope cannot be stirred except by means of a witness, someone who has already run the course indicated by the messenger, someone who has found a solution to his situation. As Mehl says: "Witnesses do not try to prove the errors or truth of a system, they do not try to analyze data . . . they describe the authority to which they submit their life and they attest that this authority is valid for their listeners."[17] The message is the proclamation of a better future, a future which is already present for the witness. He has accepted the values proclaimed and he now proclaims them to others; he has seen his own life transformed according to a new rhythm. The witness does not demonstrate a thesis; instead, he shows what has happened to him since the moment he accepted the message he now proclaims.

A message spreads to the degree that the messenger is able to make his listeners believe that they, too, can succeed in resolving their problem and in giving new meaning to their lives. The listeners surrenders to the values proclaimed when he accepts them as part of his life, but this he will not do unless the witness is able to communicate the claim, the attraction and fascination contained in those values. Such communication is impossible unless the witness has himself had such an intense experience that he cannot do otherwise than communicate it. This means that the attraction which the values proclaimed are destined, by their very nature, to exercise, can be explained and can become real only when embodied in a witness, from whom that attraction can then irradiate.

It was through such a phenomenon of radiation and communion that the message of the French Revolution was propagated, and

[16] R. Mehl, *La recontre d'autrui* (Neuchatel-Paris, 1955), p. 25.
[17] *Ibid.*

in the same way, today, that the justice underlying the Russian Revolution is communicated. When nineteenth-century political agitators sought to alter the existing regime by demanding a "constitution," it was to the French example that they alluded, to her prosperity, and her political and literary prestige. In these results they saw the rightness of the revolutionary message. In the progress made by Soviet Russia, today's oppressed peoples likewise see the strength and effectiveness of the Marxist message. These two messages have spread through a phenomenon of radiation which we may call contagious.

The Christian message

In Christianity it is a message which confronts us. This message is the proclamation of Christ dead and risen. We have here an account of events that really occurred: but what matters is not so much their truth as their meaning. Christ died and rose again for our salvation, that is, to give meaning to our lives by admitting us to participation in divine life, to the trinitarian dialogue, where human restlessness is stilled and life acquires meaning. Thus, in order to make known the true significance of all these facts, the Apostles had only one means: their life with Jesus, the contacts they had with Him for three years: eating and drinking with Him, listening to Him and seeing Him perform miracles. It was by means of these contacts that the Apostles perceived the incomparable value of His person, His status as the Word of Life (1 John, 1:1), the light of the world (John 8:12), the way, the truth and the life (John 14:6). So transformed were they by this confrontation that they could not live except in the service of the Master. No threat could silence them (Acts 4:20), no danger distress them or cause them to abandon their position. It is this commitment which surprises the Apostles' listeners and which makes them suspect a mystery. The listeners feel impelled to ask themselves who is this Christ who has so visibly transformed the Apostles, heretofore men wholly lacking in culture.

No one is impervious to this fascination. Though unmistakably opposed to the Apostles' preaching, the Pharisees could not conceal their astonishment at men so courageous as to dare anything for their Master. The Acts say: "Now seeing the boldness of Peter and John, and finding that they were uneducated and ordinary men, they began to marvel and to recognize them as having been with Jesus (Acts 4:13–14). The Pharisees felt that they were confronted by a mystery. In Iconium St. Paul's speech carried such an accent of sincerity and conviction that "a great multitude of Jews and of Greeks believed" (Acts 14:1). There were no miracles here as there had been in the case of the Apostles in Jerusalem. But the person of St. Paul must have radiated such a force that his audience did not hesitate to follow his word; and yet, at least in this first speech, his preaching of Christ was rather summary. When the keeper of the jail in Philippi saw that Paul and Silas had not run away when the earthquake set them free, he was converted: "And bringing them out, he said, "Sirs, what must I do to be saved?" (Acts 16:30). In all these examples it is the testimony of the Apostles—how they dedicate their lives so completely to the Master that they even neglect themselves and act in a way completely contrary to the ordinary—which surprises the listeners and which either leads them to the Faith, or at least to the point of considering it. In the testimony there is either an implicit or explicit invitation to follow the example of the witness, and this example is being followed or rejected according to the degree the listeners respect and need the values set forth. It is rejected by the Pharisees but accepted by the jailer at Philippi, and it causes great agitation in Gamaliel.

True and false testimony

At this point we would like to raise an objection. Is it not possible that the witness be a swindler who wants to deceive us? The answer is negative. The witness has no interest whatsoever in deceiving us: he was the first to accept the values which he proclaims and to which he is dedicated. He pays with his own person. To deceive others he would first have to deceive himself. St. Paul himself says that, had Christ not risen, he and the Christians would be "men the most to be pitied" (1 Cor. 15:19). It is, therefore, impossible to imagine a witness who wants to deceive.

However, one may object that there are false witnesses who are so clever that they can seduce the most prudent people. Our Lord Himself warns us of such possibilities when He says that the children of this world are more prudent, after their own fashion, than the children of the light (Luke 16:8). Thus we have a valid objection: false witnesses are more than a hypothesis.

We reply that the testimony has not been accepted blindly—

without discussion or guarantee of the message. This testimony attests to the presence of values which can transform the life of man, and includes the existence of proof which makes the message credible. Although it is possible to pass directly from witnessing to embracing the Faith—as was the case with the jailer of Philippi—testimony's specific task is not exactly this. Testimony must uphold the existence of values able to transform man's life, and it is therefore intended as a means of arousing in man awareness of a problem and of indicating a possible solution. It is evident that man, before committing himself, wants to understand it and to determine if the message is really credible. In this way there will be no difficulty in discerning true from false testimony.

In a passage in his *Apologeticum*, Tertullian has described precisely this task of testimony. Writing about the martyrs, he asks: "And who, after seeing the firmness of the Christian, is not moved to discover what is the ideal content of Christianity? And who, once he has found out, would not join us and, once with us, would not desire that he, too, might suffer in order to obtain complete forgiveness as the reward for his bloodshed?"[18] This is precisely the task of testimony: to induce the audience to seek out "the ideal content of Christianity," that is, to learn if God has really intervened in history. From this, seeking the judgment of credibility will derive.

In this connection, the case of Gamaliel is helpful. Confronted with the testimony of the Apostles, Gamaliel neither accepts nor rejects it: he remains doubtful, questions, and wonders if these men are in the right (Acts 5:34–39). Far from excluding apologetics, testimony renders it indispensable.

Collective testimony

There is another, more subtle objection. If the witness does not deceive, who is there to guarantee that he is not himself deceived? This objection does not concern the truth of the facts so much as their significance. Who, then, can assure us that the witness has not attributed to the facts a significance which they lack of themselves?

The answer is to be found in collective testimony. While it is possible that one individual may be deceived, or even a certain

[18] Tertullian, *Apologeticum,* c. 50.

number of individuals, it becomes less and less probable when millions accept the message and live by it, especially when accepting the message means sacrifice and renunciation.

Thus we arrive at the same conclusion: the spreading of the Gospel is not the work of individual preachers, but of the Church as a whole. Even though preachers proclaim the message, it is the Church which gives it its significance. The Christian community is essential for the spreading of Christianity.

Faith as encounter between persons

An even more urgent reason requires testimony for the spreading of faith. The object of preaching is not only a message, but a message identified with a person. The Christian message is the person of Christ. Preaching must induce an encounter between two persons, between Christ and man in his innermost being.

But just how is the encounter between persons induced? In an already quoted passage, Mouroux says: "A person cannot be understood in his entirety through a purely critical work, through the action of reason which finds and solves problems. Nor does he manifest himself in animal appetite or blind thrusts. A person can be understood by spiritual contact and through the phenomenon of communion."[19] Reason can pave the way for the encounter by showing that man needs God and it can prove the rationality of belief, but it cannot produce faith.

But how can this spiritual encounter be brought about? We have already cited St. Augustine, who claims that persons encounter each other through the phenomenon of love. Man gives himself to him who loves him first, especially, if he is a superior.[20]

The same thing happens in faith, in the encounter between God and man. God has loved us first; only then has He asked us to reciprocate this love. However, in faith God is hidden; He is not visible. He acts through a mediator who is the preacher. If faith requires a communion of love, the preacher must be its vehicle.

Here we are again concerned with testimony. The preacher must serve as witness for the love of God to man; in him we must see that God loves us. The encounter of faith is the result of this very radiation of love from God to man through the medium of the preacher, or, more generally speaking, through the Church.

[19] J. Mouroux, *Je crois en toi*, p. 47.
[20] St. Augustine, *De catechizandis rudibus*, c. 4, 7.

Here is the fundamental reason for testimony: the Church must be the bearer of the love of God. The man who sees her, who comes in contact with her life and observes the effect she has on human existence, must perceive in her the presence of God and the strength of His love. It is in this love that the Church bears God (and all mankind for the love of God), that the power of God and His love for man will have to be demonstrated. Jesus could rightfully say: "By this will all men know that you are my disciples, if you have love for one another" (John 13:35). Only in this way can that phenomenon of radiation and communion exist, without which there can be no faith.

The testimony of the Trinity

That one person can make us know another person, in his innermost being, is a fact which is verified in the Trinity. We know the three Divine Persons through the testimony that one bears concerning the other two. We know the Father through the Son, the Son through the Father, and the Holy Spirit through the Father and the Son. We know the Father through the testimony of the Son. Jesus says: "He who comes from above is over all. He who is from the earth belongs to the earth, and of the earth he speaks. He who comes from heaven is over all. And he bears witness to that which he has seen and heard, and his witness no one receives. He who receives his witness has set his seal on this, that God is true" (John 3:31–33). Jesus testifies to what He has seen with His Father (John 8:18). Nobody has seen God the Father, but we can know Him from what the only-begotten Son, who abides in the bosom of God, has testified (John 1:18). Therefore, we know the Father from what the Son says about Him.

In his turn, the Father bears witness to the Son. St. John says: "For this is the testimony of God which is greater, that he has borne witness concerning his Son. He who believes in the Son of God has the testimony of God in himself. He who does not believe the Son, makes him a liar; because he does not believe the witness that God has borne concerning his Son (1 John 5:9–10). This testimony was given by the Father when Jesus, in Baptism, was called His beloved Son (Mark 1:11; Luke 3:22); again, in the Transfiguration (Matt. 17:5); and again, on Palm Sunday (John 12:28). The testimony of the Father is also expressed in the miracles which He works for Christ (John 3:36), especially in that of the Resurrection. "The God of Abraham and the God of Isaac and the God of Jacob, the God of our fathers, has glorified his Son Jesus, whom you indeed delivered up and disowned before the face of Pilate" (Acts 3:13). Between Father and Son there is thus an exchange of testimony which strengthens both: "If I bear witness concerning myself, my witness is not true. There is another who bears witness concerning me, and I know that the witness that he bears concerning me is true" (John 5:31–32).

In addition, the Son testifies for the Holy Spirit: "And I will ask the Father and he will give you another advocate to dwell with you forever, the Spirit of truth whom the world cannot receive, because it neither sees him nor knows him" (John 14:16–17). The Spirit will render everything clear to the Apostles (John 14:26). In turn, the Holy Spirit bears witness to the Son: "But when the advocate has come, whom I will send you from the Father, the Spirit of truth who proceeds from the Father, he will bear witness concerning me" (John 15:26). The Spirit will bring honor to Jesus. (John 16:14).

As can be seen, the Divine Persons are known through an exchange of testimony which one bears to the other. In the spreading of the Faith we have the same situation. One person, the preacher, makes another person known: through his testimony, the preacher makes God—in Christ—known. It is a testimony of love which tends to arouse a response of love in him who receives it. Only another person can bring about this spiritual contact in which a person reveals himself in his innermost being. Therefore, faith is transmitted through testimony. Insofar as the preacher himself has been able to approach Christ's innermost being he is able to assist others in partaking of this intimate essence.[21]

The testimony of persecutions

We may well ask why testimony must be as radical as we have seen it described in the Acts of the Apostles. Why does the witness have to be persecuted, sometimes even to death, to the point that the highest expression of testimony is martyrdom? Persecution, as we said before, is a form of testimony.

In several texts of the Old Testament the persecution of witnesses is attributed to the fact that the will of God which they

[21] See J. Guitton, *Le problème de Jésus* (Paris, 1950), vol. I, pp. 239–243.

manifest often runs contrary to the will of men. And since men, in their pride, have never wanted to submit to God and change their designs, they sought to rid themselves of those true prophets of doom we call witnesses. The ways of the Lord are not those of men (Isa. 55:8). The Book of Wisdom quotes evil men as saying: "Let us beset the just one, because he is obnoxious to us; he sets himself against our doings, reproaches us for transgressions of the Law and charges us with violations of our training. He professes to have knowledge of God and styles himself a child of the Lord. To us he is the censure of our thoughts, merely to see him is a hardship for us, because his life is not like other men's, and different are his ways" (Wis. 2:12–15). And they conclude: "With revilement and torture let us put him to the test that we may have proof of his gentleness and try his patience. Let us condemn him to a shameful death; for according to his own words, God will take care of him. These were their thoughts, but they erred; for their wickedness blinded them" (2:21). God's prophets and His witnesses oppose the plans of unjust men, and these latter, in turn, cannot tolerate the words of witnesses or even their presence. Therefore, they try to banish them—by death, if necessary.

While not a fundamental part of the concept of testimony, persecution does emerge in the New Testament as its consequence.[22] Witnessing provokes persecution. Jesus predicts this to His disciples: "Behold, I am sending you forth like sheep in the midst of wolves. Be therefore wise as serpents, and guileless as doves. But beware of men, for they will deliver you up to councils, and scourge you in their synagogues, and you will be brought before governors and kings for my sake, for a witness to them and to the Gentiles" (Matt 10:16–18; Mark 13:9; Luke 21:12–13). He ties the persecutions of His disciples to His own: "If they have persecuted me, they will persecute you also, (John 15:20).

The motive for persecutions is to be found in the fact that witnesses proclaim to the world God's will, His plan of salvation, which cannot help but arouse Satan's opposition. The closer the relationship between God and witness, the stronger Satan's opposition and, consequently, the sufferings to which the witness is exposed.[23] In various passages of his Epistles St. Paul describes

---

[22] R. Asting, *Die Verkündigung des Wortes Gottes im Urchristentum* (Stuttgart, 1939), p. 555.

[23] Cf. Asting, *op. cit.*, p. 626–627.

with great dramatic emphasis the fate of the witness and his participation in sufferings. In the Epistles to the Romans he asks himself who could separate him from the love of Christ and answers: "Shall tribulation, or distress, or persecution, or hunger, or nakedness, or danger, or the sword? Even as it is written, 'For thy sake we are put to death all the day long. We are regarded as sheep for the slaughter.' But in all these things we overcome bacause of him who has loved us" (Rom 8:35–37). In the First Epistle to the Corinthians, he goes so far as to say that the Apostles are condemned to death and are fools. "To this very hour we hunger and thirst, and we are naked and buffeted, and have no fixed abode. And we toil, working with our own hands. We are reviled and we bless, we are persecuted and we bear with it, we are maligned and we entreat, we have become as the refuse of this world, the offscouring of all, even until now" (1 Cor. 4:11–13).

The problem of evil

To this scriptural motive, we can add another, more intrinsic one, which is linked to the very object of the message.

The preacher proclaims to men those great facts of sacred history that are symbols of God's love for man. All Revelation is summed up in St. John's text: "For God so loved the world that he gave his only-begotten Son, that those who believe in him may not perish, but may have life everlasting" (John 3:16). But an objection of undeniable strength may be voiced: If God has loved us to the point of giving up His only-begotten Son, why then the suffering? Why so many physical and moral pains? The existence of evil affords an objection against the love of God, especially when those who suffer are the innocent and the good, especially children.[24] It seems that good people should be compensated by God, whereas, on the contrary, they are the worst beset. And therefore, how can the preacher say that God loves man?

This objection, as is clear, stems from our way of perceiving love. A human father submits to every sacrifice in order to spare the children he loves all pain and suffering. God, however, acts differently. The more He loves a person, the more He exposes that

---

[24] We have already pointed out how much modern man feels the pain of children. In his novel *La Peste* Camus insists with exceptional vigor on this difficulty of modern man regarding Providence.

person to suffering. And this began with His Son in whom He is well pleased (Matt. 3:17).

However, an answer to the problem of evil is demanded. And the reply may be summed up in the very fact of who suffers, the witness who incarnates the love of God. In being persecuted, the witness shows that he is aware of this objection, that he has experienced the powers of evil in his own flesh and bones. At the same time, however, he points to a cure for evil, that is, the love of God. "And this is the victory that overcomes the world, our faith" (1 John 5:4). Whoever accepts the love of God and is united with Him in faith, overcomes evil. This is why not only persecution itself, but gladness in accepting persecution, is a part of testimony. The Apostles left the High Council filled with joy, because they had been made worthy of suffering indignities for the sake of Jesus' name (Acts 5:41). St. Paul could not contain himself for happiness in the midst of all his trials (2 Cor. 7:4).

In this sense alone, testimony becomes a mystery and poses a problem for the one who approaches the witness. He then becomes, in the midst of the visible, the witness of the invisible.

This is the task of testimony: to place the invisible in the very center of the visible. But the human person is necessary for this. The witness points his finger to Heaven: he indicates the invisible and the eternal while he lives and operates in the visible and the temporal.[25]

Christian life and the spread of Christianity

We have already noted the importance of Christian life for the spreading of the Gospel message. It is the sign which shows that Christianity comes from God. From Christian life radiates an appeal and an attraction which cause the well disposed man, searching for a meaning to life, to embrace the Faith. Why? Because he wants to undergo the same experience and obtain the same results. Christianity spreads by means of a phenomenon of radiation.

Our task, now, is to discover how experience bears out what we have established theoretically regarding the concept of the message. How did faith spread?

[25] See K. Rahner on martyrdom in *Schriften zur Theologie*, vol. II, pp. 73 ff.

In the early centuries of evangelization, Christian life was the great argument in favor of Christianity, the great motive underlying, first, the curiosity, and then the interest of all those who came in contact with it. What impressed the Gentiles was the moral transformation which the Gospel worked in those who embraced it, the love of Christians one for another, and especially the martyrdom with which many of them unhesitatingly sealed their dedication to Christ. Confronted with these facts, Gentiles were forced to ask themselves: How is this possible? What is the secret of a life so different from that which we ourselves customarily live?

These are the questions for which the pagan Diognetes sought answers in the letters now referred to by his name. He wanted to know the God to whom the Faith of Christians was directed, the nature of the worship given Him, the origin of Christians' disdain of the world and of death, and, finally, the basis for the great love that they showed one another.[26] Basically, all these problems are intertwined in the Christian life. Diognetes wanted to learn the secret of a way of life which was so different from that of the Gentiles.

Nobody should be astonished at this request. The Christian life did have an extraordinary attraction. Here the author of the letter describes it:

". . . because Christians are not different from other people, because of their native land, their language, or their dress. They do not dwell in special cities, nor use a special dialect, and their way of life has nothing special about it. The fascination of their doctrine has not grown out of their imagination or fantasies; unlike many others, they do not champion a human doctrine. They are scattered throughout Greek and barbarian cities according to the fate that befell each one; they conform to local customs in their dress, yet their food and their way of life are subject to the extraordinary and paradoxical laws of their spiritual republic. They reside in different countries, but as strangers, who have merely taken up temporary residence. All do their duty as citizens, but they endure accusations like strangers. Every foreign land is their fatherland, and every fatherland a foreign country. They marry like others, and have children, but they do not kill their

[26] *Epistle to Diognetus*, c. 1, 1.

newborn. They are made of flesh but they do not live according to the flesh. They spend their lives on earth, but they are citizens of Heaven. They obey established laws, but their mode of life excels these laws in its perfection. They love all men, and all men persecute them. They are misunderstood, condemned and even killed, and thus do they attain life. They are poor, but they enrich many. They lack everything and have an abundance of everything. They are despised and find their glory in injury. They are slandered and are in the same way justified. They are insulted and they bless in return. They are treated dishonorably and they respond with honor. They do nothing but good and they are chastised like criminals. They accept punishments joyfully, as if this would be the means of birth to a new life. The Jews make war on them as if on foreigners; they are persecuted by the Greeks and those who detest them are at a loss to say why they hate them. In short, what the soul is to the body, the Christians are to the world."[27] And he concludes: "These things cannot be the works of men; they are, rather, the effects of the power of God, the manifest proof of His coming."[28]

The conclusion is as logical as can be desired. Christian life cannot be explained without a transcendent cause: it has as its basis the truth of Christianity, that is, that God has become man and has brought a message of love which is capable of completely transforming human life.

Tertullian evokes the strength of Christian life, especially martyrdom, to explain the spread of Christianity to the pagans and the secret of the love the Christians show for one another.[29] Justin does the same when, in order to bring pagans to embrace the Gospel, he compares what Christians are before conversion with what they become after baptism.[30]

The reaction of Gentiles to the Christian life is the same as that which the life and the miracles of the Apostles evoked among the population of Jerusalem. For some of them, as for Justin, they provided a reason for conversion,[31] for others the reaction did not go

[27] *Ibid.*, c. 5–6.

[28] *Ibid.*, c. 7.

[29] Tertullian, *Apologeticum* 50, cf. c. 39.

[30] Justin, *Apologia* I, c. 4. For other examples see G. Bardy, *La conversion au christianisme durant les premiérs siècles* (Paris, 1949), pp. 146–157.

[31] Justin, *Apologia* II, c. 12.

beyond surprise,[32] while, for a third category, Christian strength in the face of death was no more than "theatrical affectation" or a form of "folly."[33] The attitude of Jesus' listeners and of the Apostles is continued in those who listen to the Apostles' successors. Preaching, however, is always effective because it provokes a decision.[34]

The testimony of the converts

What happened in antiquity is still happening today. Where does the path which leads to the conversion of our contemporaries begin, how is it made more profound? Only through the phenomenon of Christian life as experienced and lived to the hilt. Sometimes we discover this experience at the beginning of the road, at other times it takes place in a phase of evolution, or, sometimes, in the decisive phase. It is not the only element which influences so complex and so difficult an event as conversion, but it often serves as a catalyst for the others.

Edith Stein, Husserl's famous assistant, saw her own atheism dwindle when confronted with the resignation of a Christian widow who had lost her husband in the war. Seeing the widow's strength of spirit, she was shaken. She writes: "In this, my first encounter with the cross and with the divine force which it communicates to the person who carries it, I saw, for the first time and tangibly before me, the Church born of the redeeming suffering of Christ in His victory over the sting of death. This was the moment when my disbelief collapsed and Christ rose resplendent before me, the Christ in the mystery of the cross."[35]

[32] This is the case with the pagan Galenus. "Hi tamen (Christians) interdum talia faciunt, qualia qui vere philosophantur. Nam quod mortem contemnunt, id quidem omnes ante oculos habemus; item quod verecundia quadam ducti ab usu verum venerearum abhorrent. Sunt enim inter eos et feminae et viri, qui per totam vitam a concubitu abstinuerint; sunt etiam qui in animis regendis coercendisque et in acerrimo honestatis studio eo progressi sint, ut nihil cedant vere philosophantibus." The text is quoted by Harnack (*Die Mission und Ausbreitung des Christentums in den ersten drei Jahrhunderten,* 2nd ed. [Leipzig, 1906], vol. I, pp. 183–184).

All through the quoted volume, Harnack points out the influence which the Christian life exercised on the spread of Christianity in the first centuries. See especially Chapter V.

[33] Marc Aurel (*Thoughts,* 11. 3), Eppithetus (*Diss.,* Book V, 7).

[34] See also what Justin says about the negative reaction of the pagans. (*Apologia* II, chap. 2.)

[35] Edith Stein, *Teresa Renata a Spiritu Sancto* (Nürnberg, 1948), p. 22.

For Adolf Bormann, the son of the notorious Nazi, the encounter with Christian life and the aura which it spreads came while he was contemplating suicide following the defeat in war and the humiliation of his fatherland. Hidden in the house of Catholic peasants, he made a casual contact with a Catholic priest. Here is his reaction: "When that priest addressed words of comfort to me, I felt his strength inspire peace, calm and love within me. Behind this man there was the assurance of faith, not lies. For the first time the thought struck me that it probably had been a crime to imprison priests."[36] This thought finally led the young atheist to conversion and eventually to the priesthood.

For the Indian philosopher, Chuni Mukerji, the Christian life was decisive for his own conversion and as a sign of Christianity's divine origin. In the search for a more perfect life, he had passed from complete indifference to the religiosity of Bramo Somay, then to Unitarianism, and finally to Anglicanism. But when he came in contact with Catholic life, he felt sure that his spiritual vicissitudes would end in Rome. "What induced me to be subject to Rome?" he asked himself, and answered: "I can answer immediately: the admirable example of missioners, fathers, brothers and sisters: the constant and marvelous example of greatness of soul which we encounter in the whole Catholic world, and with it the perfect organization of the Catholic Church."[37]

In our days, just as in the first centuries of the Church, faith spreads in the same way: by means of persons who have perceived the meaning of Christ in their lives, who have permitted Christ to penetrate that life and who have dedicated themselves to His service. From them issues a call, a particular charm, which attracts some to the faith, and evokes in others a problem or a refusal.[38]

[36] B. Schafer, *Sie hörten seine Stimme* (Lucerne, 1950), vol. I, pp. 172–73.

[37] *Ibid.*, p. 126.

[38] Though the invitation to faith is implicit in every testimony, it is quite explicit in some. See, for instance, what is said by the author of the *Discourse to the Greek* which for some time was attributed to Justin and today is considered apocryph. After explaining the reasons which have caused him to embrace Christianity, the author tells the pagans: "Come close to Jesus, my Greeks, so that you may partake in an insuperable knowledge. Let yourselves be instructed in a divine doctrine and become disciples of an incorruptible souverain. Do not recognize heroes which bring disaster to peoples. Our King, the Divine Word who is constantly helping us, does not want

The insufficiency of the language

Before concluding this chapter on the necessity of testimony, we must cite an argument which comes from the means used by preaching, that is, the word. It is commonplace among scholars to point out that the word alone is not enough to provoke an encounter between persons in their intimate life: it is impersonal, and expresses only what they have in common but not what is exclusively theirs. Gusdorf speaks of "ontological" inadequacy in this regard. The Greeks, and after them the Scholastics, noted this insufficiency very clearly when they defined the word as *signum conceptus.* The concept, the idea, is of a universal nature and cannot express something intimate or particular. Gusdorf says: "From my thought I can manifest only the exterior, the superficial. The basic meaning always escapes because this is not an idea, or a thing, but an attitude which is properly mine, the intention of my whole life. This horizon cannot be explained and, even so, it is in reference to it that the meaning of everything that I can say is established."[39] Experience proves that there are men who exercise great influence on their listeners by their word. But as soon as these men set words to paper, they lose their effectiveness. It would seem that efficacy does not arise from words but from the person who pronounces them.

The efficacy of the word has its limitations: the word lacks a means of access to the innermost being. Gusdorf continues: "The explicit teaching of a master counts less than the testimony of his attitude, the charm of a gesture or a smile. The rest is silence, because the last word, the *maître mot,* of a man, is not a word. The most common communication between men is an *indirect communication,* which operates in spite of language, with the

---

robust bodies or noble descendence, but a pure soul, adorned by sanctity. The proof of our King are His divine actions, because it is a force which pervades the soul which, though it does not make us poets, or philosophers or able creators, but makes immortals out of us mortals, gods out of men and lifts us from the regions of the earth far beyond those of Olympus. Come close, let yourselves be instructed. You are like me because I, too, was like you. See what has seduced me: the inspirational character of the doctrine and the power of the word" (MG 6, col. 237). For the Greek apologists and the missionary intent of their writings see V. Monachino, "Intento pratico e propagandistico nell'apologetica greca del II secolo," *Gregorianum,* 31 (1951), fasc. 1–2.

[39] G. Gusdorf, *La Parole* (Paris, 1956), p. 76.

help of chance, and is often opposed to the very meaning of language."[40]

So with faith. Here, too, it is a question of putting the innermost being of one human person in contact with that of another, that is, Christ. For this purpose the simple word, if isolated from the person, is insufficient. But even in the person himself the word remains ineffective if it does not come from an "effort of life." In Christian life this force implies that one has found and tasted of Christ's intimacy. A man who has never discovered this intimacy cannot bring others to its discovery.

Experience confirms the difference between the preaching of a saint and that of an ordinary preacher. And yet they say the same things. And it can even happen that from a literary standpoint the saint speaks less fluently. The classic example of this is the Curé of Ars. When he spoke, he converted his listeners; but now that his sermons can be read in print, they appear to be rather poor. When he spoke, his words derived from an "effort of life" and were therefore able to "seal a communication" with Christ.

Thus, in order that the word of the preacher may be a vehicle for faith, it must come from his own commitment to find everything in Christ. Thus the testimony of his life, of his sanctity, is an indispensable factor for the efficacy of his preaching. It shows the divine origin of his message, it proves that in the Church God Himself is speaking. It is this testimony which shows the degree to which the message is necessary if man is to find a meaning in existence. If Christ is the light of the world, it is demonstrated in the transformation which He causes in those who listen to the Church and believe in Him.

[40] *Ibid.*, p. 83.

CHAPTER X

Efficacy of Preaching

W E ARE NOW ready to investigate the efficacy of preaching. We know that there are two distinct questions, one concerning the nature of this efficacy, and the other, the way in which this efficacy is expressed. We have already demonstrated that the manner can only be *ex opere operantis*, because preaching is a word directed to man, presenting a message and requiring an answer. It cannot impel action unless it is understood. While we have also spoken of efficacy *ex opere operato*, it was only by way of analogy with that of the sacrament. Preaching is a word to which an answer, of whatever kind, must be given.

Now we must explain this efficacy and show why preaching is a word which necessarily requires an answer. What is there about preaching that does not permit man to remain indifferent?

A word of testimony

We have already said that preaching is testimony, a bearing witness to the decisive facts in life, the proclamation of a message of salvation. The object of this message is God insofar as He is Savior, insofar as through the Incarnation, Death and Resurrection of His Son—wherein man was freed from the consequences of original sin—He has saved him and restored him to His friendship.

The object of preaching, consequently, is quite specific. God is not an ordinary object, not only because He is the Creator of everything, but also and above all because He is truth and supreme goodness—that truth and goodness which are the objects of human intelligence and will. In preaching there is something objective, something real, a special dynamism, a force of attraction which spontaneously draws to itself man's intelligence and will, which cannot attain their object except *sub specie veri et boni*. If we further consider that in preaching God is also the subject, that is, the One who presents Himself to man and offers him salvation, we can well understand all the force with which preaching is charged. The efficacy of preaching consists in the power of God, in the *dynamis* of His person, in the attracting force of the truth and goodness which are identified with Him. Drawn by a fascination and charm which they cannot resist—since God is the ultimate reason for their interior dynamism—human intelligence and will turn spontaneously to this object. But in the order of providence in which we live, God has not shut Himself off from man in such a way that He can be reached only by reasoning; God has become a historical person, Jesus Christ, whom St. Paul calls "the image of the invisible God" (Col. 1:15), and in the Epistle to the Hebrews a Son who is "the brightness of his Father's glory" (Heb. 1:3). In Christ, truth and supreme goodness have assumed a face and a figure and have discarded the abstractness and impersonalism of philosophical analysis. The Word Incarnate is the truth (John 14:6) and goodness (Luke 18:19). Therefore, it is possible to say that the attracting power of truth and of the supreme good is identified with the attracting power of Christ, with the charm of His person. It is He who attracts man and it is towards Him that man, unconsciously perhaps, is going: He alone has the words of eternal life (John 6:69); He alone is "the way, and the truth, and the life" (John 14:6); He alone is "the light of the world" (John 8:12). Thus, Christ possesses an attraction which in its turn elicits an orientation towards Him on the part of man.

A text from St. John

In this connection it seems important that we examine a well-known passage from the Fourth Gospel in which Jesus, speaking of Himself as the bread of life, stirs scandal in the hearts of many of His listeners and surprises even His own disciples: "But Jesus said to them: 'I am the bread of life. He who comes to me shall not hunger, and he who believes in me shall never thirst,' . . . The Jews, therefore murmured about him because he had said, 'I am the bread that has come down from heaven.' And they kept saying, 'Is this not Jesus, the son of Joseph, whose father and mother we know? How, then, does he say, "I have come from heaven"?' " (John 6:35, 41–42). Reacting to these murmurs, Jesus said to them: "Do not murmur among yourselves. No one can come to me unless the Father who sent me draw him, and I will raise him up on the last day. It is written in the Prophets, 'And they all shall be taught of God.' Everyone who has listened to the Father, and has learned, comes to me; not that anyone has seen the Father except him who is from God, he has seen the Father" (John 6:43–46).

In general, theologians explain the attraction of the Father as being founded on inner grace. Outward grace—in the form of preaching—already existed, they say. But Jesus' listeners did not believe Him. The Master attributes this lack of faith to the absence of attraction on the part of the Father. In order to believe, different from preaching, inner grace is necessary; lacking inner grace, we cannot assent to the revelation proposed to us externally.[1]

It is our personal conviction that this opinion is incomplete. If those who listened to Jesus' claim about being the bread of life lacked the means of accepting it, that is, if they lacked the necessary internal grace consisting of attraction to the Father, Jesus could not reproach them so seriously. If no grace is given for believing, or insufficient grace, the blame cannot be laid at the door of man's incredulity. That nothing is, in fact, lacking on God's part can be deduced from the words which Jesus applies to the prophecies, according to which we are all taught by God. If this is the case, everyone can listen and believe. Nothing is lacking on God's part. If in spite of this some do not come to Christ as believers, it can be explained only by admitting that in the teaching of God the Father through the Incarnate Word, something is present that not all can understand, namely, the powers

---

[1] The opinion which sees the attraction of the Father in internal grace is shared also by modern exegetes. See among others: J. M. Lagrange, *Evangile selon St. Jean,* 4th ed. (Paris, 1927), pp. 179–181; L. Bouyer, *Le quatrième evangile* (Tournai, 1955), pp. 126–128; R. H. Lightfoot, *St. John's Gospel* (Oxford, 1956), p. 160; C. K. Barrett, *The Gospel according to St. John* (London, 1958), p. 245; A. Wikenhauser, *Das Evangelium nach Johannes* (Regensburg, 1957), pp. 126–128.

of attraction. If some men do not perceive it and some are not attracted by it, it is the fault of men. The attraction is there, and all who wish may experience it.

As a consequence, we must admit that in addition to the internal grace which is required for faith, there must also be an attractive force which is inherent in the very Word of Jesus—in His preaching—which has to be recognized if one seeks to believe in Him.

The nature of the attraction

What is this attraction comprised of?

In order to be attractive, an object must possess something desirable, something to which man can aspire because it answers a need, a necessity, because it fills a void. Now the object which is presented us in preaching is the most desirable imaginable. Christ is the synthesis of all values which man needs and to which he aspires.

In his commentary on the Johannine verse cited above, St. Augustine puts it succinctly: "Do not expect to be attracted without the participation of your own will; the soul is attracted by love."[2] If one objects that attraction deprives a person of freedom, St. Augustine replies that this is not true. Man is also attracted by pleasures, such as Virgil describes in his second eclogue.[3] If man, then, is attracted by pleasure—which is an object aroused in him—and can follow it without losing his freedom, how much more truly can we state the following words: *trahi hominem ad Christum qui delectatur veritate, delectatur beatitudine, delectatur justitia, delectatur sempiterna vita, quod totum Cristus est.*[4] Everyone, he says, is attracted towards some object by the love or pleasure it evokes in him. Therefore, the man who loves beauty, truth, beatitude, justice and eternal life is spontaneously attracted by Christ, who incarnates these realities within Himself. The attraction is spontaneous and leaves man perfectly free. The object of preaching is therefore attractive of itself: in it is all the charm of truth, goodness and life.

But to feel the attraction of an object we have to desire what it contains, have to love it in some way. Where there is no need or

[2] St. Augustine, *In Joann Ev.*, tract. 26, c. 6, 4; ML 35, col. 1608.
[3] Virgil, *Egloga*, 2, 65.
[4] St. Augustine, *In Joann. Ev.*, tract. 26, c. 6, 4, ML 35, col. 1608.

no love, there is no attraction. If man neither loves nor seeks truth, beauty, goodness or eternal life, he does not feel their charm when they are presented to him, and the attraction these values possess will remain without effect on him. Precisely this happened to those who heard Christ speak of Himself as bread from heaven. They took offense because such bread did not interest them and, consequently, they did not understand. "Give me a man who loves," continues St. Augustine, "and hears what I say. Give me one who desires, who is thirsty, who walks abroad in this depressing solitude, sighing after the source of eternal peace: Give me such a man and he knows what I say. But if I talk to a cold heart he does not know what I say. Such were those who whispered among one another."[5]

Here is how the Father teaches and attracts: by presenting us an object, Christ, who synthesizes in Himself all the realities toward which man feels attracted and in which he is interested. And the Bishop of Hippo concludes: "Videte quomondo trahit, pater: docendo delectat, non necessitatem imponendo: ecce quomodo trahit."[6]

The attraction is thus the Word of God, the teaching of the Father, in which He talks to us and presents us with a fascinating object on which to focus the love of a soul thirsting for truth, goodness and life. It is for this reason that St. John has placed the text about attraction within the speech about the bread of life. It is because we desire this bread that we come to Christ; this is why we believe in Him as soon as the Father presents Him; because we desire eternal life, the words of Christ are accepted.

We may conclude that the attraction of the Father is inherent in His Word, that the appeal of truth and goodness, the appeal of Christ is the object of His magisterium. In speaking, God presents His Son, the Word Incarnate, for our salvation; He presents Him as the one who attracts our mind and our heart, as the one who has the words of life everlasting. The appeal of Christ is bound up with the Word of God in preaching. It is a supernatural appeal which requires the possession of internal grace to be recognized.

---

[5] These are St. Augustine's words: "Da amantem et sentit quod dico, da desiderantem, da esurientem, da in ista solitudine peregrinantem atque sitientem, talem et scit quid dicam. Si autem frigido loquor, nescit quid loquor. Tales erant isit qui invicem murmurabant" (*ibid.*, col. 1608).

[6] *Ibid.*, col. 1610.

The opinion of St. Thomas

St. Thomas Aquinas also understands the external attraction which stems from the object. In a commentary on the same text of John (6:44–46), he distinguishes various ways in which one may be attracted by the Father.

The first is *persuadendo ratione*. Thus the Father attracts men toward Jesus by demonstrating that Christ is His Son, either by means of an internal revelation, as happened in the case of Peter near Caesarea of Philippi (Matt. 16:17), or through miracles, as happened to those who believed after having seen the extraordinary thing that Jesus worked. But he could also attract men towards the Son *alliciendo*, that is, by means of a mysterious power which made them recognize Christ as the Son of God.

There is also a third mode of attraction, which the Angelic Doctor describes in these terms: "Sed trahuntur etiam a Filio admirabili delectatione, et amore veritatis, quae est ipse Filius Dei." And after having quoted St. Augustine, who expresses himself in the same terms, he concludes: "Ab isto ergo si trahendi sumus, trahamur per dilectionem veritatis."[7]

The tenor of the text indicates that it is a question of exterior grace, of an appeal that emanates from the Son of God and attracts man, who is by nature oriented towards truth. But the Angelic Doctor is even more explicit. He continues: "Sed quia non solum revelatio exterior, vel obiectum virtutem attrahendi habet, sed etiam interior instinctus impellens et movens ad credendum, ideo trahit multos pater ad filium per instrictum divinae operatonis moventis interius cor hominis ad credendum."[8] According to St. Thomas, an internal attraction parallels the external attraction that derives from the object. The Father's internal attraction moves man towards the object to be believed. Further on, the great Doctor posits the absolute necessity of attraction for belief. Without attraction, it is as impossible to believe as it is impossible to rise without help from below. Therefore, anyone who is not attracted cannot believe, and this negative reaction cannot be counted as a sin. For His part, God extends this attraction to everybody. If a man does not believe, it is that man's own fault.[9] Such reasoning tells us that the Jews, in not accepting the Word

[7] *Ibid., In Joannis Evangelium,* c. 6, lect. 5, 3.
[8] *Ibid.*
[9] *Ibid.*

of Jesus about the bread of life, were responsible for the sin of
incredulity as, having the grace of attraction, they did not feel it.
Therefore, according to the Evangelist, the attraction which they
lack can only be the exterior kind that comes from the object: and
this attraction is not felt because of the impediments they interpose.

But in what way is this attraction exercised? St. Thomas quotes
St. Augustine: "Modus utem attrahendi est congruus, quia trahit
revelando et docendo."[10] The Father attracts by presenting a
fascinating object.

For St. Thomas as well as for St. Augustine, the internal grace
which God gives to every man without exception because of
His universal salvific will is not sufficient for belief, but a certain
attraction stemming from the values which Christ Himself incarnates is also necessary. From Christ a particular fascination
emanates which guides the intelligence and the will. But this
fascination can only be felt by him who experiences a need and
desire for them. If these are lacking, one does not believe even
though internal grace is present. The Jews whom Jesus addressed
about the bread of life did not believe, even though internal grace
was present, because they had no desire for this bread from
Heaven. For them Jesus was only the son of Joseph and His words
could do nothing other than scandalize. But the Apostles believed
because, so far as they were concerned, Jesus had words of life
everlasting (John 6:69).

The efficacy of preaching consists, therefore, in the power of
attraction of the person of Jesus, who is both the subject and the
object of preaching. He is the light of the world (John 8:12), the
way, the truth and the life (John 14:6). From Him stems a fascination, the fascination of truth and of life, which cannot fail to
attract the man who seeks to quench his thirst for truth and goodness. For St. Jerome this fascination is so great that the following
of Christ becomes rational even when no miracles are performed.
The splendor of the divinity which transfigures the face of Christ
is similar to a magnet that can attract iron.[11]

[10] *Ibid.*, c. 6, lect. 5, 5.

[11] Here is what St. Jerome says: "Certe fulgor ipse, et majestas divinitatis
occultae, quae etiam in humana facie relucebat, ex primo ad se videntes
trahere poterat aspectu. Si enim in magnete lapide et succinis haec esse vis
dicitur, ut annulos, et stipulam, et festucas sibi copulent, quanto magis
Dominus omnium creaturarum ad se trahere poterat quos volebat" (*Comm.
in Ev. Matt.*, L. I., c. v. 9; ML 26, col. 57).

Truth and sanctity incarnate

Here we must raise another objection. If the efficacy of preaching consists in the appeal contained in truth and goodness, how can the fact that there are those who do not believe be explained? Human will and intelligence, through their intrinsic dynamism, are oriented toward truth and goodness. How can man reject them? If man acts only as a consequence of his tendency toward the good and true, how can we explain that he may oppose the preaching of an object which is both good and true?

In commenting on St. Augustine and St. Thomas, we have already observed that positive response to the invitation of God depends on the desire—of an implicit nature, at least—which we have for the values which he represents. But this response demands clarification. If man cannot act except in the direction of the good and true, he will not be free with respect to Christ, who in preaching presents Himself to man as the incarnation of these values.

The answer is to be found in the very nature of faith. It so happens that truth and goodness do not present themselves with full clarity, as will happen one day in the intuitive vision, but in a whole complex of visible signs. These signs, though they render truth and goodness concrete and thus accessible to men, also conceal them. During the Incarnate Word's time on earth, Christ's humanity was the sign, a transparent one, of course, the most transparent of all those which have made the divine visible, because His humanity was substantially united to His divinity. Since the Ascension, when the Word became invisible, the good and the true have been brought to us by the Church in which Christ mysteriously prolongs Himself and continues to live. He said to the Apostles: "He who hears you, hears me; and he who rejects you, rejects me; and he who rejects me, rejects him who sent me" (Luke 10:16). Truth and goodness are incarnate in the Church; there they are presented to us "in forma Ecclesiae."

This fact changes the relationship of intelligence and human will with respect to these values. Their incarnation into a visible sign—Christ and the Church—is accomplished by means of signs which cannot adequately express their reality and, therefore, their power of attraction. As a consequence, they are made to appear limited. With regard to them, man retains his freedom of choice. Instead of accepting, he can reject them. In this perspective we can understand the strength of the moral factors, so strongly emphasized by St. Augustine: Christ is accepted in the measure in which we love the values incarnate in Him.

Under the circumstances, the truth and goodness incarnate in Christ and continued by the Church present a "scandalous" aspect which Jesus Himself stressed when He said that "blessed is he who is not scandalized in me" (Matt. 11:6). This explains why preaching is always effective and yet man can still refuse to accept it. As far as preaching presents truth, goodness and life—the fundamental values—man cannot help but react and be interested in them. But when these values are presented "in forma Christi" or "in forma Ecclesiae"—that is, incarnate in a person which delimits them—there can be no obligation on man to assent. He will assent or dissent according to the degree that he desires the values presented. The Apostles accepted; the Pharisees refused.

The testimony of life

Under these circumstances one can understand not only the necessity for internal grace, but also the necessity for testimony by the preacher and the Church. Only internal grace can bring man to view the subject presented him in preaching—the plan of salvation elaborated by God—as something that lends the human personality great value, instead of punishing it. With all its demands, hard as they may seem, Christianity is the highest realization of man's most profound aspirations. It is in God that human life has its center, and it is in him alone, the infinite object, that man's thirst can be quenched. Only the internal attraction of the Father, the anointing of the Spirit and its testimony, can confirm us in our belief that to accept the divine offer made through the medium of the Church's word is the greatest of goods. And even these are accomplished in a mysterious and inexplicable fashion.

At the same time we realize the necessity of external testimony. While drawing us toward the mysterious action of internal grace, God must also visibly demonstrate how He offers us His friendship. Thus, what externally appears to be the sacrifice of our personality is actually anything but mortification and renunciation. In the transformation which faith effects in those who accept it, there is visible proof that God does not request mortification, but development of our personality, and there is visible proof, too, that the cross is the way of life.

In present-day life the man of faith has become the symbol of the presence of God in the world and of the transforming power of His love. He is, in fact, the exact opposite of what, logically, he should be. St. Paul gives us a most impressive picture of the transformation which faith works in believers: "We give no offense to anyone, that our ministry may not be blamed. On the contrary, let us conduct ourselves in all circumstances as God's ministers, in much patience; in tribulations, in hardships, in distresses; in stripes, in imprisonments, in tumults; in labors, in sleepless nights, in fastings; in innocence, in knowledge, in long-sufferings; in kindness, in the Holy Spirit, in unaffected love; in the word of truth, in the power of God; with the armor of justice on the right hand and on the left; in honor and dishonor, in evil report and good report; as deceivers and yet truthful, as unknown and yet well known, as dying and behold, we live, as chastised but not killed, as sorrowful yet always rejoicing, as poor yet enriching many, as having nothing yet possessing all things" (2 Cor. 6:3–10).

These men who were called "the refuse of this world" (1 Cor. 4:13) enjoy the purest peace, a peace which no tribulation or persecution can take from them. Even in death they are happy, to the point that they desire death as the greatest good (Phil. 1:23).

How can we avoid recognizing that Christ is the only one who can save man and give meaning to his life?

Now, the appeal which characterizes Christ—the fascination of goodness and of the highest values to which man can aspire—is transferred through Christ to the Church. In the degree to which the Church is capable of communicating the attraction of Christ and the values which He embodies, the proclamation of the Gospel achieves its aim when it confronts man with the problem of his destiny and forces him to make a decision. In this task she will never be a wholly luminous sign—without shadows—of Christ. The sign is by nature defective and, even though perfected, its intrinsic deficiency can never be entirely eliminated. There will always be a need for internal grace: possessing it, man will always be capable of recognizing the presence and action of Christ in the Church.

External grace as vehicle for internal grace

We might say that external grace, the word of the preacher, is the vehicle for internal grace. We have already seen how Suarez states this, along with other preachers of the seventeenth century. God attracts man, makes him a witness and teaches and illumi- nates—all by means of the preacher. It is not a case of there being the word of the preacher on the one side, and on the other, God, who attracts man to Himself if man can respond to the mes- sage of grace. It is solely a case of the action of God, His attrac- tion and His teaching being explained through the word of the preacher.

All this becomes clear when one remembers that it is God who speaks through man in preaching. If, in order to believe, we need God's light, truth and blessing, that our hearts may be opened, all this is achieved through the human word. This is the means God employs to bring man to a decision regarding the salvation which He offers him. God enlightens man, attracts him, shows him the sweetness of consent to truth, by talking to him through the mouth of the preacher. The preacher is God's real representative in the world, the one who renders Him present, the one who makes Him understandable through the attraction of truth and sanctity. At the same time, the preacher is the one who stirs opposition and rejection in those who are not disposed to do God's will. St. Paul can quite rightly say of the Apostles, and then of their successors in the office of preaching: "For we are the fra- grance of Christ for God, alike as regards those who are saved and those who are lost; to those an odor that leads to death, but to those an odor that leads to life" (2 Cor. 2:15–16).

As a consequence of all this, it can be stated that the action of Christ is linked to the Church to the point where, if the Church does not fulfill her role as an instrument, the action of God is not communicated. "You are the salt of the earth; but if the salt loses its strength, what shall it be salted with? It is no longer of any use but to be thrown out and trodden underfoot by men" (Matt. 5:13). But the true salt of the earth, as the true light of the world, is Christ (John 8:12). If the Apostles are also this light, it is because Christ's light shines through them. But if the Apostles' light does not shine, men cannot see their actions nor can they glorify the Father who is in Heaven (Matt. 5:16).

God illuminates man, but this illumination comes from Christ and radiates through His Apostles. God is witness to the fact that we are children of God, but this testimony passes through Christ and is, in turn, continued in the Church.

The nature of efficacy of preaching

If now, at the end of our discussion, we wish to describe the nature of the efficacy of preaching, we can say that it is ontologico-psychological. Ontological, because it is inherent in the object which is preached, that is, God in Christ, supreme truth and goodness, and because it thereby possesses a force, an energy which must necessarily exert influence on the intelligence and will of men.

On the other hand, this object is not presented by itself, but under the "forma Christi" at first, and after the Ascension, under the "forma Ecclesiae." It is presented by way of a limited sign which makes it appear as truth and goodness, but as limited truth and goodness. We also know that because of the assistance Jesus promised His Church, this sign, this divine vehicle, will be clear enough not to obscure totally the reality it contains. The sign will be clear to the extent that the eye which perceives it is benevolently disposed. Through this sign the person of Christ approaches closer and tries to attract men towards itself. It is an ontological appeal, the appeal of a person.

At the same time we must speak of psychological efficacy. Even though the force of attraction is inherent in the object, it cannot be explained, at least not in general, except through the person of the preacher, or the Church. The Word of Christ is repeated through the lips of the Church and it assumes the Church's limitations. In the measure that the Church reveals herself as a more or less apt instrument, the Word of Christ exercises more or less fascination. The perfection of the agent cannot be explained if the instrument employed is unfit for the task assigned. In other words, the Church serves the cause of God in two ways: first, by erecting no obstacles and, secondly, by bearing witness, as we have said. In this sense we may say that the efficacy of preaching is also psychological. Through her life, the Church influences the listener by making him more or less ready to heed the call of the values embodied in Christ.

Here, we are touching the very mystery of the Incarnation. God becomes man; in so doing, He is obliged to take on all the limitations of human nature, except sin. Just as the humanity of Christ influenced the attributes of the Word, so the Incarnation of the Word of God in the word of man influences the efficacy of the latter. Therefore, we may speak of an ontologico-psychological efficacy.[12]

When the efficacy of preaching is thus conceived, the way Holy Scripture expresses it becomes clear. Preaching is really a word of faith, of grace, of truth, of reconciliation and of salvation. The strength which emanates from it sanctifies because it unites with God, reconciles because through union with God it re-establishes a friendship which was lost, saves because it produces in man a desire to return to the Savior, and generates life because it governs and approaches close to the mainspring of life itself.

Thus the difference between preaching and sacrament is easily explained. Preaching produces faith and creates the premise for the reception and efficacy of the sacrament. In the latter God Himself acts, causing a radical transformation in man, whereby, through infusion of sanctifying grace, or its increase, he becomes an adopted son. But this sanctifying action has been made possible by the fact that preaching has brought man closer to God. Preaching establishes the first contact with God, a contact which may lead to friendship if man accepts God's invitation, or to condemnation if he refuses. But the message must first be understood if man is to be obliged to make a decision. Therefore, preaching can act only *ex opere operantis.*

[12] See also what Schillebeeckx has written on the subject in "Parole et sacrement," *Lumière et Vie,* 9 (1960), pp. 32 ff.

CHAPTER XI

Preaching and Adaptation

F ROM THE problem of testimony we now pass directly to that of adaptation, for testimony requires adaptation.

The close relationship between testimony and adaptation is innate in the nature of the message. The message is relative, and it is directed to others for whom, through the testimony of committed persons, it bears witness to the values which are decisive for life. To do this, testimony must be noticed, must make an impression, must strip man of his indifference, and must put him face to face with the problem of his own life.

Mentality

But to reach this goal, testimony must overcome many obstacles. Human beings do not live in a pure state but in social and mental structures which determine their thought and actions to a degree which is not negligible. Guitton says: "Persons are the result of a community which thinks and acts in them: The community awakens the person by means of language; it proposes not only the words but also the concepts, modes of reasoning, and symbols. Just as we cannot think without employing the usual signs which communication imposes on us, so we must also accept these conceptual structures which are the beliefs, the habits, dogmas, traditions and ways of expression."[1] Persons live in predetermined

[1] J. Guitton, *Le problème de Jesus et les fondements du temoignage chretien* (Paris, 1948), vol. I, pp. 190–191.

mentalities, and the testimony to be received must pass through these mentalities, these modes of reasoning in which man thinks and lives.

On the other hand, a message cannot be understood unless something in the person to whom it is addressed is awaiting it. Guitton says concerning this: "A message which would be a complete surprise would shock, but not teach us; 'waves of anticipation' are necessary both to assure that the message is good and to guarantee that it may be recognized as such. When I tell a story, I must adapt it to the needs of the group."[2] In order that we may recognize an important message as important, it is not only necessary to adapt ourselves to the mentality of the persons to whom it is directed, but also to discover in these people 'pierres d' attente,' that is, needs—at least potential ones—which can be fulfilled by the message to be communicated.

To sum up what we have said above: there is no fixed way in which the message must be presented. It is subject to constant adaptation according to the mentalities contacted and among which it is expected to spread.

These considerations apply most strongly to a message as universal and as vital to man's whole existence as the Christian message. It does not have a sacred language: Jesus has not written anything; He has only spoken and ordered man to bear witness to what He said, promising the Apostles the assistance of the Holy Spirit to guarantee the truth of the transmission (Matt. 28:19; Acts 1:8). Every epoch, every nation, every mentality must have its own mode of expressing the message of Christ: it must be translated into the languages of all peoples and all cultures.

Undoubtedly, Christ foresaw the need for adaptation when He gave the Apostles the mandate to preach the Gospel to the whole world. How many cultures, how many mentalities are there among men! So, even though the Gospel, the Good Tidings of salvation, does not change because its object, Christ, is the same today, tomorrow and always (Heb. 13:8), it still must be actualized and translated according to the various mentalities and cultures in which men live.

This intrinsic need of the message always to be actualized anew brings to the foreground the problem of Christianity's insertion

[2] *Ibid.*, p. 191.

into history, that is, the problem of the relationship between science and faith. This is a perennial problem for all ages, but in some epochs, such as primitive Christianity and modern times, it has been felt with particular sharpness and drama.[3]

Before we focus our attention on adaptation in preaching, it will first be necessary to clear up some notions.

The notion of adaptation

What, then, is adaptation?

In general, adaptation means the establishment of some sort of meeting-ground between two beings, a case of placing a means in relationship to an end.[4] Thus we say that a mother "adapts" the dress of an older child to a younger one by making the necessary alterations; we adapt the frame of one picture to another, or a living room to a study. In these examples, adaptation consists in making a thing designed to serve one purpose, serve another as well. This is obviously impossible without a few changes which, while they don't alter the nature of a thing, suit it for another purpose.

Based on this general concept, adaptation of the Christian message requires that the message be so preached that it will induce a desire for conversion, as in missionary preaching, or a deepening of this desire as in catechetical or homiletic preaching. The same message preached twenty centuries ago by Christ and the Apostles, and adapted to the Jewish and Gentile mentality of the Roman Empire, must be preached today in a way that fits the mentality and culture of the people of our era.

But is this adaptation theologically justified? Are these latent desires, these needs of man, which the Christian message assumes are there to be perceived and accepted by men of all times and all cultures—are they truly present? Could there be within man a preparation for the message? On the other hand, can a message be adapted without being changed or even destroyed?

The theological principles of adaptation

In a Protestant theology that remained faithful to the principles of the Reformation it would be impossible to speak of adapta-

[3] See also our article "Lezioni del modernismo," *Humanitas,* 12 (1957), 349–361.

[4] Charles De Koninck, *Problèmes de l'adaptation en apostolat* (Tournai-Paris, 1949), p. 1.

tion or preparation for faith. The Word of God is sovereign and can never be adapted to serve the ends of man. Original sin has corrupted human nature so badly that it can do nothing that could serve as preparation for grace. God enters the soul without any preparation, without any merit on the part of man himself, solely as a form of God's grace. This position is held today by Karl Barth.[5]

The Catholic position, on the other hand, holds itself aloof from all excesses, either of Pelagian or of Protestant coloring. It teaches that while human nature has been corrupted, to some degree, by original sin, it still retains the capacity for doing good, as well as a certain relationship with divine things. Even if fallen from the dignity with which God surrounded it in creation, even if wounded in its natural gifts and weakened, it retains its relationship with God, its ultimate goal, and its ability to work some good. Not every act of fallen man, even when he lacks grace of faith, is sin.

This position is as far from that Pelagian optimism and exaggeration which recognized no difference between human nature before and after the Fall, as it is from Protestant pessimism, which asserts complete and radical decadence. In the problem discussed here, the Catholic position admits the possibility of a preparation for faith, as well as the existence of a healing grace for all men without distinction, a grace which elevates and renders possible cooperation with grace and preparation for faith. So far as each and every man is concerned, the basic capacity to receive the message of salvation and to adhere to it is part and parcel of the Catholic stand.

If, therefore, a preparation for faith is possible and legitimate, the specific nature of Christianity—as a divine vocation rather than a need of human nature—must be recalled. Christianity con-

---

[5] However, a reaction against the extreme position of Barth is afoot today, and it seeks to rediscover and re-evaluate the function of natural theology in the preparation of faith. The most important of these theologians is Emil Brunner with his works *Der Mensch in Widerspruch* (Berlin, 1937), Beilage III, *Zum Problem der natürlichen Theologie unter der Anknüpfung* pp. 541–553, and "Die Christliche Lehre von Gott," *Dogmatik* (Zurich, 1946), vol. I, pp. 109–111. In the same vein is H. Schreiner, *Die Verkündigung des Wortes Gottes* (Hamburg, 1949), c. 6. The author refers directly to the discourse of Paul in Athens. For these authors see Schurr, *Wie Heute Predigen?*, p. 126, n. 19.

sists of a call to the trinitarian dialogue, which, by nature, is essentially supernatural and which no creature can need, in the ordinary sense. Christianity is a calling from above, not from below. This means that if a preparation for faith is possible, it cannot be such that it will reduce Christianity to a natural need, to something required by man to realize his own ends. Christianity is not the answer to our problems—even though it includes that answer—but a free gift of God, an act of love through which He permits us to participate in His divine nature. Yet, if Christianity is not something natural, it is not violent either: grace does not destroy nature but elevates it. In accord with this principle, it is permissible to seek in human nature these "pierres d'attente" of the Christian message. A well understood humanism might be an excellent preparation for the Gospel. If preaching seeks to avoid estrangement from life, it must pay attention to it. Even if there is only one Gospel, only one message of salvation, there are various ways of approaching it and making it one's own. The task of pre-evangelization, which is destined to prepare the way for evangelization, consists in searching for these "pierres d'attente."

False adaptation

But if there is a true and legitimate theological adaptation, a false and unacceptable one also exists. And it is false and unacceptable because it could lead to alteration and destruction of the message.

Any adaptation would be false which would make concessions on essential points of doctrine or morals. There are certain truths of faith such as, for instance, the Trinity, the sacraments of the Holy Eucharist and Penance, the dogma of Hell, which may irritate certain men in certain cultures in a special way. It is clear that that adaptation would be wrong in which a truth were denied or passed over in silence in order to get the message accepted. We know quite well that silence about a problem is not equivalent to solving it.

It would be equally wrong to consider that adaptation legitimate which, in deference to a certain philosophy, attempted to interpret the Christian message in a manner contradictory to its revealed and supernatural character, or in any way that would be opposed to the interpretation of Christ's Church. While Christianity may not have a philosophy of its own, it is by no means indifferent to all philosophies and to some it can never be reconciled. As a supernatural religion, Christianity would make no sense according to an idealistic or materialistic vision of the truth. For this reason the Church recommends Thomistic philosophy, wherein the rational bases of faith find a justification which satisfies the intelligence.

Finally, as far as adaptation is concerned, we must always remember that Christianity is not only a supernatural religion, but that to a human nature corrupted by original sin, it may even appear as something stupid and scandalous (1 Cor. 1:23). Man tends naturally to accept or reject ideas according to opinions he already holds, and in so doing he eliminates everything which he cannot understand or which seems disagreeable to him. In speaking of the limits of adaptation, Schurr points out that the central event in Christianity is not the Incarnation but the cross, and that the question is not one of planting God in the world but of uprooting the world to plant it in God.[6] If human nature can serve as a preparation for Christianity, it can also serve as an obstacle. When, then, is there a true adaptation? There can be no other reply but this: when, given the integrity of the message with all its doctrinal and moral ingredients, it is so presented that it will elicit a response in the one to whom it is directed, that is, a positive reaction, or negative or even doubtful. The Christian message cannot be considered proclaimed or promulgated if it fails to confront man with the problem of his destiny and his salvation. If preaching to Christians is in question, true adaptation requires a deepening of the conversion, both intellectually and culturally, should result.

These principles permit us to speak of a double adaptation: one, to the message which is preached, the other to the subject which the message preached concerns.

Adaptation to the message

It is evident that one cannot preach the message of the Gospel without understanding it, without knowing exactly what it consists in and which needs it seeks to fill. This comprehension is by no means simple.

[6] V. Schurr, "Die Möglichkeiten und Grenzen der Anpassung des Wortes Gottes in der Predigt an den Hörer," *Hörer und Predigt* (Würzburg, 1960), p. 238.

We know that the Christian message recorded in Scripture and Tradition was expressed in a tongue and in a mentality which differed from our own. Both the Old and the New Testament were conceived in a culture decidedly not ours. People of the Western world have lived, to a greater or lesser degree, according to a Greco-Roman cultural heritage, while Scripture belongs to the Oriental world, to the basically concrete and dynamic categories. We can understand Scripture only if we try to read it in the way it was written and the way that the progress of Oriental thinking is revealed to us in its fundamental structure. We have to study the Bible constantly in order to ferret out its content.

In addition to difficulty of comprehension, Scripture also presents another difficulty which springs from the present state of research. This field is still fluid: in spite of the efforts and progress made by scholars, we are still far from fully understanding the true meaning of more than one book of the Old Testament and perhaps, also, a few of the New Testament. It is plain to see that preaching cannot ignore scientific exegesis. Even when preaching is concerned more with the spiritual than the literal meaning of Scripture, preachers must study the results of scientific exegesis and then determine a passage's spiritual sense,[7] if they want to avoid the arbitrariness of some of the Church Fathers.

Schurr observes that one can measure the difficulty of understanding the New Testament by reading Kittel.[8] The same can be said about the Old. How often has the exegesis of the preachers been deficient![9]

The preacher is obliged to follow the progress of biblical studies particularly where books of major doctrinal or moral content are involved. Such books include the four Evangelists and the Epistles of the Apostles, because these are fundamental for understanding the message of salvation and its implications. The preacher must not ignore the constant progress in this field which frequently obliges him to revise and update certain positions. The problems regarding the first chapters of Genesis are on nearly the same

[7] See Vagaggini's remarks on the relationship between literal meaning and spiritual meaning of the Bible: *Il senso teologico della liturgia* (Rome, 1958) chap. 16.

[8] V. Schurr, *Wie Heute Predigen?*, p. 200, note 50.

[9] Bainvel has drawn up a large collection of biblical texts interpreted by preachers in the adaptive sense: *Les contresens bibliques des prédicateurs* (Paris, 1895).

plane of importance. Then we would put the Books of the Prophets. In order to avoid the risk of failing in their duty to truth, preachers must keep constantly informed about the progress of biblical science in this sector.

Another consideration which is founded on the nature of Christianity also requires a constant study of the message. As we have so often repeated, the originality and importance of a message do not lie so much in the truth of the facts or the ideas which it proclaims, as in their meaning for life. Now, this meaning is not something that we can immediately understand in all its dimensions. That Christ is the life of man, the light which illuminates his way, the friend who stands by his side and never abandons him—this can be understood right at the beginning. But it is only in time and in the course of years that His function in the life of man is revealed in all its depth. Christ, the content of the message, is a Person whom we come to know progressively. We first understand a person in general; only later do we discern the particulars. St. Paul admonishes Christians to display their unity through faith in the Son of God, and fuller knowledge of Him. Thus Christians shall attain perfect manhood, that maturity which is proportioned in the "fullness of Christ" (Eph. 4:13). This maturity in Christ is impossible to achieve without an ever more perfect knowledge of Him, stemming not only from the study of His history but from ever more frequent contact with Him in faith. In this way the preacher will avoid being a professor in the pulpit: but he will be a true preacher, that is, a herald of the Good Tidings of the love of God. In faith he will understand the true spiritual meaning of Scripture, the true significance of the divine attitudes.

Adaptation to the laws of expression

But it is not enough to understand the message. It must also be communicated, and to communicate we must make use of the laws of expression. This is another aspect of adaptation.

"There are two foundations," says St. Augustine, "upon which the study of Scripture is based: the manner of discovering what is contained therein and the manner of expressing what it contains."[10] To overcome the apathy of the listener and cause him to take a position regarding the Word of God, the preacher cannot

[10] St. Augustine, *De doctrina christiana*, L. IV, c. 1, 1; ML 34, col. 89.

get along without rhetoric. This is easy to understand. St. Augustine, the doctor of grace, says that he who speaks "with eloquence and wisdom will be more useful to his listeners than the one who speaks only with wisdom."[11] And he adds that he who speaks eloquently without wisdom should be avoided because of the danger that he may be believed because of his eloquence alone.[12] Scripture itself affords a good example of how abundantly all the resources of literature may be used. How many literary forms are to be found in the Bible! St. Augustine never tired of pointing out how well the sacred authors knew the various rhetorical styles and how much they themselves employed rhetorical devices![13]

Adaptation, it is clear, is not of equal import for missionary preaching and for preaching to men already converted. In the former case, it is the question of provoking the crisis of conversion, to make the Gentile adhere to Christ; in the latter, it is a case of initiating man into the Christian life, to its thought and morals.[14] In such an example, adaptation must necessarily be more limited in range. Christianity is a revealed religion. As such, it assumes a world of concepts and rites which *might*, and in more than one case, *must* appear new to man. Christianity needs a dictionary of its own to which the believer may be initiated. The expressions "God," "Revelation," "Grace," "Sacraments," "Church," have a certain meaning and the faithful must know it. Such adaptation has its limits. This, of course, is valid for other fields too. As long as it is the question of giving a summary notion of a subject, the common vocabulary is sufficient, but as soon as we want to perfect the knowledge, we have to have recourse to a special vocabulary.

Adaptation for the receivers

Adaptation to the message and to the laws of expression represents only one stage: adaptation extends also to those who receive the message. The Christian message, though its content is universal in appeal, was revealed in a way that was adapted to the mentality of the people for whom it was immediately destined. Hence

[11] *Ibid.*, c. 5, 7; ML 34, col. 91.

[12] *Ibid.*, c. 5, 7; ML 34, col. 91.

[13] *Ibid.*, c. 6, 9; ML 34, col. 92–93.

[14] Papal documents have recently insisted on the necessity of adaptation in the missionary apostolate. See especially *Princeps Pastorum* by John XXIII.

the necessity of translating it and adapting it to the psychological and sociological conditions of today's listeners.

To do this, the preacher must know the listeners whom he addresses, must know their psychology and how they are influenced by the laws of society, the so-called social pressures. For this purpose he should use the data which psychology and sociology place at his disposal. These sciences keep him informed about the influence of the environment on man and the underlying causes which have played parts in creating this environment. We shall not go into this, however, because we think it better to refer the reader to more profound, more specialized studies in these fields.[15]

In our opinion, what counts more in learning to know men of today is to live their lives. This does not mean that one must necessarily become a worker or a professional person, though sometimes this would prove very useful in understanding these social categories. We have in mind the lives of priests and preachers. He who lives his own life profoundly and experiences its difficulties, will be able to measure the difficulties in which his listeners find themselves. We can therefore say that the help of psychology and sociology are useful to the extent that these sciences impinge on the profound experience of one's own life. He who understands the art of a given author or a given epoch, can also understand the art of any author, of any period.

To achieve this empathy, a sympathetic understanding for the times in which we live is necessary. In love we find the secret of understanding.

The ontological adaptation

Adaptation to listeners means not only understanding their psychological and sociological condition but also their position regarding the Word of God. While preaching is aimed at "every creature" (Mark 16:16), not every creature finds himself in the same ontological condition to receive it.

Father Canizzaro singles out four different situations:[16]

[15] See also Schurr's work, *Wie Heute Predigen?*, so often quoted, in which the problem of adaptation is treated with special skill. This book is indispensable for those who want to study adaptation. See also *Macht und Ohnmacht der Religion* by B. Häring.

[16] B. Canizzaro, "La predicazione della Parola di Dio nel mistero cristiano," *La Parola di Dio nella comunità cristiana* (Milan, 1957), pp. 48–49.

The first concerns the *negative infidel*. He has either never happened to hear the Word of God, or else has never listened to it to the point that he finds himself obliged to take a position regarding it. Despite this, because of the universal salvific will he is remotely disposed to the Word. The universality of grace leads us to believe that he who does his best to conform to the natural law is given sufficient grace to attain faith and justification. How this happens is a mystery of grace. At any rate, this theological principle permits us to conclude that in addition to the normal ways of preaching there are also extranormal ones with the help of which, unbeknown to us, God will guide souls of good will to faith. St. Thomas speaks of internal inspiration, or the sending of an angel or a missionary.[17] This is not the place to hazard a hypothesis. One thing is certain: no soul which obeys its conscience will remain excluded from salvation.[18]

Then, we also find the *baptized heretic and apostate*. In spite of his denials, whether in good faith or bad, he possesses a disposition toward the Word of God arising from his baptismal character. He is already in touch with Christ and the Church and thus has a right to all the actual graces which may help him to arrive at or to regain the true Faith and his own integrity. Preachers must believe this fact and remember that in all these souls, badly disposed psychologically though they may be, there is a constant working of grace moving them toward Christ and the Church. Often it is only a question of removing an obstacle so that the truth can reveal itself in its completeness. The history of the Protestants and the return to the Faith of apostates attest to the uncertainty of these souls. Preaching must somehow reach such people and present to them the Word of God, adapted to their particular needs.

Different conditions arise in the case of the *baptized faithful*, who is in the state of sin. Not only does he have the Christian character, but also the virtue infused by faith whereby his intelligence is raised and his will moved, to listen to the Word of God. The elevation of the intelligence through the virtue of faith gives rise to a whole series of graces with which God moves man

[17] St. Thomas Aquinas, *In IV Sent.*, L. IV, dist. 25, q. 2, a. 1.

[18] For the whole problem of salvation of the unbelievers see the recent book by Santos, already quoted, *Salvacion y Paganismo* (Santander, 1960) which brings the classic by Caperan up to date.

toward penitence and the recapturing of grace. We may compare this state of mind to that of the Prodigal Son who leaves the father's house but takes with him his nostalgia. And he returns as soon as this nostalgia, sharpened by misery and hunger, becomes so acute that it overcomes shame and the other obstacles which kept him from seeing his mistakes and to take the way back.

In ideal conditions, finally, we find the *believer in the state of grace*. Not only his soul but all his faculties are supernaturally elevated and oriented toward Christ and the Church. The soul in the state of grace, says Canizzaro, "is the son who loves to listen to the voice of the Father, receives it, takes care of it, and meditates in his heart, even as St. Luke describes the Holy Virgin Mary, the perfect exemplar of every listener to the Word of God."[19]

These data, which Revelation has taught us and the Church, through her magisterium, has clarified for us, are important for the preacher. They tell him that he is not alone in the undertaking to bring souls to the union with God. With him is that mysterious something which is grace, with which he must cooperate in the sanctification of souls. The preacher is only its vehicle: the main role is played by grace; the preacher serves grace by extending his cooperation.

Preacher and lay teacher

The existence of the sacramental character and virtue of faith in the baptized believer brings us to an important conclusion, namely, the difference between the teacher of profane things and the preacher of sacred things.

The teaching of the master consists, as St. Thomas says, in helping the pupil's intelligence to perceive how the principles he already possesses apply to particular cases. Between professor and student a dialogue is established which, however, cannot transcend the intelligence of the student. There is a perfect proportion between the student's intelligence and his understanding.

In contrast, between the preacher and the listener, the limits of natural intelligence may be extended. It is not the natural capability of man but the Holy Spirit, the true teacher, who fixes these limits. The sacramental character and, even more, the virtue

[19] B. Canizzaro, *op. cit.*, p. 49.

of faith, give to the believer a certain connaturality with the Word of God, which brings to the soul a divine light that illuminates the Word and makes it understandable beyond natural limitations. St. John speaks of an anointing which keeps nothing hidden from us (1 John 2:20), and Psalm 35:10 tells us, "with you is the fountain of life."[20]

This is a truth which experience verifies. How also can we explain that simple and even ignorant men often understand the things of faith with a depth and facility which surprise learned theologians? It is the Holy Spirit who helps them understand. In his difficult office, the preacher must never forget that he is an ally and collaborator of the Holy Spirit.

Adaptation of the listeners to the message

Adaptation concerns not only the preacher: the listeners must also adapt themselves. While the listener may rightfully demand to understand the message and see its rationality, he has no right to set conditions on his acceptance. Here we have the Word of God which is sovereign and above men. If in receiving the Word man may exact guarantees, he cannot determine these arbitrarily, Scripture warns man against hardening his heart (Psalm 94 (95):8–9).

The best disposition for receiving God's Word is the humility that springs from love. In Chapter Five we spoke of the relationship between love and faith. One cannot come to faith if not through the portal of love. Love is the best disposition for reception of the Word. This love, of course, varies according to whether the one preparing to enter is a Gentile or a Christian who has already accepted it in his own life and is only letting it grow within him.

For the Gentile the love of God may be summed up in faithfulness to his conscience, in following the dictates of the natural law that is enshrined in his inmost being. The more faithful and obedient is man to this command, the better will he be disposed to listen to the Word of God, a Word which no longer speaks to him in the undetermined manner of his conscience but in a human voice which finds an echo within himself. The observance of natu-

[20] C. Dillenschneider, *Le Christ et nous ses prêtres* (Paris, 1960), vol. I, p. 209 and note.

ral law purifies man, keeps him from sinning, refines him in his spirituality, makes him feel that God is much closer, and keeps him in touch with providence. The day when a preacher presents himself to such a man to proclaim his salvation, that man will recognize the fulfillment of what he intimately and unconsciously aspired to in Revelation.[21] To these persons, so well disposed, the preacher can speak the words of St. Paul to the pagans of Athens—even though in a different context: "quod ignorantes colitis annuntio vobis" (Acts 17:23). Of these souls St. Augustine says that they are apparently outside the Church when in reality they are inside. Pius XII stated it even more precisely when he said that they are linked to the Church by an "unconscious desire."[22]

However, for Christians who have already listened to the Word of God and accepted it, the best way for them to prepare themselves is to hear it again, to cherish it within themselves, to meditate upon it and to love it. It is this love which will help man to purify his soul from sin, to pray, to recollect himself before the sermon, because God speaks only to the soul which has retreated within itself. In the supernatural order, love is the secret and the mover of everything. Just as God descended to earth toward man and addressed His Word to man for the sake of love, so man answers for the sake of love and makes the Word fruitful in himself. "He who does not love does not know God; for God is love" (1 John 4:8). We know God by the Word which He addresses to us through the preaching of the Church. Knowledge of God and love go together. The two realities are interdependent. Love makes us accept the Word and the Word is food for love.[23]

---

[21] The classic case of the well-disposed pagan is that of Cornelius the Centurion of whom the Book of Acts speaks in Chapter X. Even before he listens to the preaching of Peter, he is "timens Deum" (Acts 10:2).

[22] Encyclical *Mystici Corporis.*

[23] See the article by S. Grün, "Die Bereitung des Hörers für das Wort Gottes," *Hörer und Predigt* (Würzburg, 1960), pp. 266–301.

CHAPTER XII

The Preacher

To CONCLUDE the second part of this study, a chapter dedicated to the preacher himself would be appropriate. Though we have spoken of him constantly in the preceding pages, it will be well to consider him now as a person: in this way we will better understand his function.

The natural qualities

Above all, the preacher is a man whom God calls to be His collaborator in spreading His Kingdom on earth. As such, he must possess those same qualities which enable an instrument to perform its duties. Even though, because of God's action, preaching is supernatural, it employs a natural means, the word of the preacher. A defect or an impairment in him may well hinder, or even compromise, the action of grace.

Both the origin and the deepening of faith are included in the scope of preaching. With these general goals in mind, St. Thomas, like St. Augustine, assigns three tasks to the preacher: to instruct the intelligence, to move the emotions and to form the will of those who listen to him.[1] St. John Chrysostom requires, in addition, that he know how to defend his flock from external attacks by enemies of the Church and from disputes which arise spontaneously among the faithful. The preacher, the Great Doctor

---

[1] St. Thomas Aquinas, *Summa Theologica*, II, II, q. 177, a. 1.

says in language that bristles with military terms, must be at one and the same time "archer and slinger, general and captain, soldier and commandant, infantryman and cavalryman, sailor and garrison soldier."[2] These ends cannot be attained unless the preacher possesses certain natural qualities which can be refined and perfected, but not created by education. St. John Chrysostom opposes both those who accept ordination while lacking these qualities, and those others who are forced into becoming preachers.[3]

One might ask, with good reason, why the absence of certain natural qualities, such as, for instance, that of speaking, should not by itself exclude anybody from the priesthood. The preacher is both *dispensator verbi et sacramenti*. Should not an inability to preach also exclude the priest from administering the sacraments?

Scholars have always upheld the role of natural gifts in preaching. We may even say that, apart from the priority assigned supernatural qualities, they have insisted on them almost exclusively. St. Augustine discusses this in the fourth book of his *De doctrina christiana*, a model and an inspiration to all those who have subsequently undertaken the so-called *formal homiletic*. A classic in this sense is Father Sertillanges' "Christian Orator," which we have already mentioned. There, the noted theologian goes into minute detail to show the preacher how to develop his gifts of intelligence, will and heart, how to prepare and elaborate his sermon and how to give it style and tone. The fact that preaching is not only the Word of God but also the word of man takes on added importance in a reading of this book. In fact, if the importance of this observation is not recognized, preaching's attempt to arouse certain reactions in men will be seriously hampered if not completely frustrated. Preaching cannot deviate from the rules of discourse. For preaching, Cicero's dictum that oratory is the most difficult art is still valid.[4]

St. Gregory the Great was correct in reproaching those who give themselves to preaching without the right preparation. For the great Pope, those who lack seriousness of purpose in their preach-

[2] St. John Chrysostom, *De sacerdotio*, L. IV, c. 6.
[3] *Ibid.*, c. 7.
[4] Recently C. Tamberlani has treated this in his work *L'oratore sacro* (Rome, 1963).

ing deserve censure equally as much as those who abstain out of excessive modesty. "When one must deal with those who are unfit for preaching because they lack ability or are too young— even though, in the absence of foresight, they feel impelled to this vocation—it is necessary to warn them that the lightness with which they take on this burden may cost them any chance for advancement in the future. Such people must beware lest, by attempting the impossible on their own, they render themselves unable to do even that which they have the capacity for.[5]

The call from God

Even though natural gifts are necessary for the preacher, the supernatural ones are still the most important. These are, indeed, the preacher's true qualities while the others are merely their foundations. God has called the preacher to be His collaborator in transmitting His message to the world, in calling men to the divine life. "You have not chosen me, but I have chosen you, and have appointed you that you should go and bear fruit . . ." (John 15:16).

The Old Testament describes the vocation of some of the Prophets in dramatic terms. Isaias exclaims before the God who calls him: "Woe is me, I am doomed! For I am a man of unclean lips, living among a people of unclean lips; yet my eyes have seen the King, the Lord of hosts!" The psalm continues, "Then one of the seraphim flew to me, holding an ember which he had taken with tongs from the altar. He touched my mouth with it. 'See,' he said, 'now that this has touched your lips, your wickedness is removed, your sin is purged.' Then I heard the voice of the Lord saying, 'Whom shall I send? Who will go for us?' 'Here I am,' I said; 'send me!' " (Isa. 6:5–8).

Jeremias was destined by God to become a prophet to the world while still in his mother's womb. When the moment came to fulfill his mission, he was afraid: "Ah, Lord, God!" he said, "I know not how to speak; I am too young." And the psalm continues: "But the Lord answered me, Say not, 'I am too young.' To whomever I send you, you shall go; whatever I command you, you shall speak. Have no fear before them, because I am with you to deliver you, says the Lord. Then the Lord extended his

[5] St. Gregory the Great, *Regula pastoralis*, III, c. 25.

hand and touched my mouth, saying, See, I place my words in your mouth!" (Jer. 1:6–9).

Ezechiel's vocation is described with the same solemnity: "When I had seen it, I fell upon my face and heard a voice that said to me: Son of man, stand up! I wish to speak with you. As he spoke to me, spirit entered into me and set me on my feet, and I heard the one who was speaking say to me: Son of man, I am sending you to the Israelites, rebels who have rebelled against me; they and their fathers have revolted against me to this very day" (Ezech. 2:1–3).

It is this same force which compels the Apostles to bear witness to Christ, first in Jerusalem, and then, to the "ends of the earth" (Acts 1:8).

It is essential that the preacher know he has been called to his task if he would overcome the obstacles that confront a herald of the Word of God. The fact that he has not willingly undertaken a ministry of such difficulty assures him of God's assistance. With this aid, he can dare anything in the cause of the Lord.

"I was no prophet, nor have I belonged to a company of prophets; I was a shepherd and a dresser of sycamores. The Lord took me from following the flock . . ." (Amos 7:14). Nothing could be more reassuring to one who doubts he can measure up to the most divine ministry on earth.

In the mission assigned, the call assumes concrete shape. The preacher is commissioned by God. Jesus, the preacher *par excellence,* was commissioned by the Father. The preacher carries on the mission and makes it lasting. In sending him, the Lord gives him the same assurance he had given the Apostles, to be with them to the end of the world (Matt. 28:18–20). In moments of discouragement especially, the preacher should remember that it is not he who speaks but the Holy Spirit (Matt. 10:20).

Preaching, thus, is not just a means of achieving social distinction, nor a path to fame and high reputation, but a duty to God that must be fulfilled, a duty that demands that the Good Tidings of salvation be brought to everyone. Even if his public speaking ability puts him on par with other orators, the goals which the preacher seeks are not the usual human kind, in which he might find his own advantage. Like St. Paul, he must do all he can to subordinate himself in order that Christ may triumph.

He does not seek his own interest, or the fulfillment of his own needs—even if these are noble and worthy—but only Jesus Christ.

The man of the Bible and Tradition

To serve the Word means that the preacher must become a man of the Bible. The warning of St. Paul to Timothy to make reading, preaching and instruction his constant care (1 Tim. 4:12) is the preacher's foremost duty as well. We may even call it "quasi-professional." If the preacher is God's mouthpiece, if through him God actualizes the Revelation already made, then the preacher's first duty is to know the Word of God, to meditate upon it, and to understand it. Holy Scripture expresses this closeness to the Word in a most daring allegory. Turning to Ezechiel, the Prophet, God addresses him: "As for you, son of man, obey me when I speak to you: be not rebellious like this house of rebellion, but open your mouth and eat what I shall give you. It was then I saw a hand stretched out to me, in which was a written scroll which he unrolled before me. It was covered with writing front and back, and written on it was: Lamentation and wailing and woe!

"He said to me: Son of man, eat what is before you; eat this scroll, then go, speak to the house of Israel. So I opened my mouth and he gave me the scroll to eat. Son of man, he then said to me, feed your belly and fill your stomach with this scroll I am giving you. I ate it, and it was as sweet as honey in my mouth. He said: Son of man, go now to the house of Israel, and speak my words to them" (Ezech. 2:8–10; 3:1–4).

Holy Scripture must thus be the preacher's favorite book. St. Jerome admonishes his correspondent in the letter to Nepotianus to read Holy Scripture often and never to abandon it. Only thus could he learn what he must teach, and only thus could he acquire the necessary doctrine for exhortation or refutation.[6] He admonishes St. Paulinus of Nola in the same terms: "I beg of you, beloved brother, to dwell among these (topics treated by Scripture), to meditate upon them and not to know or seek elsewhere. Do not these appear to you as a precursor of Heaven here on

[6] St. Jerome, *Ep.* 52, ML 22, col. 533.

earth?"[7] It is actually this familiarity with the Bible, this "eating," which allows the preacher to come close to God, to know His mysteries and to see in His words His heart.[8]

We can apply to the preacher the principles set forth by St. Thomas for the study of the Bible. Commenting on the expression *scientia inflat*, he says that true knowledge is acquired "humbly without being pompous, seriously without being overbearing, generously with spontaneous communication, effectively with a good mode of operation."[9] If the Bible is studied with such dispositions, there is no danger of the preacher's corrupting God's Word.

But the preacher cannot be a man of the Bible without also being intimately linked to the tradition of the Church. Bible and Church are inseparable. The Bible is not a book so written that anybody can read it according to his whim and inclination: it is a book which God has entrusted to the Church and only she is its authentic interpreter. The assistance needed for spreading the Gospel was given by Jesus to the Apostles and their successors. It is thus impossible to study and read the Bible, and even less, to proclaim the message, without being faithful to the Church. Such faithfulness means that the preacher must interpret Scripture according to how the magisterium of the Church has explained it over the centuries, in the words of the pontiffs and the ecumenical councils, in those of the Church Fathers and the theologians. Bossuet says the Fathers teach that "the divine art of discussing Scripture and receiving authority as the mouthpiece of God, speaking on all subjects, arises from solid and serious application."[10] These aids thus not only give us the sense of Holy Scripture, but the sense of Tradition, and they help us to feel a part of the immense stream which grows larger and stronger the farther

---

[7] "Oro te, frater, carissime, inter haec vivere, ista meditare, nihil aliud nosse, nihil quaerere, nonne tibi videtur jam hic in terris regno caelestis habitaculum? . . . Discamus in terris, quorum nobis scientia perseverat in coelo" (Ml 22, col. 549). Caesarius of Arles also admonishes preachers and faithful to read the Bible. This is expressed in several sermons such as VI, VII, VIII (Corpus Christ, vol. 103, p. 36 ff.) See also the article "La missione pastorale del vescovo secondo Cesario di Arles" by Giuseppe Terraneo in *La Scuola Cattolica*, 91 (1963), 507–519, esp. 512. The same can be found in St. John Chrysostom (MG 52, col. 694).

[8] St. Jerome, *Homil. 15 in Ez.*

[9] St. Thomas Aquinas, *In 1 ad Cor. in h. 1.*

[10] Bossuet, *Notes sur le style et la lecture.*

it moves from its source. The Fathers are not only great personalities who are closer to the primitive Apostolic Tradition than we are, but as pastors they demonstrate how the Bible's dynamic pastoral aspect—which is of the greatest interest to the preacher— should be fulfilled. Not everything therein is worth imitating. The overuse of allegory is such that today's preacher would be ill advised to follow it literally.

The preacher and sanctity

Sent by God as messenger of His Word, the preacher must sanctify himself just as Jesus did (John 17:19), because only one thus purified and united to God can understand His mysteries. St. Thomas says: "Nobody can understand the office of preaching if he is not first purified from sin and perfect in virtue, as it is written of Christ, who *coepit facere et docere*.[11] The principle of *contemplari et contemplata aliis tradere*[12] which is so solemnly inculcated by St. Thomas, cannot be fulfilled without exercise of the moral virtues, indispensable for the contemplative life.[13] St. Gregory of Nazianzus formulated the same doctrine in his *seconda oratio apologetica*: "The preacher cannot move a tongue that is not educated."[14] He, who has not experienced it first himself, cannot teach others what they must do. One cannot teach unless he lives a truly religious life in contact with God.[15]

To acquire this luminous and warm notion of God, the preacher must be a man of prayer and meditation. St. Augustine has particularly insisted on this. The sacred orator, he says, must elicit reactions of intelligence, pleasure and obedience in his listeners. In achieving this he will succeed "more by means of the piety of his prayer than by means of the talented word. Thus, in praying for himself and those to whom he must speak, he will first be a man of prayer and then of words. When the hour for preaching arrives, he should lift his thirsting soul to God before speaking, so that he can return in the same measure the drink he has

[11] St. Thomas Aquinas, *Summa Theologica*, III, q. 41, a. 3, ad. 1m.
[12] *Ibid.*, II, II, q. 188, a. 6.
[13] *Ibid.*, II, II, q. 180, a. 2, e. 3.
[14] MG 35, 456.
[15] For the preaching of St. Gregory Nazianzus see the article by E. Bellini in *La Scuola Cattolica*, 91 (1963), 496–506. See also the interesting article by Tito Centi, "La predicazione in S. Tommaso d'Aquino," *Temi di predicazione*, NN. 11–12, pp. 39–47.

received or even enrich it by means of a broader distribution."[16]

The reason for this recourse to God is to be found in the fact that questions of faith and charity can, as St. Augustine says, be treated in various ways, and only God knows which way is best for the needs of the faithful. Therefore, the preacher will have to study the questions as best he possibly can, but when the hour for preaching arrives he should keep well in mind the words of the Lord: "But when they deliver you up, do not be anxious how or what you are to speak; for what you are to speak will be given you in that hour. For it is not you who are speaking, but the Spirit of your Father who speaks through you" (Matt. 10:19–20).[17] At the end of the book St. Augustine returns to the subject of prayer: "At the very moment when he is to speak to the people, or at the moment when he is dictating a sermon which is to be given to the people or read by those who can or will do so, the preacher should pray to God that He may give him the right words."[18]

Humility of the preacher

Together with prayer the preacher needs humility. He announces the "crucified Christ—to the Jews, indeed, a stumbling block and to the Gentiles, foolishness" (1 Cor. 1:23). The preacher may be embarrassed to preach on a subject which agrees so little with the pagan mentality of his contemporaries. The temptation to throw off the cross of Christ is always weighing on him too. If he does not feel within him the respect and love which is due the Word of God, he will be always tempted to abandon the Word and to seek subjects which are more interesting to him, like politics, art, philosophy or similar topics.

Preaching requires a continuing sacrifice of personality, because here the preacher is only a simple instrument, "a servant of the Word." Even though it requires eloquence, preaching consists in putting God forward and forgetting oneself. For the preacher the words of St. John the Baptist concerning Christ are wholly applicable: "He must increase, but I must decrease (John 3:30). This is not possible without the utmost humility, whereby the preacher finds it possible to disappear before the Word of God, to be nothing but an instrument of God's action toward men.

[16] St. Augustine, *De doctrina christiana*, L. IV, 15, 32.
[17] *Ibid.*
[18] *Ibid.*, 30, 63.

Humility is also needed for another reason. Preaching announces the Gospel, which saves whoever is disposed to receive it, and condemns him who refuses it. Nobody experiences the judging power of the Gospel more than the preacher. In proclaiming it, he cannot help but note the vast gulf separating him from the Gospel, nor can he fail to see how far he is from meeting its requirements. Without a goodly supply of humility the preacher would soon succumb to the temptation to strip the Gospel of its force. It is not easy to accept one's own incoherence.

Then too, a difficulty arises from the lack of success often associated with preaching, which again points up the need for humility. For any preacher not well grounded in humility, discouragement threatens constantly. "He who undertakes the task of the ministry of the Word must not heed the praises of strangers, nor become discouraged when they are not forthcoming, but must fashion his speeches to please God . . . if he is also praised by men, he must not refuse their praise . . . but if his listeners withhold such praise, he must think nothing of it, because the work of directing his teachings so that they meet with the approval of God should be enough reward for his efforts."[19]

One way in which this humility might be expressed would be in having the courage to tell listeners the truth. This is not an easy task because nobody likes to say what displeases others. But it is necessary and it demands faithfulness to one's mission. Among the things which Christ has condemned, the preacher must also speak of those things which offend the tastes of others: "The safety of the masses is to be preferred to the peace of the individual," says St. Thomas. "Thus . . . when a few imperil the safety of many, the preacher must not be afraid of offending so long as the majority derives some benefit from it. . . . Thus did our Lord teach publicly, despite the fact that it offended some (The Scribes and the Pharisees): He taught the truth that they hated, and He reproached them for their conduct."[20] And elsewhere he states that one must try not to offend anyone. "However, when scandal comes from truth, we must prefer truth to scandal."[21]

Humility exacts discretion on the part of the preacher. He cannot say what he wants to say, but must adapt himself to his lis-

---

[19] St. John Chrysostom, *De sacerdotio*, L. V., c. 5.
[20] St. Thomas Aquinas, *Summa Theologica*, III, q. 42, a. 2.
[21] *Ibid.*, ad 3m.

teners, to what they can understand, even when this means
sacrificing his knowledge and thus his personality. Often, the
Word of God is announced to the uneducated and other similar
people who do not understand its meaning and who are incapable
of following higher reasoning or of thinking deeply. In this case
the preacher must abandon such reasoning and talk in such a way
that he can be readily understood by all. This is what Jesus did.
In order to be understood by the majority of people, He spoke
in parables. When He explained the mysteries of the Kingdom of
God to the Apostles, He did not recount everything because they
were not capable of understanding it (John 16:12).[22] It is humility
which will keep the preacher from the philosophical or exegetical
discourses to which he very often desires to devote himself.

Humility is one mark of that faithfulness to the Word of God
which St. Paul says characterizes the Apostles (1 Cor. 4:2). It
is faithfulness to his mission which will cause the preacher to study
harder how to refine his natural abilities and become ever more
disposed toward the Word of God, how to make known the Bible
in its content and expression, and how to sanctify himself so that
by his own life he can show what the Word of God which he
preaches means in the concrete. All this explains that *parresia* of
which we have already spoken.

A text of St. Thomas

We want to end this chapter by quoting a text from St. Thomas
wherein he explains various images by which the preacher is designated in Sacred Scripture: "The apostle designates the office of
the preacher by various names and calls him: first, soldier in the
defense of the Church against her adversaries; second, wine-
grower, who trims away the bad and superfluous vines; third,
pastor, because he leads his subjects with his good example;
fourth, ox, because he must proceed with gravity; fifth, plower,
because he must open the hearts of his listeners to faith and penitence; sixth; thresher, because he must preach often and without
gain; eighth, architect of the temple, because he must construct
and repair the edifice of the Church; ninth, minister of the altar,
because he must fulfill himself in an office which pleases God."[23]

---

[22] St. Thomas Aquinas, *Summa Theologica*, III, q. 42, a. 3.
[23] St. Thomas Aquinas, *In 1 ad Cor.*, c. 9, lect. 1.

These designations illustrate the aims of preaching and the supernatural means which the preacher must employ to attain them. Preaching demands **faith**, demands that faith be anchored in men's hearts and that it be consolidated and defended against all detractors. This goal of the preacher can be attained by word and by example.

CHAPTER XIII

The Forms of Preaching

ALL THAT REMAINS to be discussed are the various forms that preaching assumes in its dynamism. In the present volume, the discussion will be brief, since we intend to make this topic the object of a special study.

The three moments of faith

What criterion do we apply to distinguish multiple forms? Above all, we must keep in mind those to whom the message is directed. There are three categories: pagans, catechumens, and those already Christian. Or again we may list them as persons who have not yet heard the Gospel—at least, in an adequate manner— those who have heard and accepted it, but only superficially, and finally, those who know it sufficiently well and have simply to translate it into their lives. We have, consequently, three categories of preaching: missionary, destined for the pagans; initiation, aimed at the catechumens, and formation, for those already Christian.

This criterion is rather empirical, and though it permits us to make distinctions among the various forms of preaching, it does not yield a clear indication of its nature. The true criterion, we think, should be apparent from the scope of the message's goal. This, as we have said before, is faith, the encounter with God in Christ. Thus it is possible to distinguish various forms of preaching insofar as it is possible to distinguish various forms of faith.

According to this criterion—which is wholly intrinsic—we can distinguish a missionary preaching, which has as its goal the acceptance of the Faith; a preaching of initiation, with an aim of knowledge of the Faith in all its doctrinal and moral implications; and a liturgical preaching which tries to give life to the Faith already accepted and understood. The first form, called evangelization, is directed to the pagan to make him adhere to the Faith; the second, called catechesis, is directed to the catechumens; and the third, called homily, is directed to the Christian community and takes place in the liturgy.[1] To produce faith, to know faith, to live faith: these are the three goals of faith, to which the three forms of proclaiming faith correspond.

These three forms coincide with the object of preaching, the person of Christ the Savior. A person is not immediately known at first contact. Knowledge of a person passes through three phases. Even at the first casual encounter, a current of sympathy may be established. Often, the persons involved may not even know each other's name and yet they already recognize a certain affinity for one another's company. And this, we would like to make clear, refers not only to the physical attraction established between persons of different sex which tends to reach an objective finalization, but also to a spiritual attraction, which precedes the form of love called friendship and which constitutes one of the motives that make people want to unite and live together.

The first encounter is followed by a period of friendly exchange when sympathy between two and even more people increases and becomes deeper. In this phase people become acquainted with one another's defects and good qualities, their shadows and light. Thus they discover one another not only in points of similarity, but in differences, too. They reveal themselves now as they really are, they understand what their friendship means: the combining of their destinies, whereby each becomes the keeper of the other. In this phase love, either conjugal or between friends, shows its true face: it is disclosed either as a passing infatuation or as based on a solid foundation which permits it to grow. This recognition

---

[1] We have mentioned the principal works in this sector in the footnote to our introduction. For the synthesis which follows we have leaned on the study by A. Rétif, *Foi au Christ et Mission* (Paris, 1953).

will be followed by either a commitment for life, or a separation which concludes a relation which has no foundation.

Then comes a third and final phase in which one passes from knowledge to life. It consists in the exercise of friendship and love. In conjugal love the three phases are clearly distinguishable: encounter, engagement, married life. In the first phase love is discovered; in the second, clarified and deepened; in the third, love lives.

In faith we have the same process. The first encounter with Christ takes place in missionary preaching, in which the person of the Savior is presented as the only reality which can provide man the salvation to which he aspires. On the part of a well-disposed man, acceptance and conversion follow: he adheres to one who offers to resolve his fundamental problem, that is, the problem of his end. In this case a man has 'acquired a summary and general acceptance of Christ, and having met Him in the Word of the Church, recognizes, at least implicitly, that he has encountered Him who is the true life. Conversion will be followed by a deepening of faith. He who has accepted Christ summarily wants to know in greater detail who He is and what this promised salvation consists of, and what the consequences will be on the intellectual and moral planes. The answer to this lies in the second phase of preaching, the catechesis. This leads to instruction and illumination of the intellect. Then we have finally the third phase. He who has been converted to Christ and knows what this conversion means, gives himself to Christ and lives His life. Homiletic preaching stimulates the will to accept harmoniously the duties assumed in baptism and outlined in depth in the catechism.

The distinction among the three forms of preaching is thus founded on the nature of the object and the end which the proclamation of the message should attain. Let us now say something about each individual form.

Missionary preaching or evangelization

Very common in the early days of Christianity when the conversion of the Gentiles was the principal goal, evangelization lost some of its importance when great numbers entered the Church. It was still a source of concern for the Church in the fourth and fifth centuries, when the last remnants of Greco-Roman paganism were converted. In the Middle Ages, with new people knocking at the doors of the old empire, missionary preaching came into its own again, though it is not clear whether the preachers of those times understood the originality of such a form of preaching. Their most pressing problem was catechesis, the instruction of the new peoples and their initiation to the Christian life.

Evangelization appeared as something different to the missionaries of the Renaissance, when new geographic discoveries proved that medieval theologians, St. Thomas included, were wrong in thinking that there was no corner of the earth where the message of the Gospel had not penetrated.

Today the phenomenon of dechristianization and the biblical movement have combined to focus scholarly attention once again on the problem of evangelization, not only as a pastoral necessity, but as an original form of proclaiming the Tidings. The studies so far completed, especially those of the Acts of the Apostles, permit us to reconstruct evangelization along general lines.

The general lines of evangelization

In evangelization, God's coming is proclaimed to the Gentiles. In the name of God, from whom he has received the call and from whom his word derives its authority, the Christian preacher, a true herald of God, proclaims God's will of salvation for non-Christians. This public and solemn announcement, destined for all without exception, inaugurates the last age of the world before the parousia. In view of it every man must take a position: on his acceptance or refusal depend salvation or damnation. Therefore, evangelization continues the work of Christ in the world, of Him who was sent by the Father to preach the message of salvation in such a way that it would mean life for those who accepted it and condemnation for those who rejected it.

The object of evangelization is salvation history, the story of Christ, from the first Messianic prophecies of the Old Testament, to St. John the Baptist, to the events of Christ's public life, to His death and Resurrection, to the Ascension and His return in the parousia. The most important place among the facts of salvation history is occupied by the Death and Resurrection of Christ, especially by the Resurrection, which is the center of all salvation history. The presentation of Christ carried out in evangelization is not so much theological or apologetic as kerygmatic. The Apostles are so full of Christ, so transported by their contact with Him, that they seek their listeners' adherence to Christ through sheer, contagious enthusiasm. Christ is the Lord to whom we must give ourselves, because He has loved us first and loved us unto death.

To the proclamation of Christ by the preacher comes either acceptance or rejection on the part of the listeners. It is, as we have said, a general and over-all acceptance. What is accepted is the person of Christ, in whom we see the concretization and deepest expression of the love of God for man—salvation. Only after that acceptance can one know in greater detail what Christ is and what the salvation which He offers means. To this end, catechesis, which follows evangelization, is directed. Man accepts the Word of God offered through the preacher, and gives himself to Christ.

In order to obtain the reply of faith, the word of the preacher is backed by signs whereby God shows the divine origin of that word. At the time of the Apostles, these signs were the prophecies fulfilled in Christ, the physical miracles which took place in His name, the conviction and the boldness of preachers who for the love of their Lord took upon themselves sacrifices unto death. After the apostolic epoch these signs were replaced by the moral miracle of the Church.[2] A result of accepting the word of evangelization is conversion (*metanoia*), which is accompanied by a total dedication to God and the shedding by the soul of everything which will detract from Him. Here penitence, the negative aspect of conversion, enters on the scene. To obtain conversion, the preacher does not hesitate to paint the tragic consequence of a refusal. The Word of God, though essentially directed toward salvation, can become reason for the condemnation of him who rejects it.

The key texts from the great discourses of the missionaries which we find in the Book of Acts, like that of Peter (2:14–39; 3:12–26; 10:34–43) and of Paul (13:14–52; 17:22–31; 24:24–25), will be presented differently by different missionaries, according to how well prepared their listeners are. They treat first one fact and then another before coming to the one and only true object of evangelization, which is Christ. Examples of adaptation to particular situations can be found among the apologists of the second and third centuries,[3] and then in the *De catechizandis rudibus* of St.

---

[2] See also what we said in Chapter 9 about the reasons for testimony.

[3] V. Monachino, "Intento pratico e propagandistico nell' apologetica greca del secondo secolo," *Gregorianum*, 32 (1951), fasc. 1, e 2.

Augustine[4] and in more recent times among the great missioners to China and Japan.[5] Today the increasing pagan population in the world gives missionary preaching a burning immediacy; it has, in fact, become the fundamental task of the Church in our century.[6]

Catechesis

The second form assumed by the proclamation of the message is catechesis. Whoever has accepted Christ as his Savior wants to become better acquainted both with Christ and with the salvation which He promises; he wants to know what this salvation means, and what a life lived in Christ's light demands. In order to meet this need for deeper knowledge, another presentation of the message of salvation, the catechesis, comes to the fore. Its aim is to initiate the convert into the Christian life—and this applies to catechumens who are not yet baptized as well as to those who received Baptism so young they did not understand the obligations their sponsors thereby assumed. Through catechesis, converts are introduced to the mystery of Christ by learning to recognize the signs by which this mystery is conveyed: biblical, liturgical and ecclesial signs. These signs shape the personality of the Christian and keep his way of thinking and acting in harmony with his conversion. All this implies the formation of the Christian mentality,[7] the "sensus Christi" (1 Cor. 2:12). Therefore, catechesis is not complete when instruction alone is offered: it must not only present a systematic exposition of Christian doctrine and morals, but must form the whole man, placing him close to Christ and showing him what he must think and do to remain in harmony with the total change which he underwent in conversion. But this, again, does not mean that the intellectual component in catechesis should be shoved aside. Though catechesis must be conducted in a holy atmosphere because it marks the first contact with the sacred object, its normal place is in the school.

[4] D. Grasso, "Saint Augustin évangélisateur," *Parole et Mission* 22 (1963), 357–378. In this article we tried to show how the well-known pamphlet by St. Augustine regarded evangelization as it was known at the beginning of the fifth century.

[5] J. Lopez Gay, La *"préevangelizacion,"* en los primeros años de la mision del Japón (Madrid, 1962).

[6] F. Legrand, *Le Concile oecumenique et l'évangélisation du monde* (Paris, 1962).

[7] G. C. Negri, "Problemi generali della catechesi," *Educare* (Rome, 1960) Vol. II, esp. pp. 224–229.

Christian antiquity has transmitted to us a whole series of catecheses, the oldest and most authoritative of which is the Apostles' Creed.[8] These are echoed down through the centuries by St. Ambrose, St. Cyril of Jerusalem, St. Augustine and Theodore of Mopsuestia. Later, the need for catechetics gave rise to the small catechisms of our own day, beginning with the *Catechismus ad Parochos* which was published by order of the Council of Trent, to that of Peter Canisius and Bellarmine, which gave impetus to a great number of manuals which attempt to adapt Christian initiation to the needs of the times. In modern catechesis there is a tendency to return to the approach of the Apostles' Creed and the catechesis of the Fathers. The best known work compiled along these lines is the German catechism.*

In catechesis we can distinguish a general form, common to all Christians and summed up by the knowledge of the catechism— which Liégé calls *basic catechesis*[9]—and a *specialized catechesis*, which acts with reference to predetermined aims to be attained within the sphere of Christian initiation of the catechumen to the end that he may be acquainted with the thought, the moral behavior, and the life of the community which he has entered or is about to enter. Yet within this Christian community each is called on to perform a certain function. Hence, the nature of catechesis must be such that it initiates the catechumen to this particular function. According to what we accent in catechesis, we can speak of an exclusively dogmatic, and exclusively moral, or an exclusively liturgical initiation in Christian existence. Intrinsically, catechesis is initiation into the mystery of Christ, who is the center of dogma, morals, liturgy, Bible, Church, apologetics and of all other aspects of Christian truth.

The homily

Initiation to the mystery of Christ is followed by living one's life in Christ, conforming to His thought and His morals. A third way of presenting the message corresponds to this third goal of

---

* *The Living Faith* (New York: Herder and Herder, 1959).

[8] There is a vast literature on this topic. See what Jungmann has to say in his volume *The Early Liturgy* (University of Notre Dame Press, 1958), Chapt. VIII.

[9] Liégé, "La catéchèse: qu'est ce á dire? Essai de clarification," *Catéchèse* 1 (1960), p. 41. See also the recent work by E. Fournier, *L'homilie selon la constitution de la sainte liturgie* (Brussels, 1964).

living a faith that has been accepted and understood. This is the liturgical sermon or homily which is directed to members of the Christian community.

The liturgical context within which this presentation takes place is its outstanding characteristic. Whereas evangelization may occur anywhere, especially in the marketplace, and while the normal place for catechesis is the school, the homily, an explanation of and comment on biblical texts, can be preached only in the Church and only during the liturgical action. The Church's new liturgical constitution points this out expressly: "The homily is highly recommended as part of the liturgical action; during the liturgical year the mysteries of faith and the norms of the Christian life taken from the sacred text are presented therein."[10] The reading of the Bible, as is well known, is part of the liturgy, inasmuch as it is the Word of God which produces the faith essential for worship.[11] Whereas the task of evangelization—while falling *ex officio* to the hierarchy of the Church—can be performed by anyone, and whereas catechesis can likewise be directed by anybody— even laymen having a special mandate—the homily is reserved to the celebrant of the Mass or, if he cannot do it, to the assistant priest. This means that liturgical preaching is an act of worship which must be performed by those especially authorized by the Church to do so.

This close connection between preaching and the liturgy, mentioned in the Acts (2:42; 20:7), and confirmed in the first non-testamentary documents,[12] is part of the same nature of both preaching and the liturgy. One cannot exist without the other. Actually, it is preaching which establishes the liturgical signs as symbols of a supernatural reality. Without the word, the liturgical actions and gestures would be simple actions and gestures lacking any relationship to the truth which it is their task to illustrate. And again, it is preaching which disposes us for proper reception of the sacraments. Even though the sacraments produce grace *ex opere operato*, man must act with faith, hope and charity in order to be correctly disposed for receiving them. The faith which comes from preaching is the foundation for this virtue, as it is for everything in the supernatural order.

[10] Conciliar Constitution on the Liturgy, art. 52.
[11] C. Vagaggini, *Il senso teologico della liturgia* (Rome, 1958), c. XVI.
[12] Justin, *Apologia* I, 67.

From this an important consequence for determining the homily's purpose may be derived. It must be found within the sphere of the liturgy. The homily is a means by which the liturgy realizes its proper goal, the union of the faithful with Christ, because in Him, with Him and through Him, the faithful offer God the worship which is His due. Thus union takes place through acts of faith, hope and charity, and then the reception of the sacraments. It is through the practice of these virtues that Christians who are already part of Christ's body through Baptism are joined even closer to Him, partake of His life, and are transformed in Him. Among these virtues, faith, as the basis of all three, exercises a special function, and this is true even though the most important virtue is charity, the goal to which the other two should lead. On the one hand, faith renders the practice of hope and charity possible and, on the other, it disposes man for the sacraments which are necessary for assimilation with Christ. Faith is thus the foundation of the supernatural life: before justification, it provides the first contact with God; after that, it deepens and develops it by making the theological life possible and disposing man toward the sacraments.

Preaching, as the instrumental cause of faith (Rom. 10:17), penetrates all stages of supernatural life in this way. In evangelization, it proclaims and calls to the Faith; in catechesis, it clarifies the implications of the Faith; and in the homily, it puts into motion the virtue infused in Baptism along with sanctifying grace.

The homily, therefore, cannot be reduced to catechesis. This, as we have seen, has for its first purpose the instruction and illumination of the intellect. Even if, as is only proper, catechesis requires prayer for success, its direct aim remains instruction, the initiation into the mystery. The school in which it is held is not the Church. In the homily, just the opposite occurs: the primary goal is prayer, that practice of the theological virtues which, however, cannot be achieved without intellectual consent.

Catechesis and homily

This difference between homily and catechesis helps us understand other differences between these two forms of preaching.

Catechesis, as we have observed many times, is aimed at the intellect, at instructing it and forming it to the Christian way of thinking. The homily, in contrast, is aimed at the will, at feelings, at moving the will to live according to the demands of the new life infused in man at Baptism. Because it is aimed at the intellect, catechesis is systematic. Even if it starts with the Bible in facts of salvation history, it seeks to discern the truth in them, the principles and ideas which allow one to perceive the close unity. In catechesis the facts already proclaimed by evangelization tend to be transformed into ideas and to manifest themselves as signs of God's intention in history. In the homily, the facts remain unchanged; they are manifestations of God's love and are designed to provoke an answer of love. With respect to biblical facts, the homily tends to see the affective element, more the heart than the mind of God. Hence, it is not systematic as catechesis is, but it follows the Bible more closely.

Then there is the matter of stylistic difference. In catechesis the style is didactic in that it appeals to the rational element, the intrinsic cohesiveness of Revelation, or the historical and apologetic element. In the homily the style is more lyrical and vivacious because it must move the will.

There is also a difference in the energy with which they explain themselves. Catechesis is calm and static, whereas the homily is more dynamic and disturbing. This explains the dangers to which the two forms of preaching are exposed. Catechesis risks falling into the abstruse, the abstract, the erudite, the polemical—all of which are defects of the intellect. The homily, on the other hand, easily descends to the rhetorical, or gets oversentimental and moralistic—defects of the will and emotions.

We may conclude, therefore, that catechesis and homily are two separate and distinct forms of preaching, with aims and means that are different, the one adapted to the school in which it is taught, the other to the liturgy in which one prays.

In this way transmission of the Christian message may assume three dynamic forms: evangelization, catechesis and homily.

Their differences, however, must not make us forget their basic unity. Since they are offshoots of a common nature, they have many elements in common. In evangelization we find didactic and catechetical elements: one cannot present Christ, in fact, without saying something about who He is and what He means for human life, as Peter did in the second chapter of the Acts. Nor can catechesis and homily get along without elements of evangelization. If only for teaching reasons, it is first necessary to call to mind the implications before specifying them. It is thus a question of emphasis, of one fact dominating but not excluding the others. While this dominance and the specific goal that is sought suffice to distinguish one form of preaching from another, still no form can be considered totally independent of the others. In spite of its variety, the phenomenon of preaching remains one.[13]

[13] In the practice of pastoral life the distinction between the three forms of preaching is less obvious than it appears in theory. They interlock and complete each other. Even if preaching is directed to pagans to provoke conversion, it must also be continuously proclaimed to Christians because they are in danger of backsliding. St. Paul himself gives us an example of this when in his letter to the Galatians he is astonished that his converts have already been drawn into "another Gospel" (Gal. 1:6). He calls his people 'insane' because they have let themselves be charmed by a false truth (5:8). The same can be said about catechesis. As well informed about his religion as the Christian may be, he is never enough so. In his daily life he constantly finds new problems which he must solve in the light of Christ. Catechesis is therefore not just a phase of Christian education which is done once and for all. It must constantly be brought up to date. On the function of evangelization in the life of the Church see our article "Il Kerigma e la predicazione," *Gregorianum*, 41 (1960), 424–450. This article has been translated into English in *The Word* (New York, 1964), pp. 220–248.

CHAPTER XIV

The Question of Terminology

In concluding this study, we want to touch upon a question which up to this time we have left suspended, and that is the question of terminology. Because a confusion of terms could easily influence one's understanding of a problem like preaching—at one and the same time actual and complex—the establishment of a definite terminology is imperative.

We must note here that these terms are used so loosely that scholars themselves have difficulty in understanding what each means. During the Congress of Eichstätt, the presence of experts from so many nations and of such varied outlooks made this fluidity quite apparent. To a great extent it hindered the dialogue which was among the aims of the congress.

Therefore, it is worthwhile to say a word in the final chapter of our research about attempts that have been made to bring clarity into this confusion. We shall do this by examining the terms used by scholars; we will then try to determine which terms are best fitted to describe the reality they are called upon to express.

Kerygma

Let us begin with the expression "kerygma," the meaning of which we have briefly defined in another article.[1] Here we shall treat it from the point of view of terminology.

[1] D. Grasso, "Il kerigma e la predicazione," *Gregorianum*, 41 (1960), 424–450.

For theolgians of the *Verkündigungstheologie*, the kerygma is the Christian message, the Gospel as the Good Tidings of salvation to be preached to all. Jungmann writes: "By *kerygma,* we understand the Christian doctrine as object of preaching, as foundation of Christian life, presented and put to the test in pastoral work."[2] Thus, kerygma, in this context, must be understood differently from kerygma as used in scientific theology, where it is presented as a system of knowledge. To preach the kerygma in the former context means to preach the Gospel, the pure Christian message, unfiltered by any theological categories. Though they are inseparable, theology and preaching have their own laws, and the latter cannot be reduced to a vulgarization of the former.

The same concept is found in Hugo Rahner, who understands kerygma as "the preaching of the divine truth according to the meaning with which Divine Knowledge has endowed it, that is, in precisely the way the Church, from the beginning, has preached the Revelation of God in its ordinary magisterium."[3] This definition refers to preaching that is centered upon salvation history, preaching as was carried on in the early Church in the catechesis of St. Cyril of Jerusalem, of St. Augustine and, in general, by the Fathers up to the twelfth century.

For Hofinger, "kerygma" and "message" are the same. Though he understands the significance of kerygma in its meaning of missionary preaching, he thinks such limitation to be "exaggerated."[4]

The word takes on a slightly different hue in Geiselmann. While he concedes that the technical meaning of primitive apostolic preaching—whether of the Twelve, or of St. Paul—is applicable, he does not consider it a missionary function. For the Tübingen theologian, kerygma is the proclamation of salvation history. As such, it must constitute "the norm" for both Christology and preaching. It is not, however, a special form of the latter, distinct from others.[5]

Geiselmann's meaning may serve as a bridge to the opinion of

[2] J. A. Jungmann, *Handing On the Faith,* p. 376.

[3] H. Rahner, *Eine Theologie der Verkündigung* (Freiburg, 1939), p. 10.

[4] J. Hofinger, *The Art of Teaching Christian Doctrine* (University of Notre Dame Press, 1957), p. 6 and note 1. See also Guy de Bretagne, *Pastorale catechétique* (Paris, 1953), p. 25.

[5] J. R. Geiselmann, *Jesus der Christus. Die Urform des apostolischen Kerygmas als Norm unserer Verkündigung und Theologie von Jesus Christus* (Stuttgart, 1951).

those scholars for whom kerygma means a special form of preaching, as the solemn and summary proclamation of the Christian message to non-Christians—whether pagans or Jews—for the purpose of conversion (*metanoia*). It is also understood in this sense by Dodd and Hunter, Rétif, Liégé, Hitz, Henry and others.[6] This form of preaching is also called evangelization,[7] missionary preaching,[8] or evangelization in a strict sense.[9] There are also those who call it kerygmatic preaching.[10]

In view of these different concepts the expression, *kerygmatic theology* assumes a different meaning. In the discussions provoked by the *Verkündigungstheologie*, the expression indicated an attempt at a theology of preaching which differed from the strictly scientific one. After the project was abandoned, the expression, according to Jungmann, could still be employed to describe "all the theoretical discussions and all the practical efforts which tend to underline the value of the kerygma and work toward a substantial renewal of the message in preaching, in catechesis and in worship ceremonies."[11] The author says himself that it would be more exact to speak of "kerygmatic" as embracing both catechetics and homiletics.[12]

Among German authors, kerygmatics is usually understood as the science of preaching, or as a study of theology which is as mindful of the dynamic and pastoral aspect of the Christian message as it is of the rational one.[13] Stated more simply, for those who conceive of the kerygma in its missionary function,

[6] The kerygma is thus understood by C. H. Dodd, *The Apostolic Preaching*, 3rd ed. (New York and London, 1936); A. M. Hunter, *The Unity of the New Testament* (London, 1944) (translated into French under the title *Un Seigneur, une Eglise, un salut* (Neuchatel-Paris, 1950); A. Rétif, *Foi au Christ et mission* (Paris, 1953); P. Hitz, *L'annonce missionnaire de l'Evangile* (Paris, 1954); A. Liégé, "*Evangélisation*," *Catholicisme*, IV (1956), col. 755–764; A. M. Henry, *L'Annonce de l'Evangile aujourd'hui*, (Paris, 1962), etc.

[7] See A. Liégé, "Evangélisation."

[8] See A. Rétif, *Foi au Christ et mission.*

[9] See P. Hitz, L'annonce missionnaire de l'Evangile, p. 8. The author also uses the expression "missionary preaching."

[10] G. Ceriani, "La predicazione domenicale della Parola di Dio," *La Parola di Dio nella communità cristiana* (Milan, 1956), p. 159.

[11] J. A. Jungmann, *Handing On the Faith*, p. 389 f.

[12] *Ibid.*, p. 303.

[13] J. Hofinger, *op. cit.*, p. 234 s. See also p. 239 ss.

kerygmatics in mission theology[14] or the theology of evangelization. Also uncertain and fluid is the meaning of the adjective, *kerygmatic*. When the term is not being used to describe the theologians of the *Verkündigungstheologie*,[15] it is used in connection with the words, *renewal* or *movement*, to express the dominance of content over method, the basic idea of the so-called kerygmatic movement. In sum, this means that renewal should be sought in the content rather than the method of preaching.[16] Aside from this context, when the adjective does not characterize missionary preaching, but preaching in general, it means that because preaching is the proclamation of the Gospel, it must be alive and in conformity with the personal and social reality of the Christian. In short, kerygmatic preaching is that which makes us feel that it is the word of life (Phil. 2:16), of grace (Acts 14:3), of salvation (Rom. 1:16) and of reconciliation (2 Cor. 5:19). "Kerygmatic" is the dynamism of the Gospel come alive in preaching.

Catechesis

As we transfer our attention from the meaning of "kerygma" to that of "catechesis," we find the same looseness. Even those who agree on the meaning of kerygma differ when it comes to the term, catechesis.

For Liégé, catechesis indicates "in a very general way, every manifestation of the prophetic function of the Church with regard to sanctity."[17] It is identical with the ministry of the Word and comprises both forms of evangelization: the first proclamation of salvation to non-Christians, and catechesis, properly speaking, which explains the doctrinal and moral requirements of the Christian life. The author employed the same terminology in his recent writings[18] with a few different shadings.[19]

[14] See Rétif, *Foi au Christ et mission.*

[15] J. A. Jungmann, *Handing On the Faith*, p. 388.

[16] J. Hofinger, *op. cit.*, p. 6 and *passim.*

[17] A. Liégé, *Revue des Sciences Philosophiques et Théologiques*, 39 (1955) 8.

[18] A. Liégé, *Lumière et vie*, 35 (1957), 34.

[19] In an article in *Catéchèse*, 1 (1960), Liégé distinguishes between a broad catechesis, which embraces the complete phenomenon of the transmission of the message to the Gentile, as well as the baptized, and more narrow catechesis, which restricts the transmission to those already converted. He favors the latter definition so long as the opposition does not become obdurate. (p. 38) because catechesis for converts develops evangelization.

Father Hitz is more flexible in his terminology. Frequently for him, catechesis is merely a form of evangelization, one which contains the elements of faith and Christian life. It is distinguishable from missionary preaching, or the evangelization that is directed at pagans, by its commentary, or higher religious instruction, which tries to penetrate the revealed Christian mysteries.[20] In other places, however, Hitz draws closer to Liégé by defining catechesis as "the announcement of the salvific Word of God, in which all variations of the message are included, from missionary preaching to mystagogic catechesis of the highest grade."[21] In this case, catechesis is identified with the ministry of the Word itself: the various forms of the ministry are seen as forms of catechesis.

Rétif thinks of catechesis as simply a form of preaching, one that is similar to the kerygma, and that belongs in the category of teaching. The New Testament designates this by the word $\delta\iota\delta\acute{a}\sigma\kappa\omega$. Admitting that in some cases the terms $\delta\iota\delta\alpha\chi\acute{\eta}$ and $\delta\iota\delta\acute{a}\sigma\kappa\omega$ are used interchangeably,[22] Rétif believes that $\delta\iota\delta\acute{a}\sigma\kappa\omega$ "has a specific sense of teaching, with marked doctrinal overtone, and often with a connotation of the moral attitude to be assumed."[23] Catechesis is thus a form of preaching that is different from the kerygma. While the latter, directed to pagans, tends to provoke conversion and then faith, catechesis instead instructs and calls attention to the implication of conversion. Thus it can be called, quite accurately, the preaching of Christian initiation. Rétif also speaks of the $\delta\iota\delta\alpha\sigma\kappa\alpha\lambda\acute{\iota}\alpha$, which is employed to lend depth to catechesis, and which can be obtained from the scriptural lessons.[24]

Charles Moeller distinguishes two aspects in the ministry of the Word, *preaching proper* and *catechesis*. The former, harking back to the prophetic mission of the Church, calls men to conversion. It brings the Good Tidings. Thus apostolic preaching was: "Testimony of the Resurrection in the midst of a world and an empire which were thoroughly pagan."[25] This is what others term kerygma or missionary preaching. In contrast, catechesis takes the man who is already converted and instructs him more thoroughly in

---

[20] P. Hitz, *L'annonce missionnaire de l'Evangile*, pp. 7–8.
[21] P. Hitz, *Nouvelle Revue Théologique*, 87 (1955), 902.
[22] A. Rétif, *Foi au Christ et mission*, p. 22.
[23] *Ibid.*, p. 23.
[24] *Ibid.*, p. 25 s.
[25] C. Moeller, "Théologie de la Parole et oecumenisme," *Irenikon*, 24 (1951), 315.

the mysteries of Revelation, and introduces him "into knowledge which will make his faith more luminous and fervent."[26] Reading the Bible, attending the liturgy, studying the dogmas of faith are some of the aspects of catechesis."[27] Later on, Moeller calls preaching and catechesis "two aspects of evangelization."[28]

According to the vocabulary of this author, preaching and catechesis are two aspects of evangelization: the first contains missionary preaching, which others call kerygma; the second contains all other forms of Christian initiation, including the liturgy.[29]

Congar's terminology is even more characteristic. In lay preaching he distinguishes between *testimony* and *preaching proper*. The first, which is every Christian's duty, is directed to the world which has not yet entered the Church; preaching, on the other hand, is directed to the faithful and is normally "a liturgical act which complements the celebration of the mysteries."[30] Referring to Moeller's article cited above, Congar takes note of the difference between his own terminology and Moeller's. He calls "preaching" what Moeller calls "catechesis," and he terms "testimony" what the other describes as "preaching."[31]

Jungmann's vocabulary is more outspoken. For him "preaching and catechesis are the two principal forms of the Church's teaching."[32] The first is directed toward developing and conserving supernatural life, while the second consists in a fundamental introduction to the whole complex of Christian doctrine and is generally addressed to young people who are already baptized. The problems which arose from Jungmann's "introduction" have given birth to the science of catechesis or catechistics which Jungmann considers a sister of homiletics.[33] Preaching, therefore, is a term which is ordinarily applied to homiletics alone.

A new word in preaching terminology was introduced by Henry, who distinguishes between *mission, catechesis* and *pastoral*. The first is directed toward unbelievers and has conversion as its aim. (The author himself remarks that others call it evan-

[26] *Ibid*, p. 316.
[27] *Ibid.*, p. 316 s.
[28] *Ibid.*, p. 331.
[29] *Ibid.*, p. 317.
[30] Y. Congar, *Jalons pour une théologie du laïcat* (Paris, 1953), p. 421 s.
[31] *Ibid.*, p. 421, note 125.
[32] J. A. Jungmann, *Handing On the Faith*, p. xi.
[33] *Ibid.*

gelization or kerygma.)[34] *Catechesis* imparts the rudiments of faith to converts to prepare them for Baptism, while *pastoral* represents the last stage of Christian formation. "It addresses the baptized or initiated and aims at bringing them to the perfect age in Christ. Sunday instructions, homilies, preparation for the sacraments (among them Baptism) and for the distribution of these sacraments, exhortations, education and administration of the faithful, and theological teachings are some of the pastoral works."[35] Pastoral works, then, are equivalent to ecclesial action for the baptized.[36]

The same uncertainty and looseness of vocabulary reigns among Italian theologians.

In an article on kerygmatic theology, Carlo Colombo applies the expression, evangelization, to "all the activity of the Church which is directed to the transmission and formation of faith in people."[37] The same all-inclusiveness of meaning is applied to the term "preacher." All are equivalent and indicate the ministry of the Word in all its forms.

Monsignor Grazioso Ceriani uses the same terminology in speaking of a "preaching mandate" which belongs properly to the bishop, and of a "mandate to evangelize which the priest receives."[38] He also speaks of a "gradual and organic evangelization and catechesis for adult Christians, who thus confirm their Baptism."[39]

Father G. B. Cannizzaro, O.S.B., prefers to speak of preaching to indicate the ministry of the Word, and he sees in it a general means both of generating faith in those who do not possess it, and of instructing those who have never been instructed.[40] The learned Benedictine, if we are not mistaken, includes catechesis and homiletics in the same form of preaching.

The terminology of Father R. Spiazzi, O.P., is even more com-

[34] Henry, *Esquisse d'une théologie de la mission* (Paris, 1959), p. 19.

[35] *Ibid.*, pp. 17–18.

[36] *Ibid.*, p. 21.

[37] C. Colombo, "Teologia ad evangelizzazione," *La Scuola Cattolica*, 78 (1950), 302, n. 1.

[38] G. Ceriani, *La Parola di Dio nella comunità cristiana* (Milan, 1957), p. 25.

[39] *Ibid.*, p. 28.

[40] G. Cannizzaro, "La predicazione della Parola di Dio nel mistero cristiano," *La Parola di Dio nella comunità cristiana*, p. 37.

plicated. He makes a distinction between types and forms of preaching. The types are κατήχησισ and διδασκαλία. The former is initiation in the great facts (homiletics) and the great principles (catechesis) of Christian life; the latter is a more perfect instruction for those who seek perfection. According to the function of preaching, which is either instruction or exhortation, we have *pastoral preaching* (homiletics and catechesis) and *exhortatory preaching* (which is not strictly pastoral, and which can be divided into three forms—*dogmatic, moral* and *apologetic*— depending on whether it is directed to the formation of the intellect, of customs, or the defense of the Faith). All in all, therefore, there are five forms.[41]

As we can see, the difference in terminology among those concerned with the problem of transmitting the message is considerable. One can easily imagine the resulting confusion.

Not counting its concrete forms, the transmission of the message is generally called "catechesis"[42] (Liégé, Hitz), "evangelization" (Moeller, Colombo, Ceriani); "preaching" (Cannizaro and others). Speaking of particular forms assumed by the message, we find the first presentation of Christianity to non-Christians described as "kerygma," "evangelization" or "missionary preaching" (Liégé, Rétif, Hitz); "preaching" (Moeller); or "testimony" (Congar). Religious instruction for those already converted, including the liturgical initiation, is called "preaching" (Congar), "catechesis" (Rétif) and "catechesis proper" (Liégé). The French and Italians tend to place liturgical preaching within the sphere of catechesis, while the Germans are more apt to make a distinction. In addition, the authors mentioned here reduce the forms of transmitting the message to two: the French speak of missionary preaching and of catechesis, while the Germans speak of catechesis and homiletics. Rétif speaks of a third form, διδασκαλία, Henry of three, and Spiazzi of five forms.

[41] R. Spiazzi, *Scientia Salutis, I. fondamenti teologici del ministero pastorale* (Rome, 1960), p. 261 s.

[42] Also, the recent *Directoire de pastorale catechetique a l'usage des dioceses de France* (*Catéchèse*, 14 [January 1964]) in using the word "catechesis" means the transmission of the message in any way whatsoever. Thus it can say that "every act of the Church is a bearer of catechesis."

Why this divergence?

After listing so many opinions, we might ask why theologians have not yet succeeded in reaching an agreement on terminology in a matter so important for pastoral concerns.

The main reason, we think, is to be found in the newness of the research. It is only in the last two decades that theologians have turned their attention to the problem of preaching, and questions that have arisen have not yet been outlined adequately enough to permit a definitive terminology. Lacking a theology of preaching, all who have probed these problems have made use of empirical concepts which were necessarily vague and imprecise. Or else they adopted a particular viewpoint according to whatever phase of preaching and its relationship to pastoral work was being discussed. To go a step further, it was the absence of theological thinking about ecclesial activity—or let us even say, the absence of pastoral theology—which has hindered the placing of preaching within the activity and the life of the Church.

This observation also holds true for those German scholars who, because of the establishment in their universities of pastoral chairs, had more opportunity to study preaching. They, too, had thought of the pastoral from a practical point of view, as a complex of rules for the apostolic ministry rather than as a genuine science. Thus the need for a theology of preaching has also been experienced in Germany.[43]

To this general observation we want to add another with respect to missionary preaching, the kerygma, and the varying needs which the study of preaching has revealed in different countries. The crisis of preaching is universal; it can be felt everywhere; and everywhere, a remedy for it is sought. But it was the German theologians who first began to consider it on the speculative plane. More exactly, it was Jungmann's book[44] which brought to the attention of theologians a subject which proved interesting for them as well. The impulse to research, however, was felt by the Innsbruck theologian as a result of his painful

[43] We must remember the discussions that followed the attempt to establish kerygmatic theology as distinct from scientific theology, about which we spoke in the Introduction.

[44] J. A. Jungmann, *Die Frohbotschaft und unsere Glaubensverkündigung* (Regensburg, 1936).

experiences with the Christian life as lived in some parishes. From experience he proceeded to reflection, and he concluded that preaching was not a vulgarization of theology. As mentioned before, an attempt was even made to arrive at a new theology called "kerygmatic." However, this entire movement was concerned with preaching and the spiritual life in countries which were traditionally Christian. This approach forestalled the study of biblical sources of apostolic preaching, of the kerygma, and it prevented theologians from seeing the missionary aspect of such preaching. Only the message, the Gospel, the Good Tidings of salvation in Christ were noticed; and these were the aspects which were missing from the Christian life of many faithful, as well as from preaching that had become essentially moralistic and fragmentary. The study of the apostolic kerygma was undertaken as a means of renewing Christian life, and not as a missionary function. This is most certainly the reason why missionary preaching, which is directed to non-Christians, has not found a place in the over-all treatment of German problematics. Their research found other directions in which to go.[45]

French problematics arose from different needs. It began with a Christian life that was not merely anemic; it was virtually non-existent. In certain parts of the country, dechristianization had reached the point that one could talk of paganism. Preaching, therefore, the crisis of which had been unrestrainedly proclaimed, had to deal with pagans, rather than with languid and lifeless Christians. When French scholars began to examine the Book of Acts, the classic for preaching, they did so from a missionary point of view: they wanted to know how the Apostles had presented Christ to the pagans of that time, and thus determine if the apostolic preaching would serve as a guide for modern missionaries. This explains how French scholars, in keeping with the findings of some exegetes,[46] could discern the missionary aspect above everything else in the preaching of the Apostles and the primitive Church. As a result, the kerygma, as a special form of preaching distinct from preaching to Christians, was rediscovered and inserted into the over-all problematics of preaching. Thus there

---

[45] This does not mean that the German scholars did not pay attention to missionary preaching, but only that they paid little attention to preaching in general.

[46] We refer to the research done by Dodd and Hunter mentioned above.

developed the different meanings assigned the term "kerygma" and its derivatives by the scholars mentioned above. This term, moreover, was used to modify the already-existing expressions, "catechesis" and "homiletics," on which kerygma's rediscovery shed new light. Over-all, an atmosphere of obscurity and uncertainty was generated.

There is still another reason of a philological nature for the existing confession: the lack of preciseness of New Testament terminology. The verbs most commonly used to describe the announcement of the Christian message are κηρύσσω and διδάσκω, and these have so many shadings that it is difficult to determine their exact meaning. Friedrich quotes thirty-two verbs which have a close relationship with κηρύσσω.[47]

The terminology

In establishing a terminology, we propose to use *preach* and *preaching* when referring to the transmission of the message in general. In this way, while these two terms can be applied in a general way to kerygma, catechesis, and homiletics, they cannot be considered synonymous with any one of the three individually.

These two words appear to be better suited than "catechesis" and "evangelization" for expressing the general task. In fact, "preach" comes from the Latin, *praedicare*. This, in turn, derives from the Greek κηρύσσω, which is the synonym of εὐαγγελίζω. According to Miss Mohrmann, the rendering of κηρύσσω by *praedicare* seems to be "normal," since, "on the one hand, it derives from κῆρυξ and, on the other, because *praedicare* seems to be somehow tied to *praeco*-herald."[48] She adds that even though *praedicare* is used in many different contexts and different meanings, its primordial Christian meaning is never obliterated: "the idea of the message proclaimed remains alive."[49] *Preach* and *preaching* thus express, in exact terms, the nature of the Word of God which is transmitted, its historical quality, and all the facts which God deems necessary both for the encounter with man, and for admitting man to participation in His divine life. Facts are

[47] Friederich in the *Dictionary* by Kittel, III, 682–717, spec. p. 702. See also II, 705–737, for the end.
[48] C. Mohrmann, "Praedicare-Tractare-Sermo. Essai sur la terminologie de la predication paleochretienne," *La Maison Dieu*, 39 (1954), 99.
[49] *Ibid.*, p. 100.

announced or proclaimed: in a word, they are preached, not taught. To these facts, man's faith—not his science—responds. This is apparent in the kerygma, the proclamation of Christ dead and risen. But it also holds true for catechesis and homiletics. Catechesis is indeed the development of the kerygma, of facts which without doubt contain a doctrine and a moral, but which remain only facts, the nature of which we must not forget. Even though we reason and explain in catechesis (and also in apologetics, morals, and history), we must never lose sight of these facts. The same may be said for homiletics, which is a commentary on a proclamation of biblical facts.

Preaching emphasizes one particular aspect of the facts proclaimed: their solemnity. The Christian message does not consist of simple facts, but of the most grandiose single fact that ever happened, of the *magnalia Dei*, as the Book of Acts calls them (Acts 2:11). Now *praedicare* in Latin also means "to praise," to celebrate, a meaning which appears in the ecclesiastical Latin of the fourth century.[50] This is an important observation because preaching, inasmuch as it proclaims God's great works, is true praise of the divine. Among God's works, the Incarnation and the Redemption are obviously the most miraculous. To proclaim these at the top of one's voice—as does the κῆρυξ—is the greatest praise that man can render to God.

Preaching thus becomes an act of worship, not only in conjunction with the liturgy, but at all times and in all its forms. Always and everywhere preaching glorifies God, proclaims and illustrates His great works, and invites man to recognize His grandeur and wisdom.

Finally, the term "preaching" emphasizes the instrumental function of man in the announcement of the message. The etymology of the word κηρύσσω places the herald in relationship to another, from whom he received the mandate to proclaim the Good Tidings. This is illustrated better by preaching than by human deeds. The preacher speaks not only in the name of God, because he has received his mandate from Him (Matt. 28:18–20), but he also speaks as an instrument used by God to transmit His plan of salvation (2 Cor. 5:20).

[50] Mohrmann, *art. cit.*, p. 104. Also Benedicta Droste, OSB, links *praedicare* with κηρύσσω in his study "Celebrare in der römischen Liturgiesprache," *Münchener Theologische Studien*, 26 (Munich, 1963), p. 132.

The terms "catechesis" and "evangelization," which are used by some authors, do not seem appropriate for expressing the general transmission of the message. Catechesis, as we shall soon see, is too closely linked to teaching to be able to show that the truth transmitted is not simply a system of ideas, but a story with a person as its center and its significance. On the other hand, *evangelization* recalls the first proclamation of Christianity to the Gentiles. It would be most difficult to apply that same term to the proclamation of the Word of God to catechumens and adult baptized Christians. Such people as these have already heard the Gospel.[51]

Missionary preaching or evangelization

If preaching adequately expresses the act of transmitting the Christian message, what are the terms we should employ to differentiate between its various forms?

We believe that the best word for designating that preaching which seeks to convert pagans is *evangelization*. Of course, there is no good reason why it should not also be called missionary preaching, except that kerygma—though justified in Scripture—remains a Greek word which will always sound strange to our ears. *Missionary preaching* is so general an expression that it can sometimes be incorrectly interpreted. Missionary preaching, indeed, does not characterize mission places exclusively, but constitutes a permanent aspect of the proclamation of the Word of God, as mentioned earlier. It regulates all preaching. Since we constantly make references to missionary preaching, we must never lose sight of its regulatory aspect. If we do, we may cause misinterpretations when we refer to it as "missionary preaching."[52] The expression *mission* runs the same risk. Moreover, this term is unsuitable for the very reason that it is so general. Evangelization, like preaching in general, is part of the mission of the Church, but that is not all that it is. It also comprises all the

[51] Vagaggini reports that some writers avoid the words "sermon" and "preaching" because these evoke a picture of something rhetorical and artificial). (*Il senso teologico dell liturgia* p. 665). The observation is acute, but this does not mean that we should renounce these expressions in this study.

[52] See our article "Il kerigma e la predicazione," *Gregorianum*, 41 (1960), spec. p. 439 ss.

powers conferred on the Apostles for the spread of the Kingdom of God in the world (Matt. 28:18-20).

The term, *evangelization*, besides accurately expressing the proclamation of the Gospel to pagans, is not so closely linked to the missionary proclamation that it could not be extended to indicate the permanent function of preaching itself. As we can see, these are implications which might or might not be accepted by the reader.

Nor do we think that missionary preaching should be described as *testimony*. Even though testimony often takes place in missionary preaching, it does not belong there exclusively, but can occur as a result of the proclamation of the message under any of the forms mentioned. Preaching is testimony (Acts 1:8) because it proclaims the facts of salvation history, facts whose significance for man is to be found not only in their truth but also in their meaning for life. The Death and Resurrection of Christ, the central themes of apostolic preaching, interest us not only because they happened, but because they happened for our salvation. The importance of these facts can only be expressed by the person who can illustrate their significance in his own life. This, as we have said before, holds true for all preaching. In evangelization, catechesis or homily, the preacher always remains a witness: he is a preacher only to the degree in which he is witness to the facts he proclaims. This can also be said for laymen who are preachers and who, by virtue of this office, participate in the power of the Church's magisterium.

The catechesis

We think, however, that the term *catechesis* may cause confusion when used to describe preaching of Christian initiation. The corresponding Greek word is κατηκεῖν, which in the New Testament in general, and in St. Paul in particular, means instruction about the content of faith (Gal. 6:6), or the deepening of knowledge already acquired (Luke 1:4).[53] The other word used in the New Testament is διδάσκω, and this means to instruct "with marked doctrinal overtones and often with a connotation of the proper moral comportment to be adopted."[54] Rétif observes that catechesis is imparted from a sitting position, the attitude of the

[53] *Kittel*, III, p. 640.
[54] A. Rétif, *Foi au Christ et mission*, p. 7.

schoolmaster rather than the herald, who stands and calls out at the top of his voice.[55]

Of the two verbs cited, κατηκεῖν describes the reality of religious instruction much better. Etymologically, it means, "to resound." It thus includes the notion of oral teaching by a master's voice. Above the catechumen is the master, the διδάσκαλος (1 Cor. 12:28; Eph. 4:11). But the most important point, it seems to us, is the one made by etymology. Here we find the concept that in religious instruction, unlike secular, that which is communicated is not something man can discover by his own efforts, but something supernatural, the knowledge of which comes *ex auditu* (Rom. 10:17). The catechumen is not one who discovers by means of the Socratic method, and who expresses what he has discovered within himself. He is rather the one to whom knowledge is imparted from the outside; his attitude is that of a listener.

What the term "catechesis" fails to express is that religious instruction is not simply a communication of ideas, but rather, the transmission of facts and actions that are intended to become principles of thought and moral conduct. But this deficiency resides in the nature of preaching itself, of which catechesis is merely one form. For this, too, the term "preaching" is preferable to any other for describing the phenomenon of the transmission of the message.[56]

But a whole series of particular catecheses enters the sphere of catechesis, and these help to shape the religious education of each and every individual, not only with respect to the commitment all hold in common, but also with regard to the specialized tasks each Christian is called upon to perform during his life.[57] Among these forms of catechesis there is also the one which Rétif calls διδασκαλία, and which he distinguishes from the kerygma as well as from διδαχή, or simple catechesis.

According to the same author, while the διδαχή confers "the moral and doctrinal teaching," either in preparation for, or after Baptism, the διδασκαλία "contributes first to the deepening of this formation, thanks above all to the lessons of Scripture and of

---

[55] *Ibid.*

[56] Kittel's *Dictionary* tells us that in the New Testament διδάσκω can also mean "give notice of something" (III, 639) as in Acts 21:21.

[57] Liégé distinguishes between a whole listing of different catecheses (*Catéchèse*, 1, 40s).

Christian thinking."[58] This means that in the *didaché* as well as in the *didascalia* there is a prevalence of the intellectual element of instruction, with the difference being that in the first-mentioned instance it is elementary, while in the second it is more profound. But the purpose of both is always in the sphere of instruction. Theology itself is a superior sort of catechesis. It is a question of a distinction within catechesis itself.

The homily

We now come to the third form of preaching, the liturgical. How can we find a specific term? It is usually called *homily*, a Greek word transposed into modern languages. Though it originally described the discourse of a pope or bishop during Mass, it is now also applied to the explanation of the Gospel by a simple priest.

Basically, the homily is a familiar kind of speech between members of the same community, wherein all social differences disappear, and only the appellation "brother in Christ," remains. The Church is the society of the "called ones"—called by the Word of God to constitute a new people of God on earth in preparation for the eschatological society. It is to this community that the priest addresses the Word and the will of God in order that it may respond with prayer and charity. This is the meaning of the familiar discourse employed in one place in the New Testament (Acts 20:11) where the expression *homily* appears. The Latin counterpart is the word *sermo*,[59] used by the Father to denote liturgical preaching.

The word *homily* seems proper to us, both because it describes a familiar kind of speech and because it distinguishes liturgical preaching from catechesis, wherein the figure of the master appears. In the homily the head of the assembly speaks to brethren among whom there are no differences, and not to pupils for the purpose of exhorting and instructing them.

However, an expression to describe the action of the one who gives the homily is still lacking. We must fall back on a circumlocution: to give a homily, or to explain the Gospel.

[58] A. Rétif, *Foi au Christ et mission*, p. 26.

[59] Mohrmann tells us that after the fourth century *sermo* becomes the most common term for preaching, either catechetical, exegetic, or patristic. If one wants to stress pastoral preaching, that which was directed to the assembly of people in Church, it was called *sermo popularis* (*La Maison Dieu*, 39 [1954], 105 ff.).

Conclusion

At the end of this book we would like to summarize briefly the conclusions at which we have arrived.

1) The starting point of this study was the preaching of the Apostles. We have tried to point out the object of their preaching by examining the expressions used for it in the New Testament. We have particularly examined the concept of mystery used by St. Paul in his Epistles, a concept which allows us to show the full function of preaching in salvation history. For the Apostle the mystery is the plan of salvation, thought out by God at the beginning of time and destined to be revealed at the fulness of time. At its center is the person of Christ dead and risen. Revelation is therefore essentially God's intervention in time and space to call man to salvation, to participation in the divine nature and to the trinitarian dialogue. Christianity is a message of salvation, the announcement of God's salvific plan to call man to divine life. This message is identified with Christ, who is not only the herald of the message but its content itself. He does not indicate a *way* for salvation: He Himself is salvation. Here is to be found the originality of preaching as a form of communication. It is not teaching, properly speaking—though it is analogous to it—but the proclamation of Christ the Savior. The object of preaching actually is not an object but a subject.

2) Continuing our examination, we saw that this subject is not only a historical person dead and risen centuries ago, and whose

message preaching now proclaims, but a Person who is present, and acts, in preaching. Christ is not only the One about whom we speak, but the One who speaks, who addresses man in order to explain to him His plan for salvation. This is a fact which the New Testament helps us to establish, and which is confirmed in the patristic tradition, especially in St. Augustine. It is basically a reflection of the doctrine of the Mystical Body, of the presence of Christ in the Church, the primordial sacrament of salvation. It was only through Scholasticism that the concept of the causality of God suffered loss of meaning. Under the influence of Aristotelian philosophy the intellectual element of Revelation came to overshadow the historical one. The accent is no longer on God's intervention in history but rather on the truth revealed by Him. Thus the concept of the message of Christianity proper is apparently being replaced by a concept which makes of it a metaphysical revelation. To put it another way, from being a word directed to man to invite him to salvation, preaching becomes a word said by man to propel him toward the search for God. The *Deus desiderans* of Scripture and Tradition, especially the Augustinian tradition, become a *Deus desideratus*. Preaching changes into a sacred discourse, *into oratio salutem animae persuadens,* according to the definition by Alan of Lille. Anti-Protestant polemic was the cause for a continuation of theological speculation along these lines, because it required that theologians distinguish, as best they could, preaching from the sacraments. But in spite of this, the concession of the causality of God stayed not only with a few theologians of the Counter-Reformation, but also with the preachers. Today's Bible research and theology of faith make this clear. It is God who speaks in preaching.

3) But in order to reach man, the voice of God needs a vehicle, a voice in which to sound. Thus there is not only a principal causality in preaching, a Word said by God, but also an instrumental causality, a word said by man. God speaks through the means of man. Thus preaching becomes an essential function of salvation history. It establishes a relationship between God and man. In God's eyes the present phase of history serves to announce to all men the salvific design of God. The parousia will arrive only when the message has been proclaimed to the end of the world.

Besides this intellectual dimension there is also a dynamic dimension in preaching. It is a means, a vehicle of grace, a true

virtus Dei in salutem omni credenti (Rom. 1:16). The word not
only proclaims salvation, it confers it: it is an effective word which
does what it says. What it confers is faith, the foundation of the
supernatural order, and with faith, eternal life, which purifies
from sin. By producing faith it generates the Church, the community of the faithful, and it makes this faith grow by developing
to maturity the life of grace in the faithful. The efficacy of preaching, however, is not one-sided: it saves those who accept it and
condemns those who refuse it.

Preaching thus is the means and the place for the encounter
with God, because it is in the Church that God speaks and calls
man. Preaching is the *hodie* of God, the most decisive event in
man's life, a fact which changes his position on earth radically.
Sacred history did not come to an end with the death of the
Apostles but continues in the history of the Church.

The close connection between preaching and faith explains
its necessity and its pre-eminence among the ministries of the
Church. As vehicle of faith, it is as necessary as faith itself: it is
the foremost duty of bishops.

4) Preaching as vehicle of faith and grace has thus a certain
sacramentality. In it, under the visible sign of the human word,
a supersensible reality is present and acts just as in the sacraments.
It is God Himself, whose presence can be perceived only through
faith. It is a mystery of faith and at the same time also of humility;
the vehicle which God has chosen is not only fragile like a word,
but it is a means which has nothing sublime in its fragility. At the
beginning of this mystery, in this union between the visible and
invisible, stands God Himself, who wanted His Gospel to be
spread by the human word, and has adapted Himself to human
psychology. Therefore, there is no preaching without the *missio
canonica:* nobody can preach who has not received his mandate
from God and from the Church to which He has communicated
His powers. The faculty of preaching is a part of the priesthood
of the New Testament. To have faculties over the sacraments, the
New Testament priest must also have them over faith, without
which the sacraments are not effective. The same person must
be minister of the Word and of the sacrament.

5) To the announcement of the message, man replies with
faith, which is the encounter between God and man in their intimacy. In order for the encounter to take place, the love of God

which is manifest in all salvation history must be communicated to man. If preaching is the vehicle of faith, it must also be the vehicle of love. This commitment is essential to faith, because it alone can bring about the communion of faith without which man cannot stay with God. From faith comes conversion, which means a change, a disengagement from everything which once meant life, a demand for orientation around a new center. Conversion implies a triple dimension: one, theological, faith to which man clings; second, sacramental, which consists in baptism in which man is reborn into a new mode of existence; and third, moral, which includes a new behavior, a new style of life in keeping with the change which takes place in man.

6) At the end of Chapter V we were able to define preaching: the proclamation of the mystery of salvation made by God Himself through His legitimate representatives in view of faith and its deepening in Christian life. Finally, we pointed out the dimensions of preaching: sacred historico-biblical, Christocentric, ecclesial, liturgical and eschatological.

7) In the second part of this book we examined the nature of preaching itself, seeking to determine in what the efficacy which Scripture ascribes to preaching, consists.

Above all, we have discussed the analogy between preaching and the sacraments by pointing out their differences and their similarities.

Taking up the question of efficacy, we have seen that the problem which interests scholars most is the way in which the two realities are effective, that is, how they influence the production of grace. After citing the opinions of various theologians, we have arrived at the conclusion that in preaching, in addition to efficacy *ex opere operantis,* there is also another which we might call *ex opere operato.* This means that it is so powerful that it can strip man of his indifference and force him to take a position regarding the salvation which was announced to him. In this sense preaching is by its very nature always effective through an inner *dynamis* which nobody can avoid. This means that there is a double efficacy: the word which brings a message can act *ex opere operantis* on its own, but inasmuch as it also has a particular content it acts *ex opere operato,* that means through an inherent force. Therefore, the part of the minister is much more important than in the sacraments. While, in the latter, the minister has nothing to do but follow the sacramental rite, in preaching he must make understandable the message which he announces. His instrumentality is important.

9) In order to plumb the nature of this instrumentality, we have examined the concept of testimony, the expression by which the Acts express the mandate of Christ to preach the Gospel in all creation (1:8). The analysis has reached the conclusion that a service of the Word, the commitment of a person, is necessary for the efficacy of the Word: this is generally called sanctity. This is not limited to the preacher but extends to the whole Church. Sanctity is not only a fact which helps preaching achieve its efficacy, but a factor which imposes a condition. There is no preaching when there is no sanctity. On the one hand, it is a sign that the word of the preacher appears as forthcoming from God; on the other, it demonstrates the meaning of this word for the life of man.

10) At this point it was possible to confront the problem of the nature of efficacy of preaching. It comes from the very object which is preached, that is, God, truth and supreme good, and therefore endowed with a particular charm which spontaneously attracts the intelligence and the will of man. In the present order of providence this charm is identified with Christ in whom God has appeared to man. From Christ emanates a particular attractiveness. This triggers a response in the intelligence and the will of man which want to be directed to it. The fact that goodness and supreme truth are incarnate in a limited sign (Christ and the Church) makes it possible for man to retain his liberty. When they are presented in preaching, he is free to accept or reject it according to whether he needs the values with which Christ is identified.

11) This efficacy can be defined ontologically-psychologically. It comes from the object itself, but needs not only internal grace but also human testimony, the commitment of the person, which clearly shows that accepting Christ does not mean renouncing one's personality, but the exploiting of it. The man who accepts Christ, who dies and rises with Him, is a true man, a man saved, one who is fully conscious of his end. The importance of the psychological factor explains the importance of one's behavior.

12) Speaking about the forms preaching assumes in its dynamism, we confined them to three: evangelization, catechesis and homily. The first is the evangelical message presented to the

pagans to convert them; the second, for catechumens, to initiate them into the Christian virtues; the third, for the Christian community, to admonish them to live according to the Faith which they have embraced. These three forms correspond to the three specifications of faith.

13) The study ends with a discussion of terminology. We have proposed the name of *preaching* for proclaiming the Christian message in general. For the concrete forms assumed in its dynamism: *evangelization,* for preaching which is directed to non-Christians; *catechesis* for catechumens or persons similar to them; and *homily,* for that directed to the Christian community.

Bibliography

The works which treat preaching only incidentally are not included here.

Alfaro, J., "Cristo glorioso, Revelador del Padre," *Gregorianum,* 39 (1958), 222–271.

"Persona y gracia," *Gregorianum,* 41 (1960), 5–29.

"Fides in terminologia biblica," *Gregorianum,* 42 (1961), 463–505.

"Supernaturalitas fidei iuxta S. Thomam," *Gregorianum,* 44 (1963), 501–542, 731–787.

Alszeghy, Z., "Die Theologie des Wortes Gottes bei den mittelalterlichen Theologen," *Gregorianum,* 39 (1958), 685–705.

Alszeghy, Z., and Flick, M., "Il problema teologico della predicazione," *Gregorianum,* 40 (1959), 671–744.

Il Vangelo della grazia. Florence, 1964. Pp. 242–245.

Anta, Jares J., *La predicacion cristiana en la doctrina de San Vincente Ferrer.* Astorga, 1962. (Dissertation)

Arnold, F. X., *Dienst am Glauben.* Das vordringlichste Anliegen heutiger Seelsorge (Untersuchungen zur Theologie der Seelsorge, Band 1). Freiburg, 1948. *Grundsätzliches und Geschichtliches zur Theologie des Seelsorge; das Prinzip des Gottmenschlichen* (Untersuchungen zur Theologie der Seelsorge, Band II). Freiburg, 1949.

Glaubensverkündigung und Glaubensgemeinschaft. Düsseldorf, 1945. *Wort des Heils als Wort in der Zeit, Gesammelte Reden und Aufsätze.* Trier, 1961.

Asting, R., *Die Verkündigung des Wortes Gottes im Urchristentum dargestellt an den Begriffen "Wort Gottes," "Evangelium" und "Zeugnis."* Stuttgart, 1939.

Augustoni, L., "Das Wort Gottes als kultisches Wort," *Anima,* 10 (1955), 272–284.

Avelino, Esteban Romero A., *Predicaciòn viviente al dia.* Madrid, 1956.

Barsotti, D., *Il mistero cristiano e la parola di Dio.* Florence, 1954.

Barth, K., *Dogmatique I: La doctrine de la Parole de Dieu.* Geneva, 1953–1954.

Dogmatics in Outline. New York, 1959.

Parole de Dieu et parole humaine. Paris, 1936.

Bea, A., "Valeur pastorale de la parole de Dieu dans la liturgie," *La Maison Dieu,* 47–48 (1956), 127–148.

Bellini, E., "La predicazione in San Gregorio di Nazianzo," *La Scuola Cattolica,* 91 (1963), 496–506.

Berbuir, E., "Wort und Sakrament," *Der Mensch vor dem Worte Gottes.* Maria Laach, 1953. Pp. 35–49.

Betz, Joh., "Wort und Sakrament. Versuch einer dogmatischen Verhältnis-bestimung," *Verkündigung und Glaube* (Festgabe für F. X. Arnold, edited by Theodor Filthaut and Joseph Andreas Jungmann). Freiburg, 1958. Pp. 76–99.

Blomjous, J., "Basic Links Between Liturgy and Catechesis," *Teaching All Nations* (edited by Johannes Hofinger and Clifford Howell). Freiburg and New York, 1961. Pp. 223–235.

Bopp, L., "Die Heilsmächtigkeit des Wortes Gottes nach den Vätern," *Theologie und Predigt* (Ein Tagungsbericht, edited by Otto Wehner and Michael Frickel). Wurzburg, 1958. Pp. 190–226.

Bornkamm, G., Art. Μυστήδιον in *Theol. Wörterbuch,* 4, col. 809–834.

Bouyer, L., "Prédication et mystére," *La Maison Dieu,* 16 (1948), 12–33.

Brinktrine, Joh., "Beiträge zur Katholischen und reformatorischen Lehre vom Worte Gottes," *Theologie und Glaube,* 54 (1964), 224–230.

Brox, N., *Zeuge und Märtyrer.* Munich, 1961.

Bühlmann, W., "Adapting Catechesis to Missionary Conditions," *Teaching All Nations.* Freiburg and London, 1961. Pp. 59–72.

Bultmann, R., "Der Begriff des Wortes Gottes im Neuen Testament," *Glauben und Verstehen,* I. Tübingen, 1954. Pp. 268–293.

Bussi, N., "Il contenuto della catechesi come mistero cristiano," *Il contenuto della catechesi* (Proceedings of the Third National Convention of the Friends of Catechesis). Turin, 1963. Pp. 47–61.

Cannizzaro, B., "La predicazione della Parola di Dio nel mistero cristiano," *La Parola di Dio nella communità cristiana* (Atti della VI settimana nazionale di aggiornamento pastorale tenutasi a Roma dal 10 al 14 Settembre 1965). Milan 1957. Pp. 31–50.

Carrier, H., *Psycho-sociologie de l'appartenance religieuse?* Rome, 1960. "La collaborazione delle scienze umane al servizio della pastorale," *La Pastorale oggi* (Atti del I Congresso internazionale di teologia pastorale di Friburgo). Milan, 1962. Pp. 203–216.

Centi, T., "La predicazione nel pensiero di S. Tommaso d'Aquino," *Temi di predicazione,* 11-12, quaderno II, pp. 39–47.

Cerfaux, L., Le Christ dans la theologie de S. Paul. Paris, 1954. Spec. Pp. 229–242 and 303–328.

"Témoins du Christ d'aprés les Actes," *Recueil Cerfaux*, Vol. II. Gembloux, 1964. Pp. 157–174.

Ceriani, G., *Introduzione alla teologia pastorale*. Rome, 1961.

"La predicazione domenicale della parola di Dio nel 'assemblea liturgica della communità cristiana," *La Parola di Dio nella communità cristiana*. Milan, 1957. Pp. 141–168.

Charlier, L., "Le Christ, Parole de Dieu," *La Parole de Dieu en Jésus Christ* (opera in collaborazione). Paris, 1961. Pp. 121–139.

Colombo, C., "Teologia ed Evangelizzazione," *La Scuola Cattolica*, 78 (1950), 302–324.

Colson, J., "Le collège apostolique et l'Evangélisation primitive," *Mission sans frontières*. Paris, 1960. Pp. 63–117.

Congar, Y., "Le Saint Esprit et le Corps apostolique réalisateurs de l'oeuvre du Christ," *Revue des sciences philosophiques et théologiques*, 36 (1952), 613–625; 37 (1953), 24–48.

"Théologie de l'Eglise particulière," *Mission sans frontières*. Paris, 1960. Pp. 15–52, spec. pp. 28–34.

Cordovani, M., *Corso di predicazione*. Milan, 1930.

Cullmann, O., Christ and Time. Philadelphia, 1950.

Daniélou, J., Parole de Dieu et Mission de l'Eglise," *Le prêtre ministre de la Parole* (Union des oeuvres catholiques de France: congrès de Montpellier 1954), pp. 41–54.

"La catéchèse dans la tradition patristique," *Catéchèse*, 1 (1960), 21–34.

"Le kérygme selon le Christianisme primitif," *L'annonce de l'Evangile aujourd'hui* (Rapports du IV colloque de *Parole t Mission* présentés par A. M. Henry). Paris, 1962. Pp. 67–86.

Davis, Ch., "The Theology of Preaching," *The Clergy Review*, 45 (1960), 524–545.

Deden, D., "Le mystère paulinien," *Ephemerides Theol. Lovanienses*, 13 (1936), 403–442.

Delanglade, J., "Essai sur la signification de la parole," *Signe et Symbole* (opera in collaborazione). Neuchatel, 1946. Pp. 13–48.

De La Potterie, I., "La notion de témoignage dans St. Jean," *Sacra Pagina*, vol. II. Paris-Gembloux, 1959. Pp. 192–208.

Delcuve, J., "Forme metodi e movimenti particolari dell'attività pastorale riguardanti la catechesi," *La Pastorale oggi*. Milan, 1962. Pp. 126–140.

Dewailly, L. M., *Jèsus Christ, Parole de Dieu*. Paris, 1945.

Dodd, C. H., *The Apostolic Preaching and Its Development*, 8th ed. London, 1956.

"Le kérygme apostolique dans le quatrième Evangile," *Rev. d'histoire et de philosophie rel.*, 31 (1951), 265–275.

Dreher, B., "Kerygmatische Predigt," *Lebendige Seelsorge*, 14 (1963), 107–114.

Die Osterpredigt. Freiburg, 1951.

Dunas, N., "Pour une proposition kérygmatique de l'Evangile aujoud'hui," *L'annonce de l'Evangile aujoud'hui.* Paris, 1962. Pp. 223–314.

Duployé, P., *Rhétorique et Parole de Dieu.* Paris, 1955.

Dupont, J., "La parole de Dieu suivant S. Paul," *La parole de Dieu en J. Christ.* Paris, 1961. Pp. 68–84.

Dürr, L., *Die Wertung des göttlichen Wortes im A. T. und im Antiken Orient.* Leipzig, 1938.

Durwell, F. X., *La résurrection de Jèsus mystère de salut,* 2nd ed. Le Puy-Paris, 1954.

Eilers, E., Gottes Wort. Eine Theologie der Predigt nach Bonaventura. Freiburg, 1941.

Elchinger, L. A., "The Bible and Catechesis," *Teaching All Nations,* New York, 1961. Pp. 137–152.

Etspüler, P. J., *Das göttliche Wort im Künder der Christlichen Warheit nach dem hl. Bonaventura.* Porto Alegre, 1961.

Feuillet, A., and Grelot, P., "Parole de Dieu," *Vocabulaire de théologie biblique.* Paris, 1962. Col. 750–758.

Fendt, L., *Homiletik. Theologie und Technik der Predigt.* Berlin, 1948.

Fesenmayer, G., "Die Schaffung der Hörerkentnis und des Hörerverständnisses in der Predigtausbildung und Fortbildung," *Hörer und Predigt.* Würzburg, 1960. Pp. 332–351.

Bibelpredigt im Aufbruch. Freiburg, 1963.

Flatten, H., "Missio canonica," *Verkündigung und Glaube* (Festgabe für F. X. Arnold). Freiburg, 1958. Pp. 123–141.

Fleckenstein, H., "Die Predigt von heute im Urteil der Hörer," *Theologie und Predigt.* Würzburg, 1958. Pp. 12–20.

"Förderungen an eine zeitgemässe Verkündigung," *Mittelalterliches in der Kirche von heute?* (Studien und Berichte der Kath. Akademie in Bayern). Würzburg, 1962. Pp. 59–80.

Flick, M., "Riflessioni teologiche sulla crisi della predicazione," *La Civiltà Cattolica,* I (1960), 225–234 and 487–495.

Floristan, C., "La palabra y el sacramento en la acciòn pastoral," *Scriptorium,* 8 (1961), 288–327.

Florit, E., "La predicazione e il culto della Parola di Dio nelle comunità apostoliche," *La Parola di Dio nella comunità cristiana.* Milan, 1957. Pp. 51–63.

Fournier, E., *L'Homilie selon la constitution de la sainte liturgie.* Brussels, 1964.

Friederich, G., Art. εὐαγγελίζομμι εὐαγγελίον, *Theol. Wörterbuch* 2, col. 705–735.

Art. κηρύσσω κήρυγμα, *Theol. Wörterbuch* 3, col. 705–717.

Fries, H., "Vom Hören des Wortes Gottes. Eine Fundamentaltheologische Überlegung," *Einsicht und Glaube.* Freiburg-Basel-Vienna, 1962. Pp. 15–27.

Gastgeber, K., *Gotteswort durch Menschenwort* (Wiener Beiträge zur Theologie). Vienna, 1964.

Geiselmann, J. R., *Jesus der Christus. Die Urform des Apostolischen Kerygmas als Norm unserer Verkündigung und Theologie von Jesus Christus.* Stuttgart, 1951.

Gélineau, J., "L'annonce de la Parole de Dieu dans le mystère du culte," *La Parole de Dieu en J. Christ.* Paris, 1961. Pp. 202–209.

"Mediantibus signis salus nobis revelatur," *Il contenuto della catechesi.* Turin, 1963. Pp. 183–205.

Gerards, J., "Die Not der Predigt," *Not und Auftrag der Verkündigung* (Eine Aufsatzreihe zur Predigt heute). Aachen, 1950. Pp. 9–24.

Ghilardi, M., "Catechesi e Liturgia," *Rivista liturgica,* 48 (1961), 101–113.

Giblet, J., "La théologie johannique du Logos," *La Parole de Dieu en J. Christ.* Paris, 1961. Pp. 85–119.

Girault, R., "La prédication est mystère," *La Maison Dieu,* 39 (1954), 7–22.

Gewiess, J., *Die Urapostolische Heilsverkündigung nach der Apostelgeschichte.* Breslau, 1939.

Grasso, D., "Lo stato attuale della catechesi," *La Civiltà Cattolica,* III (1960), 573–587.

"Il kerigma e la predicazione," *Gregorianum,* 41 (1960), 424–450.

"Evangelizazione, Catechesi, Omilia. Per una terminologia della predicazione," *Gregorianum,* 42 (1961), 242–267.

"Nuovi apporti alla teologia della predicazione," *Gregorianum,* 44 (1963), 88–118.

"The Core of Missionary Preaching," *Teaching All Nations.* Freiburg and London, 1961. Pp. 39–58.

"Saint Augustin évangélisateur," *Parole et Mission* (1963), 357–378.

"The Catechist as Witness," *Worship,* 38 (1964), 157–164.

Groppo, G., "Appunti sul concetto di educazione nella Bibbia," *Orientamenti Pedagogici,* 10 (1963), 219–233; 649–667; 870–882.

Grün, S., *Verkündigung in der Glaubenskrise der Zeit.* Würzburg, 1956.

"Die Bereitung des Hörers für das Wort Gottes," *Hörer und Predigt.* Würzburg, 1960. Pp. 266–302.

Guardini, R., *Das Wesen des Christentums.* Würzburg, 1938.

Guitton, J., *Le problème de Jèsus et les fondements du témoignage chrétien.* Paris, 1950. Pp. 153–178.

The Problem of Jesus: A Free-Thinker's Diary. New York, 1955.

Günthör, A., *Die Predigt. Theoretische und praktische theologische Wegweisung.* Freiburg-Basel-Vienna, 1963.

Gusdorf, G., *La Parole.* Paris, 1956.

Haensli, E., "Verkündigung heute aus lebendigen theologischen Einsichten," *Fragen der Theologie heute,* edited by J. Feiner, J. Trütsch, and Fr. Böckle. Einsiedeln, 1958. Pp. 463–484.

"Neuste Versuche einer Theologie der Predigt in kritischer Sicht," *Theologie und Predigt.* Würzburg, 1958. Pp. 272–308.

Hamer, J., "La crise de la prédication," *La Revue Nouvelle,* 29 (1959), 137–147.

"Parole de Dieu ou parole sur Dieu dans la pensée de Karl Barth," *La Parole de Dieu en Jèsus Christ.* Paris, 1961. Pp. 281–287.

Händler, O., *Die Predigt.* Berlin, 1949.

Hardawirjana, R., *Notio praedicationis in epistolis paulinis.* Roma, 1961. (Diss.)

Häring, B., "La conversion," *Pastorale du péché (Bibliothèque de théologie. Serie II: Théologie morale).* Tournai, 1961. Pp. 65–145.

Haselden, K., *The Urgency of Preaching.* New York, 1963.

Heimerl, H., *Laien im Dienst der Verkündigung.* Vienna, 1958.

Hengsbach, F., "Die Predigt als Verkündigung des Wortes Gottes," *Die Predigt in unserer Zeit,* edited by F. M. Rintelen. Paderborn, 1946. Pp. 62–79.

Henry, A. M., "Le kérygme dans le ministère de la parole," *L'Annonce de l'Evangile aujoud'hui.* Paris, 1962. Pp. 87–116.

Hitz, P., *L'annonce missionnaire de l'Evangile.* Paris, 1954.

To Preach the Gospel. New York, 1963.

"Théologie et catéchèse," *Nouvelle Revue Théologique,* 77 (1955), 897–923. Condensed in English: "Theology and the Ministry of the Word," *Theology Digest,* Winter (1958), 3–7.

"Die erneuerte Predigt," *Seelsorge zwischen gestern und morgen.* Freiburg, 1961. Pp. 229–240.

Hofinger, Joh., *The Art of Teaching Christian Doctrine.* Notre Dame, 1962.

Holstein, H., "Prédication apostolique et magistère," *La Parole de Dieu en J. C.* Paris, 1961. Pp. 157–169.

Hörer und Predigt. Ein Tagungsbericht, edited by O. Wehner and M. Frickel. Würzburg, 1960.

Jacob, E., *Théologie de l'A. T.* Neuchatel-Paris, 1955. Pp. 103–109.

Jungmann, J. A., *Die Frohbotschaft und unsere Glaubensverkündigung.* Regensburg, 1936.

The Good News and Its Proclamation (synopsis translation of *Die Frohbotschaft*). New York, 1961

Handing on the Faith. A Manual of Catechetics. New York, 1959.

Katechetik. Freiburg, 1955.

"Liturgie et histoire du salut," *Lumen Vitae,* 10 (1955), 281–288.

Glaubensverkündigung im Lichte der Frohbotschaft. Innsbruck-Vienna-Munich, 1963.

Kampmann, Th., "Das Wesen der Christlichen Predigt," *Liturgie, Gestalt und Vollzug* (Festgabe für Joseph Pascher). Munich, 1963. Pp. 154–170.

Kappler, E., *Die Verkündigungstheologie* (Studia friburgensia 2). Freiburg, 1949.

Karrer, O., "Das Wort Gottes in der Heilsökonomie," *Anima*, 10 (1955), 250–256.

Koch, R., "Die Verkündigung des Wortes Gottes in der Urkirche," *Anima* (1955), 256–265.

"Témoignage d'après les Actes," *Masses Ouvrières*, 129 (April 1957) and 131 (June 1957). Pp. 16–30 and 4–25.

"Die Theologie des Hörens nach dem Altem Testament," *Hörer und Predigt*. Würzburg, 1960. Pp. 66–99.

"Predigt und Heilsgeschichte," *Monatschrift für Pastoraltheologie*, 51 (1962), 13–25.

Larcher, C., "La parole de Dieu en tant que révélation dans l'A.T.," *La Parole de Dieu en Jèsus Christ*. Paris, 1961, Pp. 35–67.

Lackmann, M., *Der Christ und das Wort*. Graz-Vienna-Cologne, 1962.

Latourelle, R., *Théologie de la révélation*. Paris, 1963.

Leenhardt, F. J., "La signification de la notion de parole dans la pensée chrétienne," *Revue d'histoire et de philosophie rel*, 35 (1955), 261–273.

Léonard, A., "La parole de Dieu, mystère et événement, vérité et présence," *La Parole de Dieu en Jèsus Christ*. Paris, 1961. Pp. 11–32.

Leuba, J. L., "Signe et symbole en théologie," *Signe et symbole*. Neuchatel, 1946. Pp. 137–178.

Lerle, E., *Die Predigt im Neuen Testament*. Uelzen, 1956.

Liégé, A., "Contenu et pédagogie de la prédication chrètienne," *La Maison Dieu*, 29 (1954), 23–37.

"De la parole à la catéchèse," *Lumière et Vie*, 36 (1957), 56–72.

"Evangélisation," *Catholicisme*, 4, col. 755–764.

"La catéchèse, qu'est-ce à dire? Essai de clarification," *Catéchèse*, 1 (1960), 35–42.

"Le ministère de la parole: du kérygme à la catéchèse," *La Parole de Dieu en Jèsus Christ*. Paris, 1961. Pp. 170–184.

"Le catéchuménat dans l'edification de l'Eglise," *Parole et Mission*, 1 (1958), 31–54.

Lilje, D., "Was und wie sollen wir heute predigen?," *Die Predigt. Das Gespräch über die Predigt auf der Lutherischen Generalsynode 1957 in Hamburg*. Berlin, 1957. Pp. 9–23.

Lotz, J. B., "Wissenschaft und Verkündigung," *Zeitschrift für Kath. Theologie*, 62 (1938), p. 465 ss.

Lopez, Gay J., *La preevangelizaciòn en los primeros años de la missiòn del Japòn*. Madrid, 1962.

Maggiolini, S., *La predicazione nella vita della Chiesa.* Brescia, 1961.
"La Parola di Dio nella costituzione conciliare 'de sacra liturgia'," *La Scuola Cattolica,* 92 (1964), 154–177.

Mailhiot, B., "La psicologia religiosa scienza ausiliaria dell 'azione pastorale," *La Pastorale oggi* (Proceedings of the Fribourg Congress). Milan, 1962. Pp. 217–227.

Marlé, R., "La téologie bultmanienne de la Parole de Dieu," *La Parole de Dieu en Jèsus Christ.* Paris, 1961. Pp. 268–280.

Marxen, W., *Exegese und Verkündigung.* Munich, 1957.

McKenzie, J. L., "The Word of God in the Old Testament," *Theological Studies,* 21 (1960), 183–206.

McVann, J., *The Canon Law on Sermon Preaching.* New York, 1940.

Mehl, R., *Le rencontre d'autrui.* Neuchatel-Paris, 1955.

Mete(le)della catechesi (Proceedings of the Second Convention of Friends of Catechesis). Turin, 1961.

Mistero(il)pasquale nella catechesi (Proceedings of the First Interdiocesan Catechetical Congress of Ascoli Piceno). Ascoli Piceno, 1964.

Moeller, C., "Théologie de la parole et oecuménisme," *Irenikon,* 24 (1951), 313–343.

Mohrmann, C., "Praedicare-Tractare Sermo. Essai sur la terminologie paléochrétienne," *La Maison Dieu,* 39 (1954), 97–108.

Mollat, D., "Evangile," *Dict. de spiritualité,* 4, col. 1745–1772.

Mouroux, J., *I Believe: The Personal Structure of Faith.* New York, 1959. *Je crois en toi.* Paris, 1949.
Le mystère du temps. Paris, 1961. Spec. p. 196 ss.

Murphy, O'Connor J., *Paul on Preaching.* London-New York, 1963.

Nebreda, A., "La préparation du message," *Lumen Vitae,* 16 (1961), 419–436.
Jalones para una preevangelizaciòn en Japòn (diss.). Estella, 1964.

Negri, G., "Problemi generali della catechesi," *Educare. Sommario di scienze pedagogiche,* vol. II. Rome, 1960. Pp. 217–291.
"Le basi teologiche della catechesi," *Il contenuto della catechesi.* Turin, 1961. Pp. 81–100.

Olivier, B., "Les conditions d'authencité de la prédication actuelle," *La Parole de Dieu en Jèsus Christ.* Paris, 1961. Pp. 210–223.

Oldani, L., "La legislazione della Chiesa sulla predicazione," *La Scuola Cattolica,* 78 (1950), 325–333.

Parodi, B., *La catechesi di Sant'Ambrogio.* Genoa, 1957.

Parola(la)di Dio nella comunità cristiana. Atti della VI settimana nazionale di aggiornamento pastorale di Roma. Milan, 1957.

Paulin, A., *St. Cyril de Jérusalem catéchète.* Paris, 1959.

Petit, F., *Proclamer la Parole. Ce qu'enseigne la Bible sur la prédication.* Paris, 1963.

Peterson, E., "Le martyre et l'Eglise," *Dieu vivant,* 5, pp. 17–31.

Peuchmaurd, M., "Le prêtre ministre de la parole dans la théologie du XII siècle," *Recherches de théologie ancienne et médioévale*, 38 (1961), 52–76.

"Mission canonique et prédication," *Riv. Cit.*, 30 (1963), 122–144 and 251–276.

Prédication et prédicateurs (Cahiers de la *Nouvelle Revue Théologique*). Tournai, 1947.

Procksch, O., "Wort Gottes im Altem Testament," *Theol. Wörterbuch*, 4, col. 89–100.

Pohlmann, C., "Die theologische Konzeption der Barockpredigt," *Theologie und Predigt*. Würzburg, 1958. Pp. 258–271.

Prümm, K., "Zur phänomenologie des paulinischen Mysterion," *Biblica*, 37 (1956), 135–161.

Rahner, H., *Eine Theologie der Verkundigung*. Freiburg, 1939.

Rahner, K., "Wort und Eucharistie," *Schriften zur Theologie*, Band IV. Einsiedeln, 1960. Pp. 315–355.

Hörer des Wortes, 2nd ed. Munich, 1963.

Ratzinger, J., "Christozentrik in der Verkündigung," *Trierer Theol. Zeitschrift*, 70 (1961).

Regan, A., "The Word of God and the Ministry of Preaching," *Studia Moralia* I. Rome, 1963. Pp. 389–449.

Rengstorf, K. H., Art. διδάσκω, διδάσκαλος, *Theol. Wörterbuch* 2, col. 138–168.

Rétif, A., *Foi au Christ et Mission d'après le livre des Actes*. Paris, 1953. "Pour une catéchèse dans l'évangélisation," *Lumière et Vie*, 46 (1960), 80–88.

Ries, Joh., *Krisis und Erneuerung der Predigt*. Frankfurt, 1961.

Rigaux, B., and Grelot, P., "Révélation," *Voc. de théologie biblique*. Paris, 1962. Col. 925–935.

Ritter, K. B., "Kirche des Wortes und Kirche des Sakramentes," *Die Katholizität der Kirche*, edited by H. Asmussen and W. Stählin. Stuttgart, 1957.

Robben, E., *Il problema teologico della predicazione*. Rome, 1962.

Robert, A., and Starcky, J., "La parole divine dans l'A. et le N.T.," *Suppl. au Dict. de la Bible* 5, col. 425–497.

Rochol, Gärtner I., "Die psychologischen-pädagogischen Grundlagen der Glaubensverkündigung," *Im Dienste des Glaubens*. Trier, 1962. Pp. 3–188.

Rock, A., *Unless They Be Sent. A Theological Study of the Nature and Purpose of Preaching*. Dubuque, 1953.

Roguet, A. M., "Les sources bibliques et liturgiques de la prédication," *Le prêtre ministre de la parole* pp. 97–114.

Sartori, L., "La mentalità di fede come fine proprio della catechesi," *Le mete della catechesi*, Turin, 1960. Pp. 37–75.

Schädelin, A., *Die rechte Predigt*. Zürich, 1953.

Schelkle, K. H., *Jüngerschaft und Apostelamt. Eine biblische Auslegung des priesterlichen Dienstes*. Freiburg, 1957. Pp. 57–83.

Schillebeeckx, E., "Parole et sacrement dans l'Eglise," *Lumière et Vie*, 9 (1960), 25–45.

Schlier, H., *Die Verkündigung im Gottesdienst der Kirche*. Cologne, 1953.

Wort Gottes. Eine Neutestamentliche Besinnung. Würzburg, 1958.

"Die Stiftung des Wortes Gottes nach dem Apostel Paulus," *Theologie und Predigt*. Würzburg, 1958. Pp. 170–189.

Art παρρησία, *Theol. Wörterbuch*, 5, col. 869–884.

Schmaus, M., "Der Theologische Ort der Kirchlichen Verkündigung," *Liturgie und Gestalt und Vollzug* (Festgabe für Pascer). Munich, 1963. Pp. 286–296.

Wahrheit als Heilsbegegnung. Munich, 1964.

Schnackenburg, R., *Die Kirche im Neuen Testament*. Freiburg, 1961.

Schneyer, J. B., "Die Heilsbedeutung der Predigt in der Auffassung der Katholisschen Prediger," *Zeitschrift fur Kath. Theologie*, 84 (1962), 152–170.

Schreiner, H., *Die Verkündigung des Wortes Gottes*. Hamburg, 1949.

Schorn, A., "Das Wort Gottes bei den Vätern," *Vom Hören des Wortes Gottes*, edited by J. Gulden and R. Scherer. Freiburg, 1948. Pp. 19–34.

Schurr, V., *Wie heute predigen?* Stuttgart, 1949.

"Situation und Aufgabe der Predigt heute," *Verkündigung und Glaube*. Freiburg, 1958. Pp. 185–208.

"Anpassung des Wortes Gottes an die Hörer," *Hörer und Predigt*. Würzburg, 1960. Pp. 303–331.

Schurmann, H., *Aufbau und Struktur der neutestamentlichen Verkündigung*. Paderborn, 1949.

Semmelroth, O., "Theologische Deutung der Verkündigung des Wortes Gottes," *Catholica*, 14 (1960), 270–291.

Wirkendes Wort. Zur Theologie der Verkündigung. Frankfurt, 1962.

Seumois, A., *Apostolat*. Rome, 1961.

Sloyan, G., *Shaping the Christian Message. Essays on Religious Education*. New York, 1958.

Smolders, D., "L'audace de l'apôtre selon S. Paul. Le thème de la parresia," *Collectanea Mechlinensia*, 43 (1958), 16–30 and 117–133.

Soiron, Th., *Die Verkündigung des Wortes Gottes*. Freiburg, 1943.

"Der Prediger und der Hörer," *Not und Auftrag der Verkündigung*, edited by J. Gerards. Aachen, 1950. Pp. 25–40.

Spiazzi, R., *Verbum salutis, Storia e teologia della predicazione*. Rome, 1963.

"Ciò che permane e ciò che muta nella predicazione," *La Parola di Dio nella comunità cristiana*. Milan, 1957. Pp. 113–130.

Spicq, C., "Le mystère chrètien," *Les Epîtres pastorales.* Paris, 1947. Pp. 116–125.

Sprache und Predigt. Ein Tagungsbericht, edited by M. Frickel. Würzburg, 1963.

Stanley, D., Christ's Resurrection in Pauline Soteriology. Rome, 1961.

Strathmann, N., Art. μάρτυς, μαρτυρέω, *Theol. Wörterbuch*, 4, col. 492–685.

Taddei, N., *Predicazione nell'epoca dell'immagine.* Turin, 1964.

Theologie und Predigt. Ein Tagungsbericht, edited by O. Wehner and M. Frickel. Würzburg, 1958.

Torres, Capellàn A., "Palabra y revelaciòn," *Burgense*, 1 (1960), 143–190.

Tremel, Y. B., "Du kérygme des apôtres à celui d'aujourd'hui," *L'annonce de l'Evangile aujourd'hui.* Paris, 1962. Pp. 19–54.

Trépanier, B., "L'idée de témoin dans les écrits johanniques," *Rev. de l'Université d'Ottawa*, 15 (1945), 5–63 (special section).

Turck, A., *Evangélisation et catéchèse aux deux premiers siècles.* Paris, 1962.

Ubieta, J. A., "El Kerygma apostolico y los Evangelios," *Estudios Biblicos*, 18 (1959), 21–61.

Vagaggini, C., *Il senso teologico della liturgia.* Rome, 1958. Spec. c. XXIV.

Vajta, V., *Die Theologie des Gottesdienst bey Luther.* Stockholm, 1952.

Van Caster, M., *L'homme en face de Dieu.* Paris, 1958.

Van Imschoot, P., *Théologie de l'A.T.*, 2 vol. Paris-Tournai-Rome-New York, 1954 and 1956. Vol. I, pp. 142–255.

Vanhoye, A., "Témoignage et vie en Dieu selon le quatrième Evangile," *Christus*, 18 (1955), 150–171.

"Verantwortete Verkündigung," *Lebendige Seelsorge*, 14 (1963) with articles by various contributors.

Verdonc, E., "Phénoménologie de la parole," *La Parole de Dieu en Jèsus Christ.* Paris, 1961. Pp. 251–267.

Verrièle, A., "Le plan de salut d'après S. Irénée," *Revue des Sc. rel.*, 14 (1934), 493–524.

Vetter, A., "Der hörende Mensch," *Hörer und Predigt.* Würzburg, 1960. Pp. 13–33.

Volk, H., "Das Wort Gottes in der Seelsorge," *Universitas* (Festgabe für Albert Stohr), Vol. I. Mainz, 1960. Pp. 255–264.

Von Balthasar, H. U., "Parole et histoire," *La Parole de Dieu en Jèsus Christ.* Paris, 1961. Pp. 227–240.

Warnach, V., "Menschenwort und Gotteswort. Zur Phänomenologie und Theologie der Sprache," *Liturgie und Mönchtum*, Folge 3, Heft 12 (1953), 14–34.

"Wort und Sakrament im Aufbau der christlichen Existenz," *Liturgie und Münchtum*, Heft 20 (1957), 68–90.

William, M., "Kerygma und die Denkformen der Gegenwart," *Verkündigung und Glaube.* Freiburg, 1958. Pp. 142–154.

Wingren, G., "Die Sakramente und die Predigt als Träger des fleischgewordenen Wortes," *Die Leibhaftigkeit des Wortes* (Koeberle Festgabe). 1958. Pp. 375–386.

Die Predigt. Goettingen, 1959.

Wyder H., *Die Heidenpredigt* Gütersloh, 1954.

Index

267

Priesthood and preaching, xxiv, 75–
78
Prümm, K., 8

R

Rahner, H., xxviii, 234
Rahner, K., 110, 177
Regan, A., xxxiii
Religion, lack of joy in, xxvii
Renard, Mgr., 119
Rétif, A., xxii, 11, 148, 223, 235
Resurrection, center of the message,
11–12
Revelation
doctrine, 17, 33
event, 17
and inspiration, 41
Ries, J., x
Ripalda, 61–62
Robben, E., xxv
Rock, A., xxiv
Roguet, A. M., 110

S

Sacramentality of preaching, 40,
128–129
Sacred dimension of preaching,
111–113
Salvation
economy of, 17–18
history of, 13
obstacles to, 15
in New Testament, 14
in Old Testament, 14
plan of, 20
and redemption, 16
in supernatural order, 15
Santos Hernandez, A., 64, 105
Scheeben, M., xxxi
Scheler, M., xxv
Schelkle, K. H., xxii, 26, 52, 56
Scherer, R., xii, xv
Schillebeeckx, H., xxxi, 4, 26, 39,
129, 196
Schlier, H., xxv, 3, 23–25, 58, 127,
242–244

Schmaus, M., xxix, 129–130
Schnackenburg, R., 3, 50
Schneyer, J. B., xxiv, 30
Schreiner, H., 70, 200
Schurr, V., x, 134–135, 200, 202,
206
Segneri, P., 113
Semmelroth, O., xxv, xxxii, 138–
141
Seumois, A., 74
Shädelin, A., xii
Söhngen, G., xxxi, 60, 129
Soiron, T., xxxii, 70
Spiazzi, R., xxxiii, 52, 239–240
Spirituality and preaching, xiv
Suarez, F., 6, 40, 60
System, 17, 18–21

T

Tertullian, 30, 179
Testimony
of the Apostles, 148–150
collective, 171–172
combined, 155–156
of the community, 150–153
concept of, 146–148
of converts, 180–181
effects of, 150–153
and efficacy of preaching, 192–
193
and imitation of Christ, 157–158
and insufficiency of language,
182–183
of persecutions, 174–176
in philosophy of communication,
xvi, xx
and problem of evil, 176–177
reasons of, 160–183
and sanctity, 158–159
of the Trinity, 173–174
true and false, 170–171
Theophile of Antioch, 30
Thomas of Aquin, xxiv, 30–33, 51,
53, 66, 73, 76, 79, 88, 105, 132–
134, 141–144, 189–190, 207,
211, 217, 219, 220
Thomistic realism, 18

26074